THE SEA VOYAGE NARRATIVE

GENRES IN CONTEXT

THE SHORT STORY
The Reality of Artifice
Charles E. May

FANTASY
The Liberation of Imagination
Richard Mathews

BIOGRAPHY
Writing Lives
Catherine N. Parke

THE SEA VOYAGE NARRATIVE
Robert Foulke

SCIENCE FICTION BEFORE 1900
Imagination Discovers Technology
Paul K. Alkon

SCIENCE FICTION AFTER 1900
From the Steam Man to the Stars
Brooks Landon

NATURE WRITING
The Pastoral Impulse in America
Don Scheese

THE FAIRY TALE
The Magic Mirror of Imagination
Steven Swann Jones

TRAVEL WRITING
The Self and the World
Casey Blanton

THE SEA VOYAGE NARRATIVE

Robert Foulke

Routledge
New York and London

Published in 2002 by
Routledge
29 West 35th Street
New York, NY 10001

Published in Great Britain by
Routledge
11 New Fetter Lane
London EC4P 4EE

Routledge is an imprint of the Taylor & Francis Group.

Originally published in hardcover by Twayne Publishers, an imprint of The Gale Group.
This paperback edition published by arrangement with Twayne Publishers.

Copyright © 1997 by Robert Foulke.

First Routledge paperback edition 2002

Printed in the United States of America on acid-free paper.

10 9 8 7 6 5 4 3 2 1

Cataloging-in-Publication Data available from the Library of Congress.

ISBN 0–415–93894–5 (pbk)

To John P. Kendall, friend and fellow voyager,
who encouraged my interest in voyage narratives
and made sure it would be tempered by a healthy dose
of reality at sea

"An East Indiaman in a Gale" (1840) by William John Huggins.
Courtesy of the N. R. Omell Gallery, London.

General Editor's Statement

Genre studies have been a central concern of Anglo-American and European literary theory for at least the past quarter century, and the academic interest has been reflected, for example, in new college courses in slave narratives, autobiography, biography, nature writing, and the literature of travel as well as in the rapid expansion of genre theory itself. Genre has also become an indispensable term for trade publishers and the vast readership they serve. Indeed, few general bookstores do not have sections devoted to science fiction, romance, and mystery fiction. Still, genre is among the slipperiest of literary terms, as any examination of genre theories and their histories will suggest.

In conceiving this series we have tried, on the one hand, to avoid the comically pedantic spirit that informs Polonius's recitation of kinds of drama and, on the other hand, the equally unhelpful insistence that every literary production is a unique expression that must not be forced into any system of classification. We have instead developed our list of genres, which range from ancient comedy to the Western, with the conviction that by common consent kinds of literature do exist—not as fixed categories but as fluid ones that change over time as the result of complex interplay of authors, audiences, and literary and cultural institutions. As individual titles in the series demonstrate, the idea of genre offers us provocative ways to study both the continuities and adaptability of literature as a familiar and inexhaustible source of human imagination.

Recognition of the fluid boundaries both within and among genres will provide, we believe, a useful array of perspectives from which to study literature's complex development. Genres, as traditional but open ways of understanding the world, contribute to our capacity to respond to narrative and expressive forms and offer means to discern moral significances embodied in these forms. Genres, in short, serve ethical as well as aesthetic purposes, and the volumes in this series attempt to demonstrate how this double benefit has been achieved as these genres have been transformed over the years. Each title in the series should be measured against this large ambition.

Ron Gottesman

Contents

Preface

Many years ago I drifted into the study of voyage narratives through an interest in Joseph Conrad's fiction. Drifting is anathema to all seafarers, who want to control and navigate their vessels, but it does lead one into unexpected places. I found myself sitting in the reading rooms of the British Museum, the Admiralty Library, and the National Maritime Museum in London, studying the history of the British Merchant Service in the late nineteenth century. The impetus driving a literary scholar into maritime history came from otherwise admirable Conrad critics who wrote rather silly things about the action in his voyage fiction simply because they did not understand the historical and technical aspects of the sea world Conrad knew. I had enough sea experience to glimpse that world, and it enriched my reading of the fiction.

Little did I realize that I had entered the Gulf Stream of my academic life, a powerful current that would lead me back to the *Odyssey*, to a voyage exploring the ancient Mediterranean, to teaching for the Williams College Program at Mystic Seaport and the Sea Education Association at Woods Hole, both ashore and on board its vessels in the Atlantic. Nor could I have guessed that I would eventually take my own Skidmore students to sea on sailing ships as they read voyage literature. Through the years the "drifting" had become purposeful, a gradual exploration of the massive and amorphous body of writing about the sea and seafaring, loosely referred to as sea literature.

To describe sea literature as a field of study seems a peculiarly inappropriate application of the dead metaphor that separates academic territories. For the scholar, entering it is more like sailing into the Sargasso Sea, a vast expanse of the North Atlantic filled with patches of floating weed that was once mistakenly thought to entrap ships but is now known merely to harbor myriad species of ocean life. The varied fare of sea literature comes in Protean forms and guises, and it resists easy definition for two reasons. In the first place, we cannot separate fact from fiction, history or anecdote from literature. Writers about the sea seldom limit themselves to one mode of dealing with their subject, whether it be simple recording of facts, technical analysis of events, a straightforward chronicle larded with anecdotes, fictionalized autobiography, or pure invention of imagined events in a sea setting.

How then do we establish outer limits for sea literature? If they are inclusive, works will stretch out to the horizon, encompassing voyage narratives, tales about sailors afloat and ashore, poems reflecting the impact of the sea on human imagination, essays on the experience of seafaring, invented voyages to utopia or dystopia, navigational, geographical, scientific, and commercial information included in accounts of voyages of discovery, autobiographies of captains, journals kept by their wives at sea, ship biographies, accounts of shipwrecks and disasters, anecdotes of retired mariners, superstitions, sea lore, chanteys and ballads, and more. Within this potpourri it is difficult to grasp the essence of the subject: Inclusiveness leads to amorphous definition, exclusiveness to a tighter one that might limit the range of sea literature more than we would like.

Second, we usually distinguish literature from the unending strings of ephemeral words that clutter our daily lives by assuming that the text of the former has permanent value. Even a limited focus within sea literature cannot eliminate all the junk weed floating about. Voyage narratives alone compose an ancient and exceedingly abundant portion of writing about the sea, and many of them are indeed fleeting, badly written, and clearly unworthy of continued attention. In making such judgments, I use a very simple pragmatic definition of literature: the felt need to preserve a text intact. It works like litmus paper to separate out pure information, rambling anecdotes, autobiographical puffery, doggerel verse, and the like. Yet such simple intuitions about the nature of literature do not help us much in dealing with writing about the sea—not only a mélange of the superb and the inept, of the *Odyssey* and mass-market adventure stories, but also seemingly endless in variety and form. Sea writing has always been prolific, from its Greek beginnings through the many accounts of geographical discovery collected by Hakluyt in the sixteenth century to the large number of titles published by the Dolphin Book Club in the twentieth century. The very fact that a mass-market book club on sea writing can now be profitable indicates both a wide readership and an active writing industry. Interest in tall ships is burgeoning, sailors undertaking voyages around the world capture media attention, and the steady stream of new books about seafaring, both worthy and insignificant, continues.

Of course, sea literature belongs to a larger family of writing about travel that is equally amorphous and uneven in quality. It is probably the primordial form of travel writing in Western culture's amalgamation of Hebrew and Greek sources, beginning with Noah and Jonah, Odysseus and Jason. That is no surprise given the unfriendly topography of much of the ancient world, composed of barrier mountains and almost impassable deserts. The sea was fearsome and unpredictable, too, particularly along the sometimes harborless coasts of the eastern Mediterranean, but travelers usually got from place to place on it more easily than by struggling over high passes or crossing vast tracts of barren sand.

The word *voyage,* originally quite precise in its reference to travel by sea, gradually broadened to include other means of conveyance on land, and in some languages, like French, it is used to describe any trip. As other modes of travel supplanted movement by water in practical importance—stagecoaches, trains, automobiles, airplanes—it is curious that interest in writing about the sea has not waned while coaching, railroading, automobile touring, and even flying have not yet produced comparably rich and varied bodies of travel writing. Such an imbalance may change in time, especially with space exploration, but it is remarkable that public interest in the sea voyage remains strong long after flight has replaced it as the dominant mode of personal transport overseas. The basic vocabulary of the sea voyage has been transplanted wholesale to flight, and it persists in the daily idiom of many languages long after the precise meanings of sea terms have evaporated from consciousness. Even in the trendy realms of adventure travel—mountain climbing, camel trekking, white-water rafting, hot-air ballooning—interest in single-handed yacht voyages, round-the-world races, and tall-ship rendezvous holds its own.

The Modern Language Association bibliography recognizes travel literature as a genre but only in the broadest sense of that term, comparable to poetry, fiction, drama, and the like. Definitions of genre that some scholars think more useful—for example, picaresque novel, Bildungsroman, comedy of manners, elegy, emblem—distinguish formal patterns, conventions, characteristic subject matter, themes, and style more narrowly. For the reasons stated earlier, I regard sea literature, like the larger travel literature that includes it, not as a genre but as a broadly descriptive category with clear but limited usefulness. Within this category, however, sea voyage narratives do in fact constitute a central and clearly definable genre in the narrower sense of the term. That is the focus of this book—one centrally important kind of writing about the sea.

Some of the genre's archetypal features, like Noah's preparations for the flood or Jonah's multiple descents into the hold of a ship and the maw of a whale, reflect and extend human experience with unruly waters—in one case the periodic inundations of Mideast rivers and in the other the rapid onset of fierce Mediterranean storms. Such storms and encounters with savage peoples on strange shores form the basis of Odysseus's wanderings, and the tradition created by the *Odyssey* was powerful enough to demand repetition and variation in Apollonius of Rhodes's *Argonautica*, Virgil's *Aeneid*, Dante's *Inferno*, Joyce's *Ulysses*, Kazantzakis's *The Odyssey: A Modern Sequel,* and Derek Walcott's *Omeros.* Readers of Columbus's voyages will recognize some narrative elements (e.g., deception of the crew and immobilization during a storm) that stretch backward in time to the story of Jonah and forward to Melville and Conrad. Many of the voyage narratives collected by Hakluyt in the closing decades of the sixteenth century embody the quest patterns and utopian themes that reappear later in voyage fiction. After literacy spread into the middle classes in England during the eighteenth century and the novel became the dominant genre, voyage narratives borrowed its conventions and those of other popular genres. Defoe, Fielding, and Smollett particularly exploited the conventions of the picaresque romance for tales about maritime wanderers, while later Scott, Marryat, Cooper, Dana, Melville, and Conrad developed and elaborated the sea bildungsroman.

Although the focus of this study is quite narrow within the full range of sea writing, it is clearly ecumenical rather than sectarian in dealing with the boundaries of literature itself. A glance at the table of contents will reveal that the present volume encompasses voyage narratives with both historical and literary ancestry. The subject can be labeled neither "literature of the sea voyage" nor "historical voyage narratives" with any accuracy. For reasons that I will explore at some length in the opening chapter, the symbiosis between literature and history, imagination and experience, fiction and autobiography is very close and full of quite complex interactions. Those relationships give sea voyage narratives much of their power and may help to explain the longevity of the genre.

The scope of this study is also narrow, but its stretch is long. Condensing more than two millennia of sea voyage narratives into generic description, analysis, and illustration is task enough within Western culture, but such a practical contraction of horizon does not imply that sea voyage narratives are parochial rather than global in nature. Indeed, almost every coastal culture has its own traditional tales of adventurous seafaring, many of them relating astounding navigational accomplishments. While the Greeks were hugging the coasts of the Mediterranean and sailing from island to island by line of sight, Polynesian navigators spread across the vast empty spaces of the Pacific, finding tiny atolls and larger islands sometimes thousands of miles distant. Again, the exploits of privateers and pirates, whether in the Caribbean, the Philippines, the Pearl River Delta, the Red Sea, or the Barbary Coast, constitute a worldwide subgenre of voyage narratives. Examining the oral and literary traditions of voyage narratives in other cultures necessarily lies beyond the scope of this slim volume. Even within the bounds of Western culture, it must be an exploratory study rather than a thorough survey, and as such it examines only a few of the many narratives worthy of attention.

In a single lifetime, it would be impossible for anyone to encompass—much less add to—all the good scholarship surrounding Homer, Columbus, Cook, Melville, Conrad, Hemingway, and a variety of other twentieth-century writers of voyage narratives. But it is possible to ferret out what is most relevant to the shape and power of voyage narratives within this vast body of scholarship, and that is what I have tried to do.

Through the last two decades, collaboration with many other scholars interested in sea literature and maritime history has been enormously helpful in plotting the course of my own research and teaching. Among others, I am particularly grateful to Professor Emeritus Benjamin Labaree of Williams College, founder and first director of the Williams-Mystic Program in American Maritime Studies, and to Professor Briton Busch of Colgate University; they taught me much about the methods and substance of maritime history as the three of us brought our winter-term students together at Mystic Seaport each January for more than a decade. A former colleague, Professor Edward Sloan of Trinity College (Hartford), has also been very helpful through several decades as both of us designed and taught courses that brought maritime history and sea literature together. Other historians, archaeologists, classicists, and literary scholars read drafts of chapters and made suggestions as this volume began to take shape: D. K. Abass of Newport, Professor Michael Arnush of Skidmore College, Professor Keith Carabine of the University of East Anglia, and Professor William Phillips of the University of Minnesota. Three scholars with a special interest in sea literature read and commented on larger sections. Professor Bert Bender of Arizona State University combed the text for errors and noted a number of omissions. Professor Haskell Springer of the University of Kansas gave me much-needed bearings in approaching the leviathan of Melville scholarship and provided annotations on matters beyond my ken. Professor James Millinger of the Sea Education Association spent part of his sabbatical leave reviewing the entire manuscript, raised speculative questions, and furnished commentary on the balance of the whole. Professor Ron Gottesman of the University of Southern California, general editor of the series, provided astute and timely guidance throughout the writing process.

I especially thank Patricia Foulke, my wife and coauthor in many other writing projects, for her patience and self-reliance during my spells away at sea. She also took on innumerable tasks directly related to the book, including tracing and collecting illustrations from around the world and gaining permissions for both quoted texts and illustrations. In the process of selecting illustrations, we are especially grateful for the advice and help of William Ambler of the Hispanic Society of America, Philip Budlong of Mystic Seaport, David Bush of the Galveston Historical Foundation, Carla Fleming of Fleming Photography in Annapolis, Susan Danforth of the John Carter Brown Library, Charles Omell of the N. R. Omell gallery in London, David Taylor of the National Maritime Museum in London, Professor Carla Phillips of the University of Minnesota, and Carol Urness of the James Ford Bell Library. Stuart Frank of the Kendall Whaling Museum not only searched his own collection for appropriate illustrations but also suggested many other sources in this country and abroad. More than anyone else we leaned on help from Hunt Conard of Skidmore College, media specialist extraordinaire who combines photographic expertise with an intimate knowledge of seafaring gained through a voyage with the legendary Captain Irving Johnson. He understood the need for illustration in this book, created the maps and diagrams, and expertly reproduced many of its photographs and drawings. In such ways many hands helped launch this volume, and I am indebted to them for their generous assistance.

I also wish to thank the John Carter Brown Library, Brown University, where the Alexander O. Vietor Fellowship enabled me to spend the fall of 1993 in research for this book; its director, Dr. Norman Fiering, and the whole staff made work in the library's superb collection both productive and extremely pleasant. Finally, I am grateful to students in the literature of voyaging courses I taught at Skidmore for two decades. They asked taut questions, read themselves into an understanding of voyage narratives, stood their watches at sea, and in journals and papers made the connections between reading and experience that are at the heart of this book.

Acknowledgments

Some of the material in chapter 1 first appeared in "The Literature of Voyaging," the opening essay in *The Literature and Lore of the Sea*, edited by Patricia Ann Carlson (Amsterdam: Rodopi, 1986), 1–13. Quotations from *The Odyssey* in chapters 1 and 2 are taken from *The Odyssey* by Homer, translated by Robert Fagles. Translation copyright © 1996 by Robert Fagles. Used by permission of Viking Penguin, a division of Penguin Books USA Inc. In chapter 2 the passage from Tim Severin's *The Ulysses Voyage* (New York: E. P. Dutton) Copyright © 1987 by Tim Severin, is reproduced with the permission of Sheil Land Associates Ltd., London. In chapter 3 quotations on Columbus's voyage are drawn from two sources: *The Diario of Christopher Columbus's First Voyage to America, 1492–1493*, transcribed and translated by Oliver Dunn and James E. Kelley Jr. (Norman, Oklahoma: University of Oklahoma Press, 1989), Copyright © 1989 by Oliver Dunn and James E. Kelley Jr., with permission; and *The Life of the Admiral Christopher Columbus by His Son Ferdinand*, translated and annotated by Benjamin Keen (New Brunswick, NJ: Rutgers University Press), copyright © 1959, 1992 by Rutgers, The State University. Quotations related to Cook's first Pacific voyage are taken from *The Explorations of Captain James Cook in the Pacific as Told by Selections of His Own Journals, 1768–1779*, edited by A. Grenfell Price (New York: Dover Publications, 1971), with permission. Material on the pattern of romance in chapter 4 is excerpted from *An Anatomy of Literature,* by Robert Foulke and Paul Smith, copyright © 1972 by Harcourt Brace & Company, reprinted by permission of the publisher. Some of the interpretation in chapter 5 first appeared in two of my essays, "Postures of Belief in *The Nigger of the 'Narcissus.'" Modern Fiction Studies* 17:2 (Summer 1971): 249–62; and "Creed and Conduct in *The Nigger of the 'Narcissus,'" Conradiana* 12:2 (Spring 1980): 105–28.

Illustrations are reproduced here, with permission, from the following sources: jacket photo of the *Elissa,* The Galveston Historical Foundation; frontispiece photo of "An East Indiaman in a Gale" by William John Huggins, N. R. Omell Gallery, London; "Disabled in mid-ocean—firing signals of distress" and "Around Cape Horn—in a heavy sea," Mystic Seaport Museum; two photos of the *Argo* by Kevin Fleming of Fleming Photography, Annapolis, Maryland; Portolan chart of the Atlantic by Zuane Pizzigano of Venice and portrait of "Christoforo Colombo" by Leonardo Lasansky, James Ford Bell Library, University of Minnesota; drawings of the *Pinta, Santa Maria,* and *Niña* by Joaquin Sorolla y Bastida, The Hispanic Society of America, New York; photo of the *Endeavour* replica by Rick Yoerg, Milktoast Productions, Stowe, Vermont; engraving of the *Endeavour* careened and photo of the *Narcissus,* National Maritime Museum, London; "In the very heart of the Leviathanic life," "Cutting in," "The crow's nest," and "Garneray's Sperm Whaling Scene," The Kendall Whaling Museum, Sharon, Massachusetts, USA.

Chronology

750–725 B.C.	Composition of the *Odyssey*.
ca. 530 B.C.	Peisistratus, tyrant of Athens, directs that the *Odyssey* and the *Iliad* be codified as texts for public performance.
260–240 B.C.	Apollonius of Rhodes composes the *Argonautica*.
19 B.C.	Emperor Augustus orders posthumous publication of Virgil's *Aeneid*.
60 A.D.	*The Periplus Maris Erythraei* records a voyage around Africa.
874	Norsemen reach Iceland.
985	Eric the Red reaches Greenland.
1000 or 1001	Leif Ericsson reaches Newfoundland.
1488	Bartholomew Díaz rounds the Cape of Good Hope.
1492–1493	Columbus's first voyage to the New World.
1498	Vasco da Gama reaches India.
1519–1522	Magellan circumnavigates the world for the first time.
1534	Jacques Cartier's first voyage to Canada.
1577–1580	Sir Francis Drake circumnavigates the world.

1588   The Spanish Armada is defeated in the English Channel.

1598–1600   Hakluyt's *Voyages and Discoveries: The Principal Navigations, Voyages, Traffiques and Discoveries of the English Nation.*

1697   William Dampier, *A New Voyage Round the World.*

1719   Daniel Defoe's *The Life and Adventures of Robinson Crusoe.*

1720   Daniel Defoe, *Captain Singleton.*

1740–1744   Admiral George Anson circumnavigates the world.

1768–1771   Cook's first voyage in the Pacific.

1773   John Hawkesworth, *An Account of the Voyages Undertaken . . . for Making Discoveries in the Southern Hemisphere.*

1781   John Rickman, *Journal of Captain Cook's Last Voyage to the Pacific Ocean.*

1790   William Bligh, *The Mutiny on the H.M.S. Bounty.*

1798   Samuel Taylor Coleridge, *The Rime of the Ancient Mariner.*

1821   Sir Walter Scott, *The Pirate.*

1824   James Fenimore Cooper, *The Pilot: A Tale of the Sea.*

1827   James Fenimore Cooper, *The Red Rover.*

1836   Frederick Marryat, *Mr. Midshipman Easy.*

1838   Edgar Allan Poe, *The Narrative of Arthur Gordon Pym.*

1839   Charles Darwin, *The Voyage of the Beagle.*

1840   Richard Henry Dana, *Two Years Before the Mast.*

1844   James Fenimore Cooper, *Afloat and Ashore: or, The Adventures of Miles Wallingford.*

1849   James Fenimore Cooper, *The Sea-Lions: or, The Lost Sealers.*

1849   Herman Melville, *Redburn: His First Voyage.*

1850   Herman Melville, *White-Jacket or, The World in a Man-of-War.*

1851   Herman Melville, *Moby-Dick or, The Whale.*

1855   Charles Kingsley, *Westward Ho!.*

1870   Jules Verne, *Twenty-Thousand Leagues Under the Sea.*

1870   Suez Canal opens and makes steamships competitive on long-distance routes to the Far East.

1884   E. F. Knight, *The Cruise of the Falcon.*

1897   Joseph Conrad, *The Nigger of the "Narcissus."*

1897   Rudyard Kipling, *Captains Courageous.*

1900   Joshua Slocum, *Sailing Alone Around the World.*

1900   Joseph Conrad, *Lord Jim.*

1903   Joseph Conrad, *Typhoon and Other Stories.*

1903   Joseph Conrad's "Youth," "Heart of Darkness," and "The End of the Tether."

1903   Erskine Childers, *The Riddle of the Sands.*

1904   Jack London, *The Sea Wolf.*

1906   Joseph Conrad, *The Mirror of the Sea.*

1911   Jack London, *The Cruise of the Snark.*

1914   Panama Canal opened, eliminating the need for passages around Cape Horn.

1916   Sir Ernest Shackleton and Captain Frank Worsley sail from Antarctica to the Shetland Islands.

1917   Joseph Conrad, *The Shadow-Line.*

1919   Eugene O'Neill, *Seven Plays of the Sea.*

1924   Herman Melville, *Billy Budd, Sailor: An Inside Narrative.*

1927   H. M. Tomlinson, *Gallions Reach.*

1930   Rockwell Kent, *N by E.*

1930   A. J. Villiers, *By Way of Cape Horn.*

1987   Tim Severin, *The Ulysses Voyage: Sea Search for the Odyssey.*

1989   William Golding completes his trilogy, *Rites of Passage* (1980), *Close Quarters* (1987), and *Fire Down Below* (1989).

1990   John McPhee, *Looking for a Ship.*

1990   Charles Johnson, *Middle Passage.*

1990   Derek Walcott, *Omeros.*

1992   Robert Stone, *Outerbridge Reach.*

Chapter 1

THE NATURE OF VOYAGING

It is best to begin with human attitudes toward the sea because they spawn the prolific outpouring of sea writing and generate the most striking features of sea voyage narratives. Such attitudes may at first appear to be nothing but the romantic wanderlust of John Masefield's most famous lyric, "Sea Fever":

I must go down to the seas again, to the lonely sea and the sky,
And all I ask is a tall ship and a star to steer her by,
And the wheel's kick and the wind's song and the white sail's shaking,
And a grey mist on the sea's face and a grey dawn breaking.

In spite of such exuberant stanzas, Masefield also recognized the ironic dichotomies of life at sea, noting that beautiful sailing ships were filled with battered and degraded human beings:

A barquentine was being towed out by a dirty little tug; and very far away, shining in the sun, an island rose from the sea, whitish, like a swimmer's shoulder. It was a beautiful sight that anchorage with the ships lying there so lovely, all their troubles at an end. But I knew that aboard each ship there were young men going to the devil, and mature men wasted, and old men wrecked; and I wondered at the misery and sin which went to make each ship so perfect an image of beauty.[1]

For seamen, even novices like Masefield, attitudes toward the sea and seafaring are usually quite complex and contradictory, built around polarities of awe and fear, ennui and anxiety, exaltation and despair, and they often embody—simultaneously—the literary forms of romance and irony.

The sea both attracts and repels, calling us to high adventure and threatening to destroy us through its indifferent power. In *The Mirror of the Sea* Conrad untangles the intertwined bundle of human attitudes generated by the sea:

> For all that has been said of the love that certain natures (on shore) have professed to feel for it, for all the celebrations it had been the object of in prose and song, the sea has never been friendly to man. At most it has been the accomplice of human restlessness, and playing the part of dangerous abettor of world-wide ambitions. Faithful to no race after the manner of the kindly earth, receiving no impress from valour and toil and self-sacrifice, recognizing no finality of dominion, the sea has never adopted the cause of its masters like those lands where the victorious nations of mankind have taken root, rocking their cradles and setting up their gravestones. He—man or people—who, putting his trust in the friendship of the sea, neglects the strength and cunning of his right hand, is a fool! As if it were too great, too mighty for common virtues, the ocean has no compassion, no faith, no law, no memory. Its fickleness is to be held true to men's purposes only by an undaunted resolution and by a sleepless, armed, jealous vigilance, in which, perhaps, there has always been more hate than love. *Odi et amo* may well be the confession of those who consciously or blindly have surrendered their existence to the fascination of the sea. . . . Indeed, I suspect that, leaving aside the protestations and tributes of writers who, one is safe in saying, care for little else in the world than the rhythm of their lines and the cadence of their phrase, the love of the sea, to which some men and nations confess so readily, is a complex sentiment wherein pride enters for much, necessity for not a little, and the love of ships—the untiring servants of our hopes and our self-esteem—for the best and most genuine part.[2]

In this passage Conrad the writer surely heeds the rhythm of his lines and the cadence of his phrases, but he had been a seaman for nearly a quarter of a century and had serious business at

"Disabled in mid-ocean—firing signals of distress." Drawn by J. O. Davidson for *Harper's Weekly*, 10 December 1881.
Courtesy of Mystic Seaport Museum.

hand. In *The Mirror of the Sea*, the narrative that follows this passage—not fiction—tells of coming upon a dismasted sailing ship on a pleasant day at sea and snatching the exhausted and beaten crew off the deck just before the ship sinks. Conrad's anthropomorphic theme in introducing this narrative, the "unfathomable cruelty" of the sea, is by no means dated, as anyone who has followed seafaring disasters in the last few years knows—an English Channel ferry, a Baltic ferry, a Greek cruise ship off South Africa, with graphic television footage of its final plunge, and countless sinkings of supertankers, container ships, and yachts that do not make the news. In John McPhee's *Looking for a Ship*, Captain Washburn tells a truth of contemporary seafaring succinctly: "Every day, somewhere someone is getting it from the weather. They're running aground. They're hitting each other. They're disappearing without a trace."[3] (Indeed they are. During the writing of this chapter, the 450-foot Ukrainian cargo ship *Salvador Allende*, en route from Texas to Helsinki with a cargo of rice, sank in a North Atlantic gale with 65-knot winds and 35-foot seas; in this case there was a trace: two survivors out of 31 persons on board.) In the era before radio communications at sea, sinkings were more often than not mysterious disappearances. In another section of *The Mirror of the Sea*, Conrad captures the ominous uncertainty surrounding ships that simply vanish; at first they are reported overdue and then posted missing:

> How did she do it? In the word "missing" there is a horrible depth of doubt and speculation. Did she go quickly from under the men's feet, or did she resist to the end, letting the sea batter her to pieces, start her butts, wrench her frame, load her with increasing weight of salt water, and dismasted, unmanageable, rolling heavily, her boats gone, her decks swept, had she wearied her men half to death with unceasing labor at the pumps before she sank with them like a stone? (*Mirror*, 59)

The booming industry of making films about the *Titanic* reminds us of the metaphoric power of sinkings, some of which are taken to be emblematic of whole eras in history or the fragility of human enterprise.

One of the oldest emblems in sea literature is Odysseus's oar, symbolizing the unnaturalness of treading the "sea-road," as the

Homeric formula is often translated, and introducing the motif of leaving the sea forever. To complete his penance for offending Poseidon, Odysseus is told to

> go forth once more, you must . . .
> carry your well-planed oar until you come
> to a race of people who know nothing of the sea,
> whose food is never seasoned with salt, strangers all
> to ships with their crimson prows and long slim oars,
> wings that make ships fly. And here is your sign—
> unmistakeable, clear, so clear you cannot miss it:
> When another traveler falls in with you and calls
> that weight across your shoulder a fan to winnow grain,
> then plant your bladed, balanced oar in the earth
> and sacrifice fine beasts to the lord god of the sea,
> Poseidon—[4]

The theme of escaping bondage to the sea and living out of sight of it persists throughout sea literature from Homer to Conrad and is often associated with Odysseus's emblematic oar. That oar surfaces again in the refrain of "Marching Inland," a sea ballad from the Canadian Maritimes:

> I'm marching inland from the shore,
> Over me shoulder I'm carrying an oar,
> When someone asks me "What is that funny thing you've got,"
> Then I know I'll never go to sea no more, no more,
> Then I know I'll never go to sea no more.[5]

Among the reasons for going ashore and staying there, the ballad suggests it as Lord Nelson's cure for seasickness, reminds us that Columbus ran aground on the New World while trying to reach the Far East, remembers the fate of Drake and Grenville, famous sailors who never came home, and concludes with the admonition never to cast one's anchor less than 90 miles from shore.

Settling any closer might tempt one to return to the sea-road. This is precisely what Tennyson does to an older Ulysses, reversing the polarity of desire during the long and difficult voyage home. His restive Ulysses, stuck with an aging Penelope and an unimaginative Telemachus, cannot wait to quit the Ithaca he sought for a full decade:

> There lies the port; the vessel puffs her sail;
> There gloom the dark, broad seas. My mariners,
> Souls that have toiled, and wrought, and thought with me,—
> That ever with a frolic welcome took
> The thunder and the sunshine, and opposed
> Free hearts, free foreheads—you and I are old;
> Old age hath yet his honor and his toil.
> Death closes all; but something ere the end,
> Some work of noble note, may yet be done,
> Not unbecoming men that strove with gods.
> The lights begin to twinkle from the rocks;
> The long day wanes; the slow moon climbs; the deep
> Moans round with many voices. Come, my friends,
> 'Tis not too late to seek a newer world.
> Push off, and sitting well in order smite
> The sounding furrows; for my purpose holds
> To sail beyond the sunset, and the baths
> Of all the western stars, until I die.[6]

This Victorian Ulysses strikes out on a new voyage of discovery, while one of his twentieth-century successors, the hero of Nikos Kazantzakis's *Odyssey: A Modern Sequel*, also leaves Ithaca to create new havoc in the aftermath of the Trojan War and embark on a symbolic dark journey through ancient Egypt and primordial Africa toward death. These reworked heroes, one romantic and the other thoroughly ironic, reflect both the tenor of their ages and the radically different possibilities inherent in voyaging. Tennyson and Kazantzakis did not misread the *Odyssey* but simply pulled out of it the burning curiosity that launches Odysseus's adventures and usually gets him in desperate trouble.

The polarity between the urge to explore unknown seas and the longing to return home emerges most directly and poignantly in an anonymous Anglo-Saxon lyric, "The Seafarer":

> Little the landlubber, safe on shore,
> Knows what I've suffered in icy seas
> Wretched and worn by the winter storms,
> Hung with icicles, stung by hail,
> Lonely and friendless and far from home.
> In my ears no sound but the roar of the sea,
> The icy combers, the cry of the swan;
> In place of the mead-hall and laughter of men

My only singing the sea-mew's call,
The scream of the gannet, the shriek of the gull;
Through the wail of the wild gale beating the bluffs
The piercing cry of the ice-coated petrel,
The storm-drenched eagle's echoing scream.
In all my wretchedness, weary and lone,
I had no comfort of comrade or kin. . . .
Yet still, even now, my spirit within me
Drives me seaward to sail the deep,
To ride the long swell of the salt sea-wave.
Never a day but my heart's desire
Would launch me forth on the long sea-path,
Fain of fair harbors and foreign shores.
Yet lives no man so lordly of mood,
So eager in giving, so ardent in youth,
So bold in his deeds, or so dear to his lord,
Who is free from dread in his far sea-travel,
Or fear of God's purpose and plan for his fate.

(*Moods*, 27–28)

Here we have it all in simple contiguity—cold, misery, and loneliness in an environment devoid of human comfort set against renewed wanderlust and the urge to sail, tempered by justifiable fear. A few lines later the word *haunted* appears, and that is perhaps the most appropriate summary of the combined lure and dread, love and hate, that characterizes seafarers' attitudes toward the unstable ocean that mirrors an equally mutable sky. Living at this interface always holds out the possibility of extraordinary experience. Thus it is not surprising to find Coleridge's Ancient Mariner haunted by his extraordinary tale, one that he must tell to an unwilling but mesmerized wedding guest ashore, or to understand the overpowering obsession that corrupts Captain Ahab's imagination.

All of these continuities of attitude, and many more, suggest that unique qualities in sea experience may, in part, account for the shape and persistent themes of voyage narratives. Such possibilities are best approached through questions. For example, in narratives so closely related to fact, to the tedium of daily routine on board ships at sea, and in a profession that constantly demands hardheaded realism and attention to detail, why are nostalgia, romance, and meditation so prevalent? To what extent does the linearity and episodic nature of voyaging determine patterns of narration? Are there any fundamental psychological elements present in all voyage experience, and if so, what are they? Some answers emerge from my own sea experience over forty years, buttressed by wide reading in the genre.

The environment of long sea passages promotes reflection in thoughtful seafarers. Once committed to the open sea, human beings are enclosed irrevocably by the minute world of the vessel in a vast surround. That world reverses many physical and social realities. Ashore, healthy human beings desire bodily movement and gain a sense of freedom and power through it; at sea, motion is imposed upon them, with temporary but debilitating effects. Again, many individuals ashore can join and leave groups at will, but at sea all are compressed within a single, unchanging society, and one traditionally marked by a rigid hierarchy at that. It is often possible to choose a solitary life ashore, or at least regulate contact with others, but at sea the absolute isolation of the ship makes adapting to the fixed society on board unavoidable. In this fragmentary but self-contained world, seafarers have time on

"In a heavy sea." *Century Magazine,* June 1882.
Courtesy of Mystic Seaport Museum.

their hands, and they spend much of it standing watch—literally watching the interaction of ship, wind, and sea while waiting for something, or nothing, to happen. Their world demands keen senses because they live on an unstable element that keeps their home in constant motion, sometimes soothing them with a false sense of security, sometimes threatening to destroy them.

Although the vision of those at sea is bounded by a horizon and contains a seascape of monotonous regularity, what is seen can change rapidly and unpredictably. Unlike the land, the sea never retains the impress of human civilization, so seafarers find their sense of space suggesting infinity and solitude on the one hand and prisonlike confinement on the other. That environment contains in its restless motion lurking possibilities of total disorientation: In a knockdown walls become floors, doors become hatches. In Conrad's magnificent novella *Typhoon*, an obtuse but orderly Captain MacWhirr first realizes that he may lose his ship not by watching the furious seas that engulf her but by going below and finding his cabin in total disarray.

The seafarer's sense of time is equally complex. It is both linear and cyclical: Time is linear in the sense that voyages have beginnings and endings, departures and landfalls, starting and stopping points in the unfolding of chronological time; yet time is also cyclical, just as the rhythm of waves is cyclical, because the pattern of a ship's daily routine, watch on and watch off, highlights endless recurrence. Space and time have always merged more obviously at sea than they do in much of human experience. The simple act of laying out a ship's track on a chart by using positions determined on successive days connects time and space visibly. The nautical mile, spatially equivalent to one minute of latitude, is also the basis of the knot, a measure of speed in elapsed time. Until late in the eighteenth century European navigators calculated their position by deduced reckoning, measuring the number of miles they had sailed a particular course by combining time and speed. The invention of reliable chronometers made more precise celestial navigation possible by interlocking measurements of time and space in a more sophisticated way. Before the era of electronic global positioning systems, to find longitude one had to have a precise reading of the time at Greenwich, England. Then to get an accurate fix of the ship's position, one added a spatial measurement by taking the altitude of the sun at noon or of a star at dawn or dusk. What wonder that mariners tended to be reflective when they had to deal with abstract time and celestial space just to find out where they were in the watery world? Control of such world-encompassing dimensions can lead to delusions, too, when it lures seafarers into manipulating navigational reality. Like one of the competitors in a single-handed race around the world in the 1960s, Owen Browne, protagonist of Robert Stone's *Outerbridge Reach*, fabricates false positions; when Browne can no longer "pursue the fiction of lines" and is weary "of pretending to locate himself in space and time," he jumps overboard.[7]

Voyages also suggest larger patterns of orientation because they have built-in directionality and purpose, an innate teleology. We embark on voyages not only to get somewhere but also to accomplish something and, in Western culture, often to discover more about the ways human beings can expect to fare in the world. The epic voyages of Odysseus, Jason, and Aeneas were freighted with metaphor as well as adventure, and that characteristic has clung to voyage narratives ever since. In this sense voyages are a natural vehicle for the human imagination exploring the unknown, whether it be discovering strange new lands, finding out the truth about ourselves, or searching for those more perfect worlds we call utopias. These purposes and intentions, as well as tension between the lure of new experience and the desire to get home, mark every stage of Odysseus's return from the Trojan War; as he recapitulates to Penelope the whole of his extraordinary voyage, he tells the first returning seaman's yarn in the Western world. Because the *Odyssey* spawned a host of literary patterns, it became an archetype of voyage narratives in Western literature, and the basic structure of the *nostos* or return, the long and difficult voyage, recurs down through the centuries to Conrad's *Nigger of the "Narcissus,"* the sea plays of Eugene O'Neill, and William Golding's Edmund Talbot trilogy (*Rites of Passage, Close Quarters,* and *Fire Down Below*).

In addition to exploration, discovery, and return, voyage narratives assimilate and develop many other literary paradigms. One is the hunt for a big fish, perhaps best exemplified in twentieth-century literature by Hemingway's classic, *The Old Man and the Sea*. When the pursued object is overtly symbolic, like the Golden Fleece in the voyage of the Argonauts, the hunt borrows the conventions of romance and is transformed into a quest. If those engaged in a pursuit endow a part of the natural world with supernatural powers and implications, the quest turns metaphysical and often becomes tragic; the most striking example in Western literature is, of course, *Moby-Dick*, with an obsessed Captain Ahab pursuing evil that he thinks is made incarnate in the form of a white whale.

Another frequent and natural pattern for voyage narratives is the anatomy of society, in which the small world of the ship serves as a microcosm of civilization as a whole. The usual action is a sudden increase in entropy, a revolution—or mutiny in shipboard terms; *Mutiny on the Bounty* and *The Caine Mutiny* represent a whole class of narratives. Self-contained, isolated, and organized as a rigid hierarchy, the ship is also a natural setting for exploring ethical dilemmas such as the conflict between virtue and authority (in Melville's *Billy Budd*) or the degeneration of a whole society (in Katherine Anne Porter's *Ship of Fools*, which develops the medieval motif of the world as a ship). Similarly, the voyage can provide a vehicle for getting to utopia—literally no place on earth—as in Jules Verne's *Twenty Thousand Leagues under the Sea*, or to dystopias, as in three of Gulliver's four voyages.

Initiation is a third important literary pattern developed within voyage narratives. In its simplest form, an initiation at sea puts a young person (usually a boy until recent decades) into an unfamiliar situation, tests his or her worth in a crisis, and rewards those who pass muster with full acceptance as adults. This is the design of Outward Bound schools, and it is reflected in much sea literature, like Kipling's *Captains Courageous*. More complex versions of the pattern are innumerable, including Apollonius of Rhodes's *Argonautica*, Smollet's *Roderick Random*, Marryat's *Mr. Midshipman Easy*, many of James Fenimore Cooper's sea novels, Dana's *Two Years Before the Mast*, Melville's *Redburn* and *White-Jacket*, Conrad's "Youth," Jack London's *Sea Wolf*, Stephen Crane's "The Open Boat," and scores of less well known but memorable sea Bildungsromane. The multitude of examples is not surprising, since life at sea removes the inexperienced youngster from the familiarity of shoreside places and provides a full range of potential tests—storm, fire, stranding, collision, falling from aloft or overboard, disease, starvation, sinking—all threatening injury or death.

When the test becomes more menacing and the probability of failure greater, the stakes change from growing up to risking moral destruction. This is the usual case in Conrad: Marlow nearly loses his own identity during the voyage to Kurtz's Inner Station; similarly, Lord Jim discovers a fatal "soft spot" in his character when he jumps from the bridge of a steamship that he thinks is sinking, just as Captain Whalley (of "The End of the Tether") does when he continues to navigate his ship while going blind. Sometimes the protagonist is an overaged innocent, like Conrad's Captain MacWhirr or Melville's Captain Delano, who can either ignore or survive exposure to the "destructive element." The usual archetype for such a dark initiation is descent, both obvious and as natural as a ship or person sinking to the bottom of the sea. In this way descents repeat myths of visiting the underworld—Odysseus in Hades or Jonah in a whale's belly—but such myths are usually displaced (i.e., made more naturalistic) in modern literature. The central scene in the storm section of Conrad's Nigger of the "Narcissus" is a descent into the deckhouse of a nearly capsized ship to rescue its source of dissension, James Wait; in the same way, the climactic scene in Melville's White-Jacket is a spectacular fall from high in the rigging deep into the sea.

Another archetype, immobilization, represents the more subtle threat of prolonged calm or stranding on the rocks and beaches of coastlines. Coleridge's Rime of the Ancient Mariner and Conrad's Shadow-Line depend upon the powerlessness of human effort and use many images of stagnation and stillness. Similarly, stranding gives the ship back to the land that produced her in an unnatural way; waves that a hull had parted now rip it to pieces, and those who swarm over the ship are no longer builders but wreckers bent upon booty. There is a whole subgenre of sea writing about shipwrecks and disasters in coastal regions, perhaps because at those dramatic moments the power and danger of the sea impinge upon the imagination of land dwellers. Gerard Manley Hopkins captures the irony of a storm stranding—the fact that the disaster takes place within sight of safety before witnesses powerless to help—in the magnificent stanzas of "The Wreck of the Deutschland."

These patterns and their modulations occur in all varieties of voyage narrative, whether they purport to be reportorial or fictitious. An unusually close relationship exists between historical accounts of voyages and literary fictions based on them—so close that it is often difficult to determine the purpose of the narrative by looking at its structure. Is Dana's *Two Years Before the Mast* a historical journal or a semifictional Bildungsroman? Sea narratives, whether claiming to report fact or project fiction, have remarkably similar configurations. They seem to be isomorphic with the experience of voyaging itself, in the sense that a map resembles the landscape it surveys. Some of the classics of sea literature have been forged nearly whole in the smithy of experience. This fact is immediately evident when we compare "Youth" (1902) with the details of Conrad's voyage on the *Palestine* from September 1881 until she sank in March 1883 or "The Open Boat" (1898) with "Stephen Crane's Own Story" (1897) of the sinking of the *Commodore*. The subtitle of Crane's powerful story makes the connection between voyage experience and sea fiction explicit: "A Tale Intended to Be after the Fact, Being the Experience of Four Men from the Sunk Steamer *Commodore*." Such parallels lead to a central aesthetic question: Is form somehow natural or inherent in the voyage experience itself rather than imposed on it by the writer? And, to the extent that such a hypothesis applies, does built-in form somehow explain the extraordinary power of voyage narratives? Such questions loose theoretical issues of mimesis and narration that are far more unruly than Aeolus's bag of winds; they lie beyond the scope of this introduction and would keep us from ever reaching Ithaca if we faced them in general terms. But they will reappear in discussions of specific incidents and narrative sequences in the chapters that follow, where a more limited context can provide some firm and suggestive answers. And we can begin with one general principle.

Clearly, historical and literary voyage narratives are often nearly identical in structure and substance: Usually no clear demarcation exists between fact and fiction, experience and imagination. Among narrative forms, voyages cling to the inescapable realities of life at sea, on the one hand, and simultaneously project human desires and fantasies on the other. They record strenuous human enterprise, serve as emblems of the course of life, and, in ambitious narratives like the *Odyssey* or *Moby-Dick*, leap back and forth between a precise rendering of events in the sea world and moral or metaphysical interpretations of that world. Midway between literature and history lies Richard Henry Dana's classic voyage narrative, *Two Years Before the Mast*, which sometimes reads like pure reportage, sometimes like fiction, but most frequently shares the conventions of both. When Dana describes his seaman's competence and pride in sending down a royal yard, for example, this initiation rite has literary outlines but is full of detail incomprehensible to anyone lacking specialized knowledge of sailing-ship rigging. Again, when Captain Thompson flogs an innocent seaman, the incident is an accurate report of an event at sea but could be transformed into a short story without any substantial change.

Dana also develops the sea meditation, a mode of reverie found throughout voyage narratives and essays on seafaring, from the *Odyssey* to *The Mirror of the Sea* and Hilaire Belloc's *On Sailing the Sea*. The sea meditation springs from one segment in the broad essay genre; it stands with feet planted firmly in everyday reality on board ship and has a head stuffed with metaphor and fancy. Ashore the tradition flourished for centuries in authors as various as Montaigne and Pascal, Ruskin and Carlyle, Emerson and Thoreau; such writers share the impulse to connect quotidian detail with larger intuitions, either by burrowing within an observation or leaping from it in flashes of illumination. At sea the meditation or reverie is nourished by the immensity of the ocean, isolation, and ample time for reflection. With strong roots in Dana, Melville, and Conrad, it has been prolific in twentieth-century writers such as Alan Villiers, H. M. Tomlinson, John Muir, Jan de Hartog, Hilaire Belloc, Joshua Slocum, and Peter Matthiessen. Often it is intermixed with narration, momentarily suppressing the energy of unfolding events. Thus in *Two Years Before the Mast* we hear Dana musing on the barrenness of sunrise at sea, the breathing of whales, the vacuum caused by a death at sea, the beauty of ships, the boredom of gales, and dozens of other subjects. Two brief excerpts from these meditations capture the essence of the mode, a sudden stillness that suspends action without eliminating it, much like Keats's frozen movement in "Ode on a Grecian Urn":

> Much has been said of the sun-rise at sea; but it will not compare with the sun-rise on shore. It wants the accompaniments of the songs of birds, the awakening hum of men, and the glancing of the first beams

14

upon trees, hills, spires, and house-tops, to give it life and spirit. But though the actual rise of the sun at sea is not so beautiful, yet nothing will compare with the early breaking of day upon the wide ocean. There is something in the first grey streaks stretching along the eastern horizon and throwing an indistinct light upon the face of the deep, which combines with the boundlessness and unknown depth of the sea around you, and gives one a feeling of loneliness, of dread, and of melancholy foreboding, which nothing else in nature can give. This gradually passes away as the light grows brighter, and when the sun comes up, the ordinary monotonous sea day begins.[8]

* * *

Death is at all times solemn, but never so much so as at sea. A man dies on shore; his body remains with his friends, and "the mourners go about the streets"; but when a man falls overboard at sea and is lost, there is a suddenness in the event, and a difficulty in realizing it, which give to it an air of awful mystery. A man dies on shore—you follow his body to the grave, and a stone marks the spot. You are often prepared for the event. There is always something which helps you to realize it when it happens, and to recall it when it has passed. A man is shot down by your side in battle, and the mangled body remains an object, and a real evidence; but at sea, the man is near you—at your side—you hear his voice, and in an instant he is gone, and nothing but a vacancy shows his loss. Then, too, at sea—to use a homely but expressive phrase—you miss a man so much. A dozen men are shut up together in a little bark, upon the wide, wide sea, and for months and months see no forms and hear no voices but their own, and one is taken suddenly from among them, and they miss him at every turn. It is like losing a limb. There are no new faces or new scenes to fill up the gap. There is always an empty berth in the forecastle, and one man wanting when the small night watch is mustered. There is one less to take the wheel, and one less to lay out with you upon the yard. You miss his form, and the sound of his voice, for habit had made them almost necessary to you, and each of your senses feels the loss. (*Two Years*, 77)

Although sea meditations are often contained within large and powerful narrative structures—voiced by Ishmael in *Moby-Dick* and Marlow in *Lord Jim*—where they are intertwined with the advance of the story, sometimes they become the container themselves. One notable example is *The Mirror of the Sea*, growing from an impulse that Conrad describes in letters as "the wonderfulness of things, events, people—when looked back upon" and "an imaginative rendering of a reminiscent mood."[9] The impulse is emblematic, and it suppresses narrative energy throughout, with the exception of two autobiographical sections on rescuing the crew of a sinking ship ("Initiation") and a smuggling expedition along the Spanish coast ("The *Tremolino*"). Both are encased in meditation, and throughout *The Mirror* incidents become exempla; their complications are pared away and their growing room is confined by the point they are meant to illustrate. In many ways the structure of the whole book resembles that of a classical elegy on departed ships—beginning with connections between death and time, moving to shared experiences of prowess demonstrated and difficulty overcome, then to expressing grief at lives cut short, resting momentarily in two versions of completed voyages, reaching a climax with poignant reflections on the meaning of death for the speaker, and closing with the celebration of a continuing maritime tradition.

In his introduction to *The Oxford Book of Sea Stories*, Tony Tanner remarks, "I was surprised during my researches to discover how much writing about the sea is either autobiographical or historical—how we finally sailed to there, or the voyage of the Something. It almost seems as if fiction is pre-empted, unnecessary."[10] It would be easy to illustrate how closely great voyage stories by writers like Melville, Conrad, Crane, London, and Hemingway conform to the conditions and structures of experience at sea, but it may be more intriguing to glance the other way and ask how much supposedly factual accounts of real voyages are driven by narrative conventions that have their ultimate source in literature. In journals the linearity of the ship's progression is infused with human purpose, and the regularity of chronological time is compressed or expanded to dramatize shipboard events. Hakluyt's *Voyages* are filled with sea meditations, as are accounts written by later voyagers, even those with a scientific bent like Cook and Darwin.

These literary features seem even more remarkable when we consider the impetus for voyage accounts: For three centuries, from early Portuguese voyages down the west coast of Africa through Cook's exploration of the Pacific, voyage narratives had enormous economic, political, and military implications. They were gobbled up as eagerly as the latest exposés of wrongdoing in high places are now, and pirated editions, often inaccurate and sensational, set a precedent for the journalistic excesses of Fleet

Street. These were the centuries during which global geography was first being charted, and voyage narratives provided crucial intelligence that would be classified secret by most governments today. Yet map making, too, as David Fausett notes, "was suffused with fictional elements, and fiction confused with fact; both being largely dependent on hearsay reports. . . . Indeed, the transporting of 'local truths' to other places lies at the very origins of fiction; the earliest known work of which is an Egyptian fragment about a maritime adventure."[11] At the beginning of this era of global voyaging, in the accounts collected by Hakluyt, all sorts of semifantastical stories about peoples and customs in newly discovered parts of the world were accepted at face value; at the end, a cautious James Cook and his scientific entourage were annoyed at partial and inaccurate publications that preceded the authorized accounts of his voyages. Still, the streams of fiction and fact never separated entirely in the voyage narratives of later centuries and probably never will. Since such accounts are in part the maritime autobiographies of the writer, the Danas and Slocums out there cannot avoid emphasizing, suppressing, and sometimes reordering the events of their voyages. Before Robert Stone's protagonist in the fictional *Outerbridge Reach* begins fabricating his navigational positions, he asserts that the established conventions of the genre mask the truth in accounts by solitary sailors: "The authors all sounded alike. He suspected them of cribbing from each other. . . . They are writing about what cannot be fully described, Browne thought. They reduced things and provided no more than what they knew was expected" (*Outerbridge Reach*, 248).

In voyage narratives, the relationships between history and literature, autobiography and fiction, are too complicated to be unsnarled by any simple dichotomy between fact and invention. The first problem for most readers is establishing a context for interpretation. The world of commercial sailing ships has disappeared almost entirely, apart from a few remnants—the genuine tall ships and schooners converted to the sailing cruise trade and a few new experimental "windships" that hoist and furl sails by computer automation. Steamships and transatlantic liners are also relics of the more recent past, and for most readers the contemporary ocean world dominated by supertankers and container ships is remote and strange. As cruise ships grow larger and more luxurious to meet a booming demand, they remove passengers even farther from any perception of the realities of seafaring and distract them with constant entertainment. Such changes have eroded direct knowledge of the sea, ships, and seafaring among the American public, with unfortunate political and economic consequences for support of the fisheries, the merchant marine, and the law of the sea. But for readers of voyage narratives the consequences can be summed up more simply as lack of context. At the beginning of our century, Conrad could assume a partially shared context with his readers in the opening sentence of "Youth": "This could have occurred nowhere but in England, where men and sea interpenetrate, so to speak—the sea entering into the life of most men, and the men knowing something or everything about the sea, in the way of amusement, of travel, or of bread-winning."[12] Quite simply, that is no longer true, either in Britain or America.

Part of the missing context is historical, consisting of very specialized segments of knowledge totally outside the compass of the best general education one could imagine. From the fifteenth through the nineteenth centuries, such knowledge would include the objectives and methods of Prince Henry's school of navigation at Sagres, Portugal; the medieval cosmology and geography that was part of Columbus's intellectual baggage; the devastating effects of scurvy on Admiral Anson's circumnavigation and Cook's efforts to prevent it during his own voyages; the struggle to calculate longitude at sea and the development of accurate chronometers; the opening of the Suez Canal in 1870 and the subsequent decline of sailing ships as ocean carriers when steamships became more economical; the Plimsoll controversies about overloading and undermanning ships; and the systematic exploitation of crimps, who sold entrapped seamen to ships needing crew for an advance against their future wages after they had run up bills they could not pay ashore.

The missing context would also include the technological history of ships—for example, the balance between an efficient size for maneuverability and the needed size for economic return, as well as the gradual evolution from wood to iron and steel construction and from sail to steam and diesel propulsion. Another important context is linguistic: the detailed and precise technical vocabulary needed for handling complicated ships, especially under sail. Many passages in Dana are incomprehensible without such knowledge, and others in Conrad are often misunderstood for lack of it. Voyage narratives cannot be fully appreciated apart from some of this background, so their study is linked to maritime history. Other helpful and often missing contexts are experiential. Readers who have never lived at sea may not comprehend the psychological effects of the simultaneous confinement and exposure that all seamen endure. Similarly, they may not understand the physics or mechanics of seamanship well enough to interpret the meaning of what seamen do or fail to do.

Such contexts, both historical and experiential, affect our reading of voyage narratives in three important particulars: understanding the functions of nautical character types, the significance of action at sea, and the reliability of narration. From the Restoration onward, sailor types abound in anecdotes, caricatures, ballads, sketches, plays, and novels. Familiar types include the jolly tar, the picaresque rogue in naval togs, the hawse-hole captain who goes to sea as a ship's boy and climbs to command, the bully mate, the brawny bo's'n, the stowaway, the jinx, the landlubber greenhorn, the wise old seaman mentor, the ancient mariner who must tell his tale ashore, the malingerer, the handsome sailor, the coal heaver, the oiler, and others. The list is lengthy because work roles on board ship are very tightly defined, necessarily, and any elaboration or deviation is instantly noticeable. Some have become stereotypes, the butt of ridicule, like the jolly tar whose drunken revels resound throughout the world's ports, or the harsh but good-hearted hawse-hole captain who brings his sea ways and lingo ashore to the amusement of all. In Restoration and eighteenth-century drama we meet Captain Manly in Wycherly's "The Plain Dealer," Ben Legend in Congreve's "Love for Love," and a whole cast of nautical characters in Shadwell's "The Fair Quaker of Deal"—Commodore Flip, Captains Worth and Mizen, Midshipman Derrick, Jack Hatchway, and Dick Binnacle. As the novel grew in importance throughout the eighteenth century, its nautical characters included Daniel Defoe's buccaneer, Captain Singleton, and a host of figures from Tobias Smollett's *Roderick Random* and *Peregrine Pickle*—Captain Oakum, Lieutenant Tom Bowling, Jack Rattlin, Commodore Hawser Trunion, Lieutenant Hatchway, and Boatswain Pipes. In the early nineteenth century Frederick Marryat continued the tradition of the naval novel in Smollett's wake, again using young midshipman protagonists like Peter Simple and Jack Easy to survey whole shiploads of seagoing types. The nautical names of these characters reveal their springs of motivation—almost like the humours of Renaissance drama—and determine their responses to a series of encounters, both afloat and ashore. Although exaggeration often clothes these sea types in literary settings, they do grow from real persons and frequently repeated human situations at sea.

Most of the playwrights and novelists who used sailors had some experience at sea, but when Sir Walter Scott wrote *The Pirate* (1822) his unfamiliarity with seamen and ships spurred James Fenimore Cooper to write *The Pilot* (1824) as an antidote. Thus began the tradition of American sea fiction, and Cooper's 12 sea novels produced a string of memorable characters, including captains like Tuck and Daggett and seamen like Long Tom Coffin and Boltrope. More important was a sea change in the conception of character itself. The gallery of sea eccentrics who display their oddities in shore society gave way to extended portraits of multifaceted seamen who are enmeshed in a compressed and isolated shipboard society and who face not only the ills of that society but larger issues raised by precarious human interaction with the sea. In an essay recognizing the influence of Marryat and Cooper on his own work, Conrad "surrenders" to both but notes the difference between the novelist of the Royal Navy and his American counterpart: "In his [Cooper's] sea tales the sea inter-penetrates with life; it is in a subtle way a factor in the problem of existence, and for all its greatness, it is always in touch with the men, who, bound on errands of war or gain, traverse its immense solitudes."[13] Cooper only began to realize the full potential of complex characters acting within an immense, totally fluid environment of sea and sky, but others followed, including Dana's persona in *Two Years Before the Mast*, Melville's Ahab, Ishmael, and "Starry" Vere, Conrad's Lord Jim and Marlow, Hemingway's Santiago, Golding's Edmund Talbot, McPhee's Captain Washburn, and Matthiessen's Raib Avers.

In this evolution of sea fiction and nonfiction, largely begun in America but transported back to Britain as well, type characters did not disappear but were transformed. Some have important narrative functions to perform: The stowaway and the jinx serve as the intruder and the scapegoat in shipboard society, and the bully mate becomes the enforcer of rigid rules that encroach upon the crew's slender margin of freedom. Yet others, like the green hand or neophyte, become the central figures who grow to manhood at sea; they usually cross class barriers as soon as they set foot in the forecastle and need the help of the older seamen who become their mentors. This is the familiar narrative pattern of the sea Bildungsroman, seen in its simplest form in novels like Melville's *Redburn* and Kipling's *Captains Courageous*. Some highly specialized types that belong to a specific era of seafaring upset the equilibrium of shipboard society and provide the central impetus of the narrative. The malingerer (the seaman who shirked and dodged all the hard work on sailing ships because he was paid by the day no matter what he did) often became the focus of hatred tinged with envy, the disturbing role both Donkin and Wait play in Conrad's *Nigger of the "Narcissus."* The handsome sailor, on the other hand, is the very stuff of the young hero, combining physical beauty and seamanlike competence with the simple goodness of the untutored "natural man" who is undefiled by the ways of the world. He appears again and again in sea narratives and in sea experience. Dana describes one he met in Monterey:

He had been at sea from a boy, having served a regular apprenticeship of seven years, as all English sailors are obliged to do, and was then about four or five and twenty. He was tall; but you only perceived it when he was standing by the side of others, for the great breadth of his shoulders and chest made him appear but little above the middle height. His chest was as deep as it was wide; his arm like that of Hercules; and his hand "the fist of a tar—every hair a rope yarn." With all this he had one of the pleasantest smiles I ever saw. . . . He had a good deal of information, and his captain said he was a perfect seaman, and worth his weight in gold on board a vessel, in fair weather and in foul. His strength must have been immense, and he had the sight of a vulture. It is strange that one should be so minute in the description of an unknown, outcast sailor, whom one may never see again, and whom no one may care to hear about; but so it is. Some people we see under no remarkable circumstances, but whom, for some reason or other, we never forget. He called himself Bill Jackson; and I know no one of all my accidental acquaintances to whom I would more gladly give a shake of the hand than to him. Whoever falls in with him will find a handsome, hearty fellow, and a good shipmate. (*Two Years*, 134–35)

Melville had also met such men and remembered them well enough to build the characters of Bulkington and Billy Budd. In *Rites of Passage*, Golding inverts the type with Billy Rogers, also a foretopman, and gives him the clever malice of a Claggart. Clearly, in these last instances and many others, the focus has shifted from the surface appearance of sailors to their innate characteristics.

The second missing context for many readers of voyage narratives is both historical and experiential: enough knowledge of seamanship to understand the implications of action at sea. That context includes what sailors do and fail to do in moments of stress, when specific acts are most noticeable, but has far larger implications as the substance of their work. In its broadest sense, seamanship encompasses everything one must know and do to move vessels safely from one port to another. It is a learned body of knowledge derived from past experience, applied physics, naval architecture, and marine engineering; it requires many specific skills in operating and maintaining machinery, handling boats, anchors, booms, winches, and (in recent years) using electronic equipment, as well as a working knowledge of tides, currents, wave formations, weather patterns, aids to navigation, and rules of the road. Above all it is an art demanding foresight, initiative, the ability to improvise, a sense of proportion, and finely tuned judgment as seafarers deal with an unpredictable ocean. The practice of seamanship requires precision in the use of an extensive technical vocabulary, scrupulosity in the maintenance of hull, spars, sails, engines, and equipment, reliability in following established routines, alertness to changing conditions at sea, and readiness to cope with emergencies quickly and decisively. And because the sea is neither totally predictable nor tolerant of human mistakes, the practice of seamanship is often complex, demanding imagination and discrimination more than adherence to fixed rules of procedure. Conrad excoriates those who believe that technology can tame the sea in his vitriolic essays about the loss of the *Titanic*:

> The new seamanship! . . . The proper handling of an unsinkable ship, you see, will demand that she should be made to hit the iceberg very accurately with her nose, because should you perchance scrape the

bluff of the bow instead, she may, without ceasing to be as unsinkable as before, find her way to the bottom. I congratulate the future Transatlantic passengers on the new and vigorous sensations in store for them. They shall go bounding across from iceberg to iceberg at twenty-five knots with precision and safety, and a "cheerful bumpy sound," as the immortal poem has it. It will be a teeth-loosening, exhilarating experience. (*Notes*, 240)

Not many years ago I got a taste of the new seamanship in nearly identical circumstances, apart from the "cheerful bumpy sound." On a morning visit to the bridge of a transatlantic liner, I learned that we had roared through a field of icebergs at 28 knots the night before, depending upon radar to avoid them; I was also told that it would take seven miles to stop the ship at that speed.

Two brief examples will illustrate the difficulties readers face in judging acts of seamanship. One is understanding the significance of "hard driving" in sailing vessels, by no means an arcane question since ocean racers still make decisions every day about how much sail they can carry to maximize speed without risking knockdown or dismasting. In *Two Years Before the Mast* Dana both celebrates the thrill of pushing a ship to its limit and describes the mess that ensues when sails blow out and spars break. Again, in *The Mirror of the Sea* Conrad recalls a very dangerous instance of hard driving with a fair wind in thick weather; the sky cleared just as the ship had run up to the rocky coast of the Isle of Wight. Narrowly considered, how much sail to carry was a judgment call based on the captain's experience and knowledge of his ship, but such decisions were often made in wider contexts.

Captains of sailing ships had obligations and desires that were not easily reconciled: The safety of the ship, the welfare of the crew, the profit of the owner and charterer, and the progress of a career did not always mesh neatly. Conflict between these interests was normal in sailing-ship voyages during the nineteenth century. A remarkably fast passage would establish a captain's reputation and lead to a more lucrative command; it would also reduce the owner's operating costs and attract paying passengers; similarly, it would give the charterer a chance to beat competitors to commodity markets with cargo, thereby increasing its price. Yet by pressing the ship hard—carrying sail to the limits that hull and rigging would stand, and beyond—the captain risked both ship and men. Crew members gained no advantage from a fast passage because they were paid by the day. Since they had less chance of surviving their work on a deck awash with heavy seas or on wildly swaying yards aloft when the ship was driven hard, they tended to oppose a captain's penchant for "lugging sail"—no matter how much they might admire his daring. And most captains knew that pushing a ship too hard did not make her go much faster. By calculating the displacement and drag of a sailing vessel's hull, naval architects can establish its maximum speed. Beyond that maximum, additional power is counterbalanced by a sharp rise in surface friction, so no matter how much sail is "cracked on," the ship cannot overcome increased drag. Thus what seems to be a simple, everyday decision can in fact be quite complicated, with technical, professional, economic, and moral dimensions.

As a second example shows, the advent of steam and diesel power changed the terms of a captain's decisions but did not eliminate conflicts of interest. The focal point of Herman Wouk's *Caine Mutiny* occurs in the midst of a typhoon, setting the necessities of seamanship against naval orders. When Captain Queeg refuses to change the course of his destroyer until the task force commander orders him to do so, the First Lieutenant, Maryk, relieves him of command and sets a new course that has a better chance of preventing a capsize in desperate sea conditions. The situation is dramatically loaded but not contrived; four destroyers did in fact roll over in a typhoon during World War II, with the loss of many lives. In general terms, seamanship is hardly ever just a matter of knowledge, technique, and following the rules; like any craft or art, it often reveals the character of the practitioner. As the primary form of action in voyage narratives, seamanship acquires far more central human and symbolic significance, representing a modicum of power and control in the sometimes chaotic ocean universe.

Lack of historical or experiential context can mislead us in a third way. Whether we are reading Columbus or Dana, Melville or Conrad, we need to be wary about the reliability of narration for two reasons. The first is simple: We were not on board ship for the voyages they describe, and unless we have been on similar ventures we are likely to lean too heavily on what the narrator tells us. We cannot draw paradigms for shipboard life, especially in former ages, from experience in cities, towns, villages, farms—or even from expeditions into desert, jungle, or mountain terrain. Also, voyaging has always fostered fantasy, and the tradition of lying about what one has done goes back to Odysseus, who invents new and extravagant lies whenever he comes ashore to deal with strangers. That tradition persisted through the age of discovery, as a reading of many of the voyage accounts collected by Hakluyt demonstrates; the writers seldom hold to firm discriminations between fact and fantasy and often reach nonexistent islands inhabited by strange creatures. As noted earlier, voyage narratives are persistently autobiographical, whether or not they pretend to be fictional, and that leads to the second reason for wariness: The writer usually has other agendas. This is most obvious in historical voyage narratives: Columbus has to please Queen Isabella, Cook is writing an official report, Dana is taking up the cause of common seamen against captains and owners, and even the disarmingly laconic Joshua Slocum is trying to eke out a living by relating his adventures in lectures and books.

In fiction the case is more complex and the agendas more hidden, but it is noteworthy that many voyage tales have central figures like Ishmael or Marlow as participant narrators. The paradigm here is Coleridge's Ancient Mariner, who must tell his own magical tale to listeners who will not recognize its kernel of truth. Also taking us to worlds unconstrained by ordinary seafaring experience, often at the poles of the earth, Poe's narrators vanish within their own tales. Melville uses Ishmael to relate improbable sequences of events at sea after taking great care to project them from meticulously realistic descriptions. Even Conrad—intellectually and aesthetically committed to truth-telling—was far more comfortable after he had found Marlow to give him some sea room for meditation. Perhaps the common thread is the need for meditation, a form of mediation between the direct and accurate report of experience at sea and the many speculations and fancies that sea experience generates. Appearance and reality merge in strange ways at sea, leading to mistaken perceptions of human nature or nautical reality; thus we are not surprised to find Captain Delano misreading all the signs of disorder on board the *San Dominick* or Lord Jim equating a bulging bulkhead with a sinking *Patna*. As readers of voyage narratives, we need to listen to the narrating voices, whether embodied in characters or omniscient, without assuming that they convey the whole truth. The events such voices unfold have contexts of their own, either buried in details within the texts or standing outside them in the conditions of voyaging during various eras. This volume brings those contexts to bear on the interpretation of some major voyage narratives in the Western tradition.

The sea has been a "place" of extraordinary importance in the evolution of Western culture. It has encompassed human beings during major movements of expanded awareness—the Greek colonization westward through the Mediterranean during the Archaic era; the Portuguese explorations of the South Atlantic, at first tentative, then bold; the early Spanish voyages to the Indies; Renaissance circumnavigations of the world; explorations of the Pacific during the eighteenth century; polar expeditions to the Arctic and Antarctic during the nineteenth and early twentieth centuries; and undersea exploration to profound depths of the ocean in recent decades. From the Odyssey to the present, it has served as a place for literary portraits of adventure and disaster, for quests, hunts, and tests of human endurance.Throughout all centuries, unlike the land, the sea has been a constant for those who sailed on it, variable in mood but unchanging in essence: a place with a character much like that attributed to Poseidon, by turns both placid and turbulent, serene and menacing. For seafarers, these are the defining dimensions of their place, largely unchanged since the first separation of earth and water.

Chapter 2

Navigation and the Oral
Tradition: *The Odyssey*

When Odysseus finally reaches Ithaca after one decade
fighting at Troy and another wandering about the
Mediterranean, he must establish his identity and clear
his house of the pestilent suitors before he can be reunited with
Penelope. With that accomplished, the next thing he does is characteristic of the oral tradition: He tells her and retells us the tale
of his long voyage home:

He launched in with how he fought the Cicones down,
then how he came to the Lotus-eaters' lush green land.
Then all the crimes of the Cyclops and how he paid him back
for the gallant men the monster ate without a qualm—
then how he visited Aeolus, who gave him a hero's welcome
then he sent him off, but the homeward run was not his fate,
not yet—some sudden squalls snatched him away once more
and drove him over the swarming sea, groaning in despair.
Then how he moored at Telepylus, where Laestrygonians
wrecked his fleet and killed his men-at-arms.
He told her of Circe's cunning magic wiles
and how he voyaged down in his long benched ship

to the moldering House of Death, to consult Tiresias,
ghostly seer of Thebes, and he saw old comrades there
and he saw his mother, who bore and reared him as a child.
He told how he caught the Sirens' voices throbbing in the wind
and how he had scudded past the Clashing Rocks, past grim Charybdis,
past Scylla— whom no rover had ever coasted by, home free—
and how his shipmates slaughtered the cattle of the Sun
and Zeus the king of thunder split his racing ship
with a reeking bolt and killed his hardy comrades,
all his fighting men at a stroke, but he alone
escaped their death at sea. He told how he reached
Ogygia's shores and the nymph Calypso held him back,
deep in her arching caverns, craving him for a husband—
cherished him, vowed to make him immortal, ageless, all his days,
yes, but she never won the heart inside him, never . . .
then how he reached the Phaeacians—heavy sailing there—
who with all their hearts had prized him like a god
and sent him off in a ship to his own beloved land,
giving him bronze and hoards of gold and robes.

(Odyssey 23: 354–84)

At this point in reading the *Odyssey* we know the story in so much greater detail that the synopsis seems irrelevant, but if we were listening rather than reading, the repetition would be a welcome jog to memory. Text spatializes the narrative and lets us revisit any part of it by merely flipping the pages, whereas recitation demands frequent recall of material that is otherwise lost in fade-out as we keep listening. Like other oral epics, the *Odyssey* is filled with all kinds of repetitive, mnemonic devices related to its composition and fluidity—epithets, images, similes, metrical formulae—that enable an improvising teller to keep the story moving. In a recited text, those tags of oral improvisation help us to recall details of a long story as we are absorbed in transitory moments of listening attention. And it is a long story: Robert Fitzgerald estimates that Homeric performance would have taken about six sessions of four hours each.[1] In modern terms, retelling parts of the story is comparable to using melodic motifs in opera; as well as identifying characters, such motifs serve both to recall past events and to place them in new contexts of action, thereby creating resonances and amplifying the themes of the narrative.

Odysseus is a master at telling and retelling—and sometimes lying about—his adventures, first as a precaution when he meets strangers and later as a means of gaining status through the fame that has preceded him. When asked to identify himself by Arete, the queen of the Phaeacians, Odysseus circumspectly abbreviates the adventures one would expect to hear from a seafarer—the shipwrecks that brought him to Calypso's island and to the shores of Phaeacia—without directly revealing who he is (7:277–341). After the bard Demodocus has told his third story about the Trojan War before the Phaeacian court, a visibly weeping Odysseus meets a second inquiry about who he is from King Alcinous. He cannot dodge this request and unequivocally identifies himself:

> I am Odysseus, son of Laertes, known to the world
> for every kind of craft—my fame has reached the skies.
> Sunny Ithaca is my home.
>
> (9: 21–23)

Then he launches into the tale of his voyage home from Troy, beginning with the raid on the Cicones and ending with the shipwreck that brings him to Calypso's island (Books 9–12).

Thus Odysseus becomes the first-person storyteller of the largest part of the wanderings, a circuitous return from Troy to Ithaca that probably encompasses much of the central Mediterranean. In form his story is a *nostos,* a traditional oral tale of difficulties encountered by heroes as they try to return home after exploits in foreign parts. Odysseus's self-told nostos is central to the complex structure of the epic but is not the only voyage tale in the *Odyssey.* It is preceded by Telemachus's voyage to Pylos in search of his father, a rite of passage for the untested young man (Books 2–4). While in Pylos Telemachus hears the first of three overlapping versions of the heroes' return voyage; Nestor recounts the squabbles and false starts in the departure from Troy, his own speedy and uneventful return, and the fates of Agamemnon and Menelaus (Book 3). When Telemachus visits Sparta seeking further news of his father, Menelaus retells what we have just heard from Nestor in far greater detail, his own nostos of seven years voyaging through the eastern Mediterranean, in many ways an antipodal version of Odysseus's wanderings farther westward (Book 4). At the same time Menelaus tells more about the end of Agamemnon's voyage and fatal ambush, a story that recalls another part of the oral cycle, the assembly of the great fleet at Aulis in Boeotia and the difficulties associated with the voyage to Troy (*Iliad*, Book 2). He also recounts some of Odysseus's exploits at Troy and provides a glimpse of the missing hero's whereabouts wrested from Proteus. An abrupt switch to that location, Calypso's Ogygia, finds Odysseus building a boat to undertake another calamitous leg of his voyage home, one that ends in shipwreck and swimming to the shore of Phaeacia (Book 5). Thus by the time Odysseus begins telling his full tale to the assembled Phaeacians, we already know a good part of it, and we can assume that the original listeners would know much more, if not all. Within that extended first-person narration there are also further retellings, notably Circe's lengthy and detailed instructions on how to navigate the hazards ahead (12: 41–153), immediately followed by Odysseus's account of the events themselves. We are hardly prepared for the disclaimer that closes this long recitation:

> Why cover the same ground again?
> Just yesterday, here at hall, I told you all the rest,
> you and your gracious wife. It goes against my grain
> to repeat a tale told once, and told so clearly.
>
> (12: 488–91)

Even while we are reading the *Odyssey* as a text, we are always immersed in an oral world, hearing voices tell us what we already partly know once again, with variations and elaborations. The epic seems to surround us, lacking clear demarcations of before and after, reverberating always in the present tense of its telling. As modern readers alert to the distortions and lapses of first-person narration and to Odysseus's propensity for lying, we are always uneasy about the authenticity of the tale. On first reaching Ithaca he creates a false version of his wanderings, telling Athena, who is disguised as a shepherd, that he has been dropped there by Phoenicians. She chides him in a remarkable passage that connects lying and storytelling:

> Any man—any god who met you—would have to be
> some champion lying cheat to get past *you*
> for all-round craft and guile! You terrible man,

foxy, ingenious, never tired of twists and tricks—
so, not even here, on native soil, would you give up
those wily tales that warm the cockles of your heart!
Come, enough of this now. We're both old hands
at the arts of intrigue. Here among mortal men
you're far the best at tactics, spinning yarns,
and I am famous among the gods for wisdom,
cunning wiles, too.

(13: 329–39)

This is only the first of many ingenious versions of his voyage
invented by a disguised Odysseus after his return to Ithaca; the
longest, told to his old retainer, the swineherd Eumaeus, parallels
the wanderings of Menelaus (14: 220–407). Although pure fiction, nothing in it is implausible in the context of Mediterranean
seafaring in the eighth century B.C., and it connects clearly with
the legends of the Trojan expedition some five centuries earlier.
Thus experience and fiction, tradition and invention, meld in the
first extended voyage narrative of the Western world.

The complexity of multiple and fragmented narration used in
just setting forth the wanderings—not to speak of equally sophisticated techniques that order the more compressed homecom-
ing—is worthy of a Joseph Conrad or a Henry James, and it is
astounding in the fluid context of oral composition. That is probably the only way the epic did exist—as a relatively open sequence of legendary episodes that could be remolded in performance—for two centuries. There is a huge gap between its
probable date of composition (ca. 750–725 B.C.) and its codification into a single version under the direction of Peisistratus (ca.
530 B.C.), although the role that the newly imported technology
of writing might have played in its composition and transmission
is unclear.[2] Like the *Iliad*, it was part of an epic cycle dealing with
the Trojan War composed between the eighth and sixth centuries
B.C., a cycle not mentioned until the second century A.D.; meager
non-Homeric fragments of the cycle do survive. The codification
of the Homeric epics in text did not stop oral recitation, which
continued, both at the Panathenaean festival and by groups of
professional rhapsodists like the Homerids on the island of
Chios, a possible birthplace of the poet.

Two other kinds of oral tradition contribute to the substance of
the long voyage home. The first is sailor's lore—yarns, folktales,

wind magic. Denys Page argues that the framework of the wanderings rests on 10 folktales. These folktales are about barbaric peoples, like the Cyclopes who neither raise grain nor build ships; about dangers, like the rocks of the Sirens, the cliff of the monster Scylla, and the maelstrom of Charybdis; about the magic that allows Circe to turn men into swine or about the power of nature confined in a bag of winds. Page sees the folktales as "set in the real world, and blended with past and present realities.... The world of the *Odyssey* is largely a world within the experience and knowledge, or at least the belief, of its audience."[3]

Sailors' yarns represent a specialized type of folktale; they spin exaggerations around a core of sea reality, and they share the fluidity of the oral tradition. They are outlandish only in the sense that they build around places that are new and strange, and that realm includes everything beyond the Aegean and Ionian seas known to Greek seafarers in the era of the epic's composition. Only the first episode of the wanderings—the raid on the Cicones—deals with fully human beings; in the rest Odysseus and his crews encounter beasts or monsters, immortals, sorcerers, or gods—the stuff of a good yarn. Magic substances and talismans abound, from the intoxicating lotus and the spell that transforms men into swine through the veil that saves Odysseus from drowning. Yet, after noting that Aeolus is not divine, Page ascribes the bag of winds "not to folklore but to life, a particular sphere of life in which magical arts are commonly employed"; he also reminds us that *The Golden Bough* documents 50 examples of wind magic, many of them from European sources (Page 76, 74). Attempts to induce or control winds are endemic to peoples who depend on them, surviving as superstitions through every era of sailing vessels into the twentieth century. Other scholars like Erich Auerbach have tried to define the nature of realism in the *Odyssey*, both in relation to sources in myth, folklore, and legend and to qualities of physical immediacy in description and action. Auerbach perceives "a delight in physical existence" and "a savory present, a present which sends strong roots down into social usages, landscape, and daily life" smoothly combined with legendary and miraculous material.[4]

For the sailor, landscape becomes a seascape created by wind and wave interspersed with islands, reefs, and coastline. In the era before charts and compasses, unusual or prominent topo-

Unforgettable seamarks for navigators in the Aeolian Islands.
Photo by Robert Foulke.

graphic features served as primary guides for line-of-sight navigation. Just as we easily anthropomorphize memorable geological formations into the Old Man of the Mountain (New Hampshire) or the Giant's Causeway (Northern Ireland), so ancient sailors invested extraordinary shapes with monsters, giants, and demigods. The Mediterranean is loaded with striking seamarks that would catch the attention of any alert navigator: the volcanic cones of Vesuvius and Aetna; the smoke that emerges every 16 minutes from the crater of Stromboli, an island flanked by an unmistakable pillar of rock resembling a dragon; the caldera of Santorini—so deep that no anchor finds bottom; the sheer cliff at the southern end of Capri that gives that island its distinctive profile; and a host of other individuating shapes that one can navigate by scattered throughout the Aegean, Ionian, Adriatic, and Tyrrhenian seas. Even in our age of electronic navigation, British Admiralty charts and coast pilots for the Mediterranean note these "remarkable" features. As the storm at Cape Malea blows Odysseus offshore to begin his wanderings, he takes his unintended departure from one of them, the huge egg-shaped rock of Ovo that lies off the southern end of Cythera.

Many of these seamarks are associated with episodes in the wanderings and still bear Odyssean names—Monte Circeo on the Tyrrhenian coast, the Aeolian Islands north of Sicily, the cliff of Scylla that marks one side of the northern entrance to the Straits of Messina—bringing the merger of stories and navigation full circle.

Just as folktales generate material in the *Odyssey*, so do the sailing directions handed down through ancient seafaring peoples of the Mediterranean—Egyptian, Minoan, Cycladic, Mycenaean, Phoenician, and Greek. Although there is no way of establishing a firm provenance for any *periplus*[5] before it was written down, such sailing directions probably evolved through oral transmission to meet the needs of navigators and merchants. The extant written versions often combine narratives with the practical navigational material that we expect to find in coast pilots—descriptions of coastal topography, seamarks, reefs, unusual local wind conditions, harbors, anchorages, sources of food and water, even local produce available as cargo for shipment home.

A contribution of the literate culture of Egypt, the earliest extant precursor of the periplus is the written account of a merchant voyage in the late twelfth century B.C. Wenamon, a high priest from Thebes, was commissioned to sail to Lebanon for a cargo of cedar, and his voyage is primarily a story of diplomatic and political mishaps, but it is also loaded with details about trading in Syrian waters.[6] Dominating most of Mediterranean trade from that time to Homer's era, the Phoenicians were close-mouthed and left little certain evidence of their extensive commercial and navigational intelligence. They had sailed westward at least as far as Carthage and Cadiz, well beyond the boundaries of Greek knowledge, and when Odysseus tells his lies about where he has been he claims to have sailed on Phoenician ships. Written *periploi,* either extant or reported in later accounts, appeared in the sixth century B.C. Herodotus alludes to voyages around Africa and to India, and ship captains from Marseilles and southwestern Spain describe coastal voyages beyond the Strait of Gibraltar along the Atlantic coasts of Africa and Europe.[7] The seminal literary voyages of the ancient world—especially those of Odysseus and Jason—replicate the circular form of periploi. Odysseus ranges widely through the Mediterranean before returning home, and Jason traces even wider arcs

The rock of Ovo off Cythera, Odysseus's last seamark in the known world of the
Aegean Sea.
Photo by Robert Foulke.

through the Black Sea and European rivers, repeating many of
Odysseus's adventures in the latter part of his circuit.

Those with a geographical bent can track Jason's route quite
precisely from Volos in Thessaly to the Kassandra Peninsula and
the island of Lemnos, through the Dardanelles, the Sea of Mar-

mara, and the Bosporos into the Black Sea, then along its southern shore to Colchis in Georgia, where Jason procures the golden
fleece with Medea's help; in 1987 geographer-adventurer Tim
Severin retraced this route in a replica of the Argo.[8] Jason's circuitous route home varies with each version of the story, starting
within the boundaries of each writer's geographical knowledge
but soon stretching beyond it to rivers that do not exist or to
impossible portages between ones that do. This blurred vision is
often attributed to Odysseus's voyage as well, but that is only
half the truth. Like Jason's voyage to Colchis, the voyage to Troy
and the first part of the voyage home can be tracked with geographical, navigational, and even meteorological precision worthy of the best periplus, combined with the dramatic tensions
embedded in the whole Trojan expedition.

As described in the Catalogue of Ships in Book 2 of the *Iliad*,
Agamemnon has assembled a vast fleet of 1,200 ships in the cove
of Aulis in Boeotia (near Chalcis). According to various traditions,
either strong headwinds or a calm kept the fleet and its restive
warriors at anchor for a long time awaiting the favorable wind
needed for the passage to Troy. That delay would be crucial in
any attempt to sail northeastward across the Aegean to Troy before
the prevailing summer Etesian winds (now called "meltemi") set
in, and it provided the seed of Agamemnon's troubles as later
tragedians told his story.[9] These winds would be dead against the
fleet's course to Troy, and they get stronger and more frequent as
the summer progresses, often blowing two or three weeks at a
time with only brief periods of respite before the next onslaught.
The voyage track from the cove of Aulis to Troy first passes
through the strong currents of the narrow strait between mainland Greece and the large island of Euboea at Chalcis, moves
northwestward through the Gulf of Euboea, turns northeast at
Cape Kinaion through the Orei and Trikeri Channels past the
Gulf of Volos, then continues northeastward through the
Northern Sporades and across the Aegean to Lemnos and the
beachhead below Troy, where the Scamander River flows into the
Dardanelles.

The first legs of the voyage home from Troy are described with
equal geographical and navigational precision. The nostos starts
from the beachhead below the city and moves to the nearby
island of Tenedos, where Odysseus changes his mind about

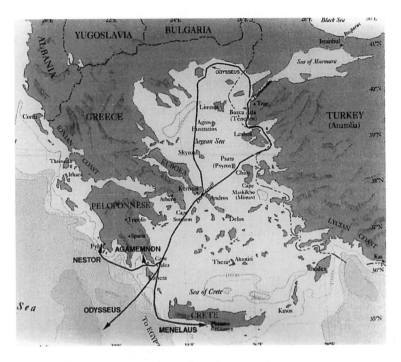

Routes of the Greek heroes returning from Troy.
Map by Hunt Conard, Skidmore College.

returning with Menelaus and decides to rejoin Agamemnon's fleet, which has not yet left the beach. In the fleet that is putting to sea, there is a heated debate over whether to coast the shore of Asia Minor or to cross the Aegean directly. Nestor, Menelaus, and Diomedes worry about their homeward course:

> Late in the day the red-haired Menelaus joined us,
> overtook us at Lesbos, debating the long route home:
> whether to head north, over the top of rocky Chios,
> skirting Psyrie, keeping that island off to port
> or run south of Chios, by Mimas' gusty cape.
> We asked the god for a sign. He showed us one,
> he urged us to cut out on the middle passage,
> straight to Euboea now,
> escape a catastrophe, fast as we could sail!
>
> (3: 187–95)

The *Argo,* a replica of an ancient galley used by Tim Severin in retracing the voyages of Jason and Odysseus.
Reproduction of original color photo by Kevin Fleming, courtesy of Fleming Photography, Annapolis.

This debate is particularly interesting because it pits a shorter, direct course home against a far longer but more sheltered coasting route. Sailors in open galleys were reluctant to head offshore for cogent reasons: tiny stowage space; limited rations of grain, wine, and water; virtually no sleeping space; absolutely no cover to escape the sun; long periods of strenuous rowing; sudden, unpredictable storms; and the danger of swamping in heavy seas. In addition to exposure, hard work, and partial starvation offshore, uncertainty about landfalls made coasting more attractive. With some trepidation, then, these returning warriors risk heading out to sea immediately after leaving the shelter of Lesbos rather than hugging the land as long as possible, but with a freshening northeast wind, they scoot 85 miles downwind to the Doro Strait. Had they chosen the other route, which stays inside Chios for protection, they would have had only 60 miles of open sea to reach the strait but at a more difficult heading across the wind.[10]

After the fleet passes through the Doro Strait and reaches Cape Sounion, the nostoi of the heroes diverge. Nestor gets a quick and safe passage all the way home to Pylos on the southwestern coast of the Peloponnese. After the remarkable first day's run from Lesbos to Geraistos (just beyond the Doro Strait), a continuing fair wind pushes him around the three capes of the Peloponnese in four more days. Having left Troy several days later, Agamemnon also gets a quick but disastrous passage home after being blown downwind at Malea:

> But just as he came abreast of Malea's beetling cape
> a hurricane snatched him up and swept him way off course—
> groaning, desperate—driving him over the fish-infested sea
> to the wild borderland where Thyestes made his home
> in days of old and his son Aegisthus lived now.
> But even from there a safe return seemed likely,
> yes, the immortals swung the wind around to fair
> and the victors sailed home.
>
> (4: 577–83)

A puzzling question remains: Why did Agamemnon approach Malea at all, since the infamous cape is well beyond the normal course to Mycenae through the Argolic Gulf? One answer suggests that he was wary of a direct approach to Mycenae after years of absence and planned to come in through the "back door" of his extended territories to assess the situation at home. A more probable answer lies in narrative necessity, since nostoi are usually difficult and perilous, especially for long-absent kings; three of the four principal heroes in this voyage home suffer extended hardships or disaster. The storm at Malea also reinforces parallels in the experience of Agamemnon and Odysseus and highlights the antipodal nature of their wives and their fates, a thematic contrast central to the moral system of the epic.

Menelaus is separated from Nestor and Agamemnon at Cape Sounion, where his skilled helmsman, Phrontis, suddenly collapses at the tiller and dies; the burial rites ashore delay Menelaus, causing him to miss the fair wind that had sped Nestor home. Blown downwind southeastward from Cape Malea in a fierce gale, half of Menelaus's fleet is wrecked on the virtually harborless southern coast of Crete in one of the *Odyssey*'s intensely realistic shipwreck scenes:

> Now, there's a sheer cliff
> plunging steep to the surf at the farthest edge of Gortyn,
> out on the mist-bound sea, where the South Wind piles breakers,
> huge ones, left of the headland's horn, toward Phaestos,
> with only a low reef to block the crushing tides.
> In they sailed, and barely escaped their death—
> the ships' crews, that is—
> the rollers smashed their hulls against the rocks.
> But as for the other five with pitch-black prows,
> the wind and current swept them on toward Egypt.
>
> (3: 331–40)

There Menelaus begins seven years of wandering that take him to Phoenicia, Cyprus, and Libya, and perhaps to Ethiopia and Arabia; he makes his final leg home to Sparta from Pharos, an island off the Egyptian coast where he has been windbound and wrestled with Proteus for news of other Greek warriors. Odysseus's lies about his captivity among Phoenician sailors (in Books 13 and 14) replicate many of Menelaus's wanderings. Odysseus, too, is blown downwind trying to round Cape Malea to parts unknown, although traditionally assumed to be in the central Mediterranean.[11]

> And now, at long last,
> I might have reached my native land unscathed,

but just as I doubled Malea's cape, a tide-rip
and the North Wind drove me way off course,
careering past Cythera.

(9: 88–92)

Thus Cape Malea becomes the hinge of the voyage narrative
in a number of important ways, determining or setting in motion
the final outcomes of the nostos for each returning Greek war-
rior. There many elements in the seafaring context of the *Odyssey*
come together as at a focal point. Malea is the great geographical
and navigational divide in the epic: Everything to the east of it is
well known to Greek seafarers of the eighth century B.C., whereas
much to the west is unknown. To be sure, the whole of the
Peloponnese as well as the Ionian coasts and offshore islands of
mainland Greece from Pylos to Corfu were familiar, and by 750
B.C. seafarers had some knowledge of Ischia and parts of southern Italy and eastern Sicily, yet most of the coasts and islands of
the Adriatic and Tyrrhenian Seas were still terrae incognitae.
Rounding the cape became essential as Greek cities founded
colonies in the central Mediterranean during the last half of the
eighth century. Peculiar meteorological conditions called kata-

Cape Melea in the Peloponnese, turning point in the *Odyssey* voyage.
Drawing by Jane Teller, 1987.

batic gales (intense offshore winds sliding down the mountains like avalanches), which still persist, would have made it especially difficult for galleys rigged with single square sails to pass the cape heading westward, which is precisely what the fleets returning from Troy try to do.

Whether ancient galleys could cope with those fierce gales and then make good progress to windward against prevailing westerly winds is still hotly debated by naval architects and maritime historians. Passages around Cape Malea in the ancient world were as difficult as those around Cape Horn in the nineteenth century—both capes stood as seemingly insurmountable obstacles in the path of ships headed westward for trade and colonization. To avoid duplicating his fleets or transferring them back and forth around Malea, Periander, tyrant of Corinth, proposed cutting a canal through the Corinthian Isthmus as early as the sixth century B.C. but settled for the easier solution of building the *diolkos*, a prototype of the marine railway, across the three miles of the isthmus. Julius Caesar, Caligula, and Hadrian studied the idea of a canal before Nero actually began digging, unsuccessfully, in A.D. 67. The cape was notorious among sailors, as reflected in an aphorism reported by Strabo: "When you round Cape Malea, say goodbye to your home" (8.6.20). Thus do the harsh realities of ancient seafaring blend with folktales and other sailors' lore to form the substance of the wanderings in the *Odyssey*. Finally, from a literary perspective, the diaspora of heroes at Malea and an aborted return for Odysseus are absolutely necessary to the structure of the narrative as a whole.

Clearly, up to this point in the voyage home from Troy, details of geography, navigation, even meteorology and oceanography, have been absolutely precise, but all that changes as Odysseus's wanderings begin. Two factors have generated more than two thousand years of uncertainty about the route. One is loss of knowledge about waters beyond the Aegean, the Sea of Crete, and parts of the Ionian during the Greek "Dark Age," usually defined as the three centuries between 1100 and 800 B.C. Curiously, the Mycenaean forebears of Greek seafarers in the eighth century B.C. almost certainly sailed at least as far west as southern Italy and Sicily and perhaps farther in search of metals; there was a settlement at Scoglio del Tonno, near Taranto, and Mycenaean pottery has been found on the east coast of Sicily, the

Lipari Islands, and the island of Ischia in the Bay of Naples. After the collapse of the powerful Mycenaean cities during the twelfth century B.C., that geographical and navigational information seems to have disappeared. It had to be relearned in the eighth century B.C. as the Greeks sailed westward again to repeat and extend the discoveries of Mycenaean and Phoenician seafarers.

The other factor leading to continued uncertainty about the geography of Odysseus's wanderings is the generic similarity of coastal topography in various regions of the Mediterranean. For instance, one can identify many examples of two harbor configurations prominent in the story: the double harbor separated by a peninsula and the cliffbound harbor with a hidden entrance. Both had clear practical value for seafarers, the first providing shelter against strong winds from various directions, the second preventing discovery by enemies or pirates. Some of the most powerful cities in the ancient world grew around double harbors—Halicarnassus (Bodrum) and Phocaea (Foca) in Turkey, Syracuse in Sicily, Valletta in Malta, and Carthage in Tunisia. And there are many hidden harbors scattered about the Mediterranean, among them Knidos in Turkey, Ieraki in the Peloponnese, and Bonifacio in Corsica.

At times some Homeric scholars have wanted to dismiss questions of geography out of hand, arguing that the epics belong to a literary rather than a historical world. Following Eratosthenes rather than Crates or Strabo among ancient commentators, they would maintain that the wanderings, in particular, reflect fantasy rather than reality, but a number of points argue against such an easy dichotomy. One is the non-Cartesian cast of thought in the early part of the Archaic Age (800–500 B.C.) from which the epics emerge, a cast that assimilated rather than distinguished myth, tradition, and history. Herodotus does not question the reality of the Trojan War or the existence of its heroes, and both he and Thucydides report speeches from the oral tradition that are at least partly invented rather than documented. James Romm, a scholar of ancient geography, notes that for the Greeks "*geographia* represented a literary genre more than a branch of physical science" and that "it relied on narratives as a source of information: All that was known about distant lands had to be derived from someone's report of them, and the information tended to remain embedded in these reports far longer than we might expect."[12] Although geography had not emerged as a separate branch of knowledge by Homer's time, it is reasonable to believe that he had access to some information about regions beyond the scope of his own travels, perhaps from sailors or traders operating in the maritime world surrounding him. Sharp distinctions between history and myth, information and fantasy, had not yet solidified.

The blurred time frames of the epics also argue for synthesis rather than discrimination as an effect of oral transmission. In the *Odyssey*'s case, that frame of reference stretches through five centuries—from the late Bronze Age through the Dark Ages to the early Archaic Age, from the thirteenth-century B.C. locus of the Trojan War to the probable date of composition between 750 and 725 B.C. In *The Cambridge Ancient History*, G. S. Kirk concludes: "The *Iliad* and *Odyssey* were created progressively, up to the point of large-scale composition itself, and each of the three periods contributed its share."[13]

Archaeological evidence also suggests that the Homeric epics have roots in protohistory and refer to undocumented events that were perhaps exaggerated but nonetheless characteristic of their time. What would be so unusual about a raid on a town situated in a strategic position to control shipping through the narrow strait leading from the Aegean to the Black Sea, especially if that town lay at the edge of a region rich in the metal ores needed during the Bronze Age?[14] In this light both the *Iliad* and the *Odyssey* reflect geopolitical realities of the ancient world, and it is no accident that Heinrich Schliemann, the amateur archeologist who excavated major Mycenaean cities, had a copy of the *Iliad* in his hand. He began with Troy in 1870, moved on to Agamemnon's citadel of Mycenae in 1876, and started to work on nearby "Tiryns of the huge walls" in 1884. Half a century later American archaeologist Carl Blegen used the text of the *Odyssey* to locate Nestor's palace at Pylos in 1939, and in 1983 Sarantis Symeonoglou reconfirmed a precise match between the description and relationship of landmarks in the text and the geography of Ithaca. Now he is leading a team of archaeologists in excavating what they think is Odysseus's city on the narrow, high ridge that connects the two halves of the island. No one claims that the epics are exact history, but few would deny that they contain strands of it, no matter how indirectly.

In addition to the existence of specific Mycenaean sites related to the Trojan expedition, there is also some basis for locating Odysseus's wanderings beyond Malea in the central Mediterranean. Archaeological evidence reveals an extensive network of Phoenician trade routes throughout the Mediterranean as early as the tenth century B.C. These renowned seafarers founded many trading stations in the eighth century B.C. or earlier, especially in key areas of the central and western Mediterranean like Carthage in Tunisia, Motya and Nora in western Sicily, Sulci and Tharros on the east and west coasts of Sardinia, and sites on both the Mediterranean and Atlantic sides of the Strait of Gibraltar. Recognition of their sea power recurs throughout the *Odyssey*, and some scholars even speculate that the more disastrous episodes of the wanderings reflect Phoenician scare stories designed to keep the Greeks off the sea lanes. Greek colonization of the central Mediterranean occurred by cloning from the eighth through the sixth centuries B.C.; typically, an Aegean city would reproduce a largely independent duplicate of itself, especially in Sicily and the lower Tyrrhenian coast of Italy. Examples include Pithecusae, founded by Chalcis and Eretria in the early part of the eighth century B.C., as well as Cumae (ca. 750 B.C.), both on the northern fringes of the Bay of Naples; in eastern Sicily, Syracuse, founded by Corinth and Chalcis in 734 B.C., and Naxos, below Taormina, also founded by Chalcis in 734 B.C.; on the Straits of Messina, Zancle, founded by Chalcis and settlers from Cumae ca. 730 B.C., and Rhegium, now Reggio Calabria, founded by Chalcis and Messenia ca. 720 B.C. Although the Tyrrhenian Sea was not as well known as the Aegean when the *Odyssey* was composed, Greeks were actively rediscovering and exploring it.

Yet these historical contexts cannot establish a precise voyage track beyond Cape Malea in spite of repeated attempts to do so during the last two thousand years. Discovering the route of a legendary hero whose wanderings passed through centuries of bardic elaboration before being recorded in writing is obviously a tricky business at best, but many have tried. Traditional routes date back to Strabo and Virgil, elaborated by the scholarship of Victor Berard in the late nineteenth century and retraced by sailors like Ernle Bradford in the twentieth; Berard links Odysseus's wanderings closely with the navigations of Phoenicians, and Bradford suggests some variations in the traditional route based on his own sailing about the Mediterranean after World War II.[15] Other scholar-adventurers have produced a set of possible and barely probable alternative routes. Following Samuel Butler's theory that Homer was a woman who lived in Trapani, western Sicily, L. G. Pocock's route circles Sicily with an extension as far west as Tangier.[16] Tim Severin, a geographer and navigator who has retraced the voyages of St. Brendan, Sinbad, Jason, and Odysseus, notices the disparity between the small size of Mycenaean cities and textual descriptions of their magnitude; by analogy, he scales down the wanderings, confining them mostly to the Peloponnese, western Crete, and the Ionian coast of Greece.[17] In scale this condensed route is the eastern counterpart of the Sicilian circle, but other retracers are not so modest. Mauricio Obregón, flying his plane in aerial surveys as he had in working with Samuel Eliot Morison on the Columbus voyages, extends Odysseus's voyage track from Cyprus in the east to Tangier in the west; Gilbert Pillot goes even further, plunging through the Pillars of Hercules to Madeira and Teneriffe before heading north to Ireland, the Hebrides, and Iceland.[18]

What are we to conclude from this maze of geographical theories? First, no matter how extreme or even quirky such theories may seem, they do have a common foundation: the belief that voyage narratives, even if embellished with folklore and sometimes fanciful geography, do in fact reflect the realities of seafaring in their time. Second, when Odysseus is blown downwind past Cythera, the precise geography of the voyage up to this point is replaced by an equally exact topographical narrative, continuing the sense of immediate, physical reality that readers and scholars have always noticed. Descriptions that are vivid and detailed seem to ask for geographic identification, and the rugged and memorable terrain of Mediterranean coastlines and islands provides more than a handful of potential sites. Topographical narrative is isomorphic with real places when it shares the same structure of relationships, just as a map is isomorphic with the terrain it surveys. With the text of the *Odyssey* in hand, one can find a number of sites that fit descriptions almost exactly, as well as sequences of places that match legs of the voyage.[19] Topography and text readily merge, reminding us of the general principle of reciprocal association between places and myths: Unusual places generate stories about them, and stories seek visual embodiment in landscape, just as gods are known through their incarnations.

Five generic features in the seascape of the northern Mediterranean are prolific in the text of the *Odyssey* as well: caves, straits, islands, harbors, and coastal mountains. All are associated with uncertainty, with danger and security, with help and deception, with barbarism and civility. Odysseus has to know the right things to survive in this strange world. Each of the route finders has a more or less convincing match between topography and text for the various episodes of the wanderings, but one does not have to go beyond the traditional route to illustrate remarkable similarities.[20] One of the large limestone caves on the sea side of Monte Circeo, on the Tyrrhenian coast southwest of Rome, has been named Circe's Cave, probably because it is large enough to contain Odysseus's single remaining ship and close enough to the sea for hauling it in. This immense cave with a smooth flat floor could also serve as a model for the cave in which Odysseus and Calypso lived for seven years. Many Mediterranean sea caves are huge and deep enough for galleys to enter; such caves would provide the double advantage of shelter and a hiding place from enemies.

Passages through straits are usually associated with danger, both from currents and from unfriendly inhabitants who controlled their shores. The cliff named Scylla on the Calabrian coast at the northern entrance to the Straits of Messina is pockmarked with small caves that have been associated with the many heads of the monster. On the other side of this strait lie possible remnants of Charybdis, three whirlpools that were once much stronger before an eighteenth-century earthquake altered the bottom; they are still threatening to small boats when wind and current are opposed, and particularly during spring tides. Dangerous passages with strong currents were also iconically represented by moving or clashing rocks that could crush a ship between them. The image of moving rocks is not so absurd as it may seem at first glance: Viewed from a boat struggling to maintain a safe course in a strong current or rapids, threatening rocks do indeed move in relation to that fixed perspective and may even appear to close a narrow winding channel in the distance ahead. The most notable ancient example is the Symplegades in the Bosporos, which Jason must pass through to enter the Black Sea—a tale retold in the *Aeneid*.

Islands often represent the unknown in the *Odyssey*, and many of them appear in the wanderings. The Tyrrhenian islands of Ustica and Stromboli have been associated with Aeolus; Lipari, Vulcano, and Stromboli with the wandering rocks; Malta and Gozzo with Calypso; and Capri and the Galli Islands with the Sirens. Such associations—a mere sampling of the geographical lore spawned by the wanderings—usually grow from specific physical features. The Galli Islands, for example, present a remarkable, animistic shape to the eye and a "song" to the ear; their configuration of rocks makes a continuous sea noise that might suggest the Sirens' alluring and deadly call to unwary mariners. They also lie a few miles off the Sorrento Peninsula in the main sea track along the Tyrrhenian coast and would have been noticed by sailors who depended upon seamarks for navigation.

Hidden harbors also carry a double value as secure havens and potential sources of disaster, either as traps in unfriendly territory or through the difficulty of finding and entering them. Bonifacio Harbor at the southeastern tip of Corsica is long and

Paleokatstritsa, Corfu, an exact topographical analogue to the land of the Phaeacians, including their ship turned to stone offshore.
Photo by Robert Foulke.

narrow with an entrance hidden in what looks like an unbroken line of cliffs. Once inside such a harbor, ships have perfect shelter from wind and sea but are surrounded by overhanging cliffs. In such a place the Laestrygonians might attack and destroy 11 of Odysseus's 12 ships by hurling rocks down on them. Other harbor types, especially the double harbor, are more benign. The one at Paleokatstritsa in northwestern Corfu is a perfect model for the harbor of the magical Phaeacians who receive Odysseus and ultimately carry him home, and the topography of their coastline is fully congruent with his long swim seeking a small beach among the cliffs that block his chance to come ashore.

The cannibalistic Cyclops episode involves a secure, hidden harbor difficult to find and a dangerous cave full of food on a nearby mountainside. When Odysseus and his hungry crew have been at sea for many days after leaving the temptations of the lotus-eaters, they are miraculously blown right through the nearly hidden entrance of a safe harbor on a foggy night. Ernle Bradford and L. G. Pocock, as well as their more famous predecessor Samuel Butler, believed they had found the perfect topographical configuration in western Sicily; they identified the island full of goats as Favingnana and assigned the site of the Cyclops' cave to the rugged slopes of Mount Eryx above Trapani. Euripides and Virgil placed the episode on the opposite shore of Sicily below Mount Aetna, the active volcano that dominates the entire coast. Others associate the final disastrous episode of the cattle of the sun with the slopes below Aetna.

Such prolific conflation of Mediterranean topography and Homeric text raises a question: Were these Tyrrhenian sites associated with the *Odyssey* transplanted from the Aegean by colonizing Greeks? Since we are dealing with a semifictional narrative rather than the log of a specific voyage, several plausible explanations emerge for the traditional identification of sites in various parts of the Mediterranean. Either the topography of newly discovered regions was carried back to Homer by seamen and incorporated into the epic, or the Greek colonists of the eighth, seventh, and sixth centuries B.C. brought versions of the epic with them and fitted its incidents to their new environment. No matter which explanation we may prefer, it is clear to anyone who sails Mediterranean coastlines that a magical realism shines through the text.

Apart from geography and coastal topography, that realism projects seafaring trauma in storms and in passages along unfriendly coasts. Although travel by sea was often the only practicable way to get about in a land of islands and mountainous coastline sealed off from the interior, fear of the sea is repeatedly expressed in the *Odyssey*. We see it in the warriors' debate about routes home at the outset of the return voyage from Troy, in the expectation that each storm will drown them and in the belief that those who put to sea are particularly vulnerable to the will of the gods. When Calypso suggests that Odysseus, now alone and without a single ship, make the last leg of his long voyage home in a small boat, he rebels:

> Passage home? Never. Surely you're plotting
> something else, goddess, urging me—in a raft—
> to cross the ocean's mighty gulfs. So vast, so full
> of danger not even deep-sea ships can make it through,
> swift as they are and buoyed up by the winds of Zeus himself.
> I won't set foot on a raft until you *show* good faith,
> until you consent to swear, goddess, a binding oath
> you'll never plot some new intrigue to harm me![21]
>
> (5: 192–99)

Routinely, seafarers began and ended their voyages with rites of propitiation, often a sacrifice to Poseidon. Even if they evaded storms at sea, returning to the land was not always easy. The Mediterranean is full of potential lee shores without harbors; much of the Tyrrhenian coast is exposed beach, and the south coasts of Sicily and Crete are virtually shelterless. Unbroken rock-bound coasts with jutting promontories are frequent and more ominous. When Odysseus has been shipwrecked for the last time and is swimming along the cliff-lined coast of Scheria, he anticipates and barely escapes death in the surf:

> But just offshore, as far as a man's shout can carry,
> he caught the boom of a heavy surf on jagged reefs—
> roaring breakers crashing down on an ironbound coast,
> exploding in fury—
> the whole sea shrouded—
> sheets of spray—
> no harbors to hold ships, no roadstead where they'd ride,
> nothing but jutting headlands, riptooth reefs, cliffs.

The *Argo* dwarfed by the cliffs of Gramvousa Island off northwestern Crete, one of the many unfriendly coasts in the eastern Mediterranean.
Reproduction of original color photo by Kevin Fleming, courtesy of Fleming Photography, Annapolis.

Odysseus' knees quaked and the heart inside him sank;
he spoke to his fighting spirit, desperate: "Worse and worse!
Now that Zeus has granted a glimpse of land beyond my hopes,
now I've crossed this waste of water, the end in sight,
there's no way out of the boiling surf—I see no way!
Rugged reefs offshore, around them breakers roaring,
above them a smooth rock face, rising steeply, look,
and the surge too deep inshore, no spot to stand
on my own two legs and battle free of death.
If I clamber out, some big comber will hoist me,
dash me against that cliff—my struggles all a waste!
If I keep on swimming down the coast, trying to find
a seabeach shelving against the waves, a sheltered cove—
I dread it—another gale will snatch me up and haul me
back to the fish-infested sea, retching in despair."

(5: 443–63)

Such attitudes were appropriate to embarking on a sea that still bedevils fishermen and yachtsmen with unpredictable vagaries and sudden storms. Modern seafarers in large power vessels may not appreciate the extent to which their ancient counterparts depended upon favorable winds and manageable seas and feared the reverse, which they attributed to the anger of the gods. We can reconstruct the conditions they faced by comparing ancient and modern meteorological observations.[22] And it is still possible to experience three winds that intimidated ancient Greek seafarers—meltemi, downdrafts, and katabatic gales.

Meltemi, the Etesian or "annual" winds of the ancient world, blow through the heart of the sailing season (July and August) recommended by Hesiod near the end of the eighth century B.C.[23] They are phenomena peculiar to the Aegean, consisting of very strong northerly winds during the greater part of the summer. Their direction varies from northeast to northwest, depending upon region, since they fan out from the north on curved paths throughout the Aegean. Their velocity is usually above 20 knots and sometimes reaches 35 knots or more, especially in the middle regions. Sometimes lasting as long as one to two weeks without respite, they recur frequently during a season beginning in late June and continuing through July and August into early September.

Meltemi are caused by a stagnant low pressure system over Cyprus and the Middle East, in conjunction with nearly stationary high pressure centers piling up over southern Europe, particularly in Spain, France, and Italy. Their strength comes from the steep pressure gradient (i.e., the great pressure difference between the low and the highs in a short distance); they are intensified by a slot effect between the high- and low-pressure systems, the confluence of northerly winds swirling counterclockwise around the low and clockwise around the highs. The onset of meltemi can be instantaneous, so it would not be farfetched to attribute them to gods.[24] Local fishermen predict that onset through Greek weather folklore—whether or not there is morning dew, the shape of clouds over mountains, and the behavior of birds, those timeless messengers of the gods. Meltemi are specifically alluded to in an epic simile from the *Iliad* (9: 4–8), and at the beginning of Odysseus's return after the Thracian raid, there is a fine description of a meltemi in the northern Aegean:

> Now Zeus who masses the stormclouds hit the fleet
> with the North Wind—
>   a howling, demonic gale, shrouding over
> in thunderheads the earth and sea at once—
>   and night swept down
> from the sky and the ships went plunging headlong on,
> our sails slashed to rags by the hurricane's blast!
> We struck them—cringing at death we rowed our ships
> to the nearest shoreline, pulled with all our power.
> There, for two nights, two days, we lay by, no letup,
> eating our hearts out, bent with pain and bone-tired.
>   (9: 76–84)

The mountainous land bordering much of the northern shore of the Mediterranean also unleashes two notorious winds that buffet sailing vessels: downdrafts and katabatic gales. Downdrafts occur when there is a high mountain ridge creating a lee or shelter from the strong winds of various regions—the meltemi of the Aegean, the sirocco of the Sea of Crete, the bora of the Adriatic, the tramontana of the Tyrrhenian—and a sharp drop from cliff edge to sea level, usually several hundred feet or more. Along steep coastlines, the wind coming over the mountains may have more downward force than horizontal movement; when gusts hit the sea, they radiate outward from the point of impact in all directions simultaneously, producing a circular wind structure that sailing vessels cannot cope with. (Encountering such a downdraft is comparable to sailing through the prop wash of a helicopter.) Sailors have always learned to "read" the water to windward for wind direction and strength so they can meet a powerful gust by heading into it or spilling wind from a sail, but the full force of downdrafts hits the sail before it can be read on the water. When downdrafts are very strong, they often create arcs of spume rising from the sea near their point of impact, then spurt outward as if a giant bellows were fanning them.[25] The fact that both Homeric epics contain formulaic descriptions of such circular wind patterns may be an indication of their frequency. In the *Iliad*, a gust with downdraft structure appears as an epic simile to describe Nestor's indecision during a confused rout of the Achaeans:

> As when the open sea is deeply stirred to the ground-swell
> but stays in one place and waits the rapid onset of tearing
> gusts, nor rolls its surf onward in either direction
> until from Zeus the wind is driven down to decide it;
> so the aged man pondered, his mind caught between two courses.
>
> (14: 16–20)

As Odysseus approaches the cliff-lined coast of Scheria, Poseidon's final blast has the same circular structure:

> With that he [Poseidon] rammed the clouds together—both hands
> clutching his trident—churned the waves into chaos, whipping
> all the gales from every quarter, shrouding over in thunderheads
> the earth and sea at once—and night swept down from the sky—
> East and South Winds clashed and the raging West and North,
> sprung from the heavens, roiled heaving breakers up—[26]
>
> (5: 321–26)

Yet a third pernicious wind is the key to Cape Malea's enormous influence on ancient seafaring. The mountainous slopes of certain Mediterranean shores, capes, and islands generate sudden and partly unpredictable danger for sailors to cope with in katabatic gales. Like downdrafts, they are produced by high windward shores, but there are important differences in their causes and structure. Katabatic gales generally blast down the leeward slopes of mountains 2,000 or more feet high and cover wider areas; they are linear rather than radial in structure and continuous rather than erratic; they are associated with specific regions and may last six to eight hours. Katabatic gales occur when accumulations of cooled mountain air suddenly slide, like an avalanche, down the slopes. As a light or moderate wind blows onto the shore of a mountainous cape or island, the air accumulates and cools while moving upslope on the windward side of the mountain, and the collected air mass at the top becomes colder and denser. When this air mass begins to slide (often suddenly) down the leeward side of the mountain, it gains gravitational speed as it drops. Katabatic gales commonly occur along the southern coast of Crete, on a number of Aegean islands, and at the capes of the southern Peloponnese—especially Malea.

These are the gales that drive Agamemnon, Menelaus, and Odysseus offshore at Malea; only Nestor escapes their wrath. Such gales can catch sailors by surprise because common sense tells them to seek shelter from a strong offshore wind by moving closer to the land. This is precisely the wrong thing to do: The nearer they move, the stronger the wind.[27] Tim Severin, sailing the *Argo*, ran the same gamut when he approached Cape Malea from the northeast just as the returning heroes did:

> From across the far side of the peninsula a stream of clouds came hurtling out, a sure sign that a fierce wind was blowing on the opposite flank of the cape. The clouds came streaming over the crest of the ridge like banners, twisting and turning and then ripping into shreds. I was watching the surface of the sea between the Cape and the distant shape of Cythera Island. The water was increasingly flecked with breaking waves. Clearly the gale was working up strength. Abruptly I called on the crew for a change of course. I had reached my decision. Conditions were too dangerous for a galley to proceed out into the channel, and we should try to seek shelter under the cape, even though the Sailing Directions offered no shelter. Derry got out an oar and began to pull Argo's head round, rowing with difficulty in the choppy water. We tried three times to turn the galley, and each time the wind was too much for us. As we faltered, the galley lay uncomfortably across the wind, wallowing from side to side, losing ground

as she was swept towards the open sea. We were only nine men aboard—not nearly enough to row five tons of laden galley—and it was becoming increasingly urgent to get to shelter. (Severin 71–72)

Through a combination of sail and outboard power, this crew eventually succeeded, but Severin concludes from his own experiences that Homeric seafarers probably would not have done so: "[I]f the early galleys were caught in a full-blooded Mediterranean gale, their crews did not have the strength to row their way out of trouble. They were as helpless as scraps of wind-blown chaff blown by the gale on to whatever shore lay in their lee" (Severin 59).[28]

Just so it was with Menelaus and Odysseus in the gale at Cape Malea, which is also a necessary literary turning point in the structure of the *Odyssey*. If their nostoi had ended as quickly and peacefully as Nestor's, there would be no wanderings and no story to tell. The gale provides a new departure—a starting point for navigation in the nautical sense of that word—one that creates literary advance and forestalls closure. It sets up a rhythm of delayed completion in the nostos that repeats itself with variations throughout the wanderings, most notably in the Aeolus episode, the Circe episode, and Odysseus's sojourn with Calypso. Thematically, it appears in constant tensions between curiosity and caution, temptation and discipline, the impulse to continue exploring and the desire to return home, as Odysseus encounters unexpected hazards afloat and barbarism ashore. These adventures in the unknown world occur in three phases: In the first, he leads a fleet of galleys and relies on his own wits, unsuccessfully; in the second, he commands a single remaining galley and leans on help from Athena to escape destruction; and in the third he is alone, the survivor of shipwrecks premeditated by Zeus and Poseidon, and must tap his innate strength and use help from talismans to reach Scheria. There he begins the slow process of reintegration into society that will lead him back to Ithaca, control of his house and kingdom, and reunion with Penelope.

The first phase includes the episodes in the land of the lotus-eaters, the escape from the Cyclops Polyphemus, two encounters with Aeolus, and the destruction of ships and men by the Laestrygonians. Three of these encounters pit Odysseus against barbarians who do not know the meaning of civilization as the

Greeks understand it, and in two of them the code of hospitality to strangers is inverted to cannibalism. Throughout this first phase Odysseus must survive without divine help; he recovers from a series of mistakes through clever strategems, but in the end, reduced to a single ship out of the original 12, he has lost the battle to get home with his fleet intact. In the first episode, after a wild and windy nine-day crossing to the land of the lotus-eaters, it is no wonder that the men wanted to stay ashore. Whether or not the lotus was a hallucinogenic drug, as is likely, the episode is conceived as a temptation, testing the men's will to continue the voyage. It is also the first of three respites from the rigors of sea-faring, anticipating Odysseus's longer lapses ashore with Circe and Calypso. Unlike Jason trying to pry himself and his fellow Argonauts away from the women of Lesbos, Odysseus uses the intuitive wisdom of a more experienced commander: Get the men out as fast as you can.

When he does, after a sea passage of unspecified length, the fleet reaches an island off the land of the Cyclopes. The night landing on an unseen island is harrowing, a navigator's nightmare:

> here [a snug deep-water harbor] we landed, and surely a god
>   steered us in
> through the pitch-black night.
> Not that he ever showed himself, with thick fog
> swirling around the ships, the moon wrapped in clouds
> and not a glimmer stealing through that gloom.
> Not one of us glimpsed the island—scanning hard—
> or the long combers rolling us slowly toward the coast,
> not till our ships had run their keels ashore.
>   (9: 157–65)

The episode that follows, like many in the wanderings, at first focuses on the temptation of food for sailors who want to gorge themselves after days of semistarvation at sea. But for Odysseus that focus soon shifts to curiosity, brashness, and ultimately pride as he leaves the island to "probe the natives living over there" on the mainland (9: 194). "What *are* they—violent, savage, lawless? Or friendly to strangers, god-fearing men?" (9: 195–196) What he discovers is the antipode of Greek civilization, a barbaric people without agriculture, government, and, especially, ships and sea trade:

> For the Cyclops have no ships with crimson prows,
> no shipwrights there to build them good trim craft
> that could sail them out to foreign ports of call
> as most men risk the seas to trade with other men.
>
> (9: 138–41)

Nevertheless, Odysseus decides to test Polyphemus against one of the key customs of Greek civilization—hospitality to strangers. Here Odysseus's curiosity becomes brashness and then folly, leading to the destruction of a number of his men. After the stratagem that blinds Polyphemus succeeds and the remaining men escape the cave, Odysseus commits his fatal error, this time through an excess of pride. In parting taunts to Polyphemus, he identifies himself in order to claim fame for his cleverness. The Cyclops responds by hurling rocks at the departing galley and praying to his father, Poseidon, asking that a final curse be laid upon Odysseus: that he may never get home, or at the very least

> if he's fated to see
> his people once again and reach his well-built house
> and his own native country, let him come home late
> and come a broken man—all shipmates lost,
> alone in a stranger's ship—
> and let him find a world of pain at home!
>
> (9: 590–95)

The next episode, two encounters with Aeolus, king (but not god) of the winds, explores the folklore of wind magic and brings Odysseus to the second aborted closure of his nostos. In their first encounter, Aeolus welcomes Odysseus and gives him both a bag full of adverse winds to keep tied up and a favorable west wind to get him home. Once again, as in earlier encounters with meltemi and katabatic gales, the assumption that the galleys cannot cope with strong headwinds is clear. When the fleet raises a landfall on Ithaca during the 10th day of an open sea crossing, an exhausted Odysseus, who has trimmed the sail all the way, falls asleep and thereby remains blameless for what follows. The crew's curiosity and avarice lead them to open the bag, letting loose the "storm" of adverse winds that blows the fleet back to the island of Aeolus, who this time refuses hospitality to anyone so hated by the gods.

Odysseus taunting Polyphemus, as represented on a mural in St. Anne's Gymnasium, Cracow.
Photo by Robert Foulke.

Seafarers visiting strange lands expect and often help create inhospitable receptions by their own actions, but Odysseus's men are almost blameless, if incautious, in the final, disastrous episode in this first phase of the wanderings. The fleet sails into a sheltered, hidden harbor surrounded by high cliffs, thoroughly safe from the dangers of the sea but vulnerable to those of the land. Odysseus, now partly chastened by his failures, remains wary, mooring temporarily to a niche in the cliffs near the harbor entrance to reconnoiter the situation. When a scouting party reaches the king of the Laestrygonians, he turns out to be another giant cannibal backed by tens of thousands of subjects, and the creatures immediately start hurling huge boulders and spears on the men and ships trapped in the harbor below while a helpless Odysseus cuts his mooring cable and heads out to sea to mourn his losses. In a single afternoon his fleet has been reduced from 12 ships to a lone galley.

In the second phase of his wanderings, Odysseus is gradually reduced to a man confronting nature and society alone. As he outwits Circe, confronts the dead in Hades, resists the lure of the Sirens, skirts the wandering rocks, and completes the passage between Scylla and Charybdis, he faces tests requiring more knowledge than mortal ingenuity can provide. He must lean on the gods for advice: Hermes tells him how to avoid Circe's spells, and Circe herself provides elaborate sailing directions to overcome the dangers that lie ahead. Like Jason attempting to recover the golden fleece, Odysseus must be armed with the special power of magic if he is to survive, especially in the encounter with Circe and the visit to Hades. After the Laestrygonian disaster, the demoralized and rebellious crew faces a harrowing year filled with the temptations of luxury and excess ashore, traps laid by the resourceful sorceress. Only as they are about to sail again does the accidental death of a drunken crew member suddenly jolt the men back to a sense of the threats lurking ashore, parallel to those in the land of the lotus-eaters but more severe.

The successful voyage to and from the mouth of Hades, with a tailwind both ways, depends entirely upon Circe's wind magic, but the following three episodes return Odysseus and the crew to a world that puts demands on their seamanship: They must avoid shipwreck on the rocks of an island, keep clear of an erupting volcano, and navigate a passage between a cliff and a whirl-

The lure of the Sirens.
From a drawing by Flaxman in an 1853 edition of the *Odyssey* published in London.

pool. The first test at the island of the Sirens is overlaid with the lure of knowledge; the second near the wandering rocks is purely naturalistic; and the third, sailing through a strait between Scylla and Charybdis, blends the hazards of currents and maelstroms with monsters. Thus, in these episodes, the realities of navigating merge with the exaggerations of folklore. In the final episode, after Odysseus's starving crew violates a prohibition against slaughtering the cattle of the sun, a vividly naturalistic, violent thunderstorm from Zeus smashes his last ship and drowns the crew:

> then Zeus the son of Cronus mounted a thunderhead
> above our hollow ship and the deep went black beneath it.
> Nor did the craft scud on much longer. All of a sudden
> killer-squalls attacked us, screaming out of the west,
> a murderous blast shearing the two forestays off
> so the mast toppled backward, its running tackle spilling
> into the bilge. The mast itself went crashing into the stern,
> it struck the helmsman's head and crushed his skull to a pulp
> and down from his deck the man flipped like a diver—
> his hardy life spirit left his bones behind.
> Then, in the same breath Zeus hit the craft
> with a lightning-bolt and thunder. Round she spun,

reeling under the impact, filled with reeking brimstone,
shipmates pitching out of her, bobbing around like seahawks
swept along by the whitecaps past the trim black hull—
and the god cut short their journey home forever.

(12: 435–52)

Once again, in an echo of the Aeolus episode, Odysseus is saved
from blame and destruction only because he had fallen asleep
when the violation occurred.

Astride the mast and keel lashed together, Odysseus drifts into
the third and final phase of his wanderings, alone. His ordeal is
by no means over: After the thunderstorm a south wind pushes
him back into the strait for an encounter with Charybdis; he then
drifts nine more days before washing ashore on Calypso's isle,
where he remains for seven years before building a boat and
putting to sea again. As he nears the coast of Scheria, Poseidon's
final storm wrecks him again, and the goddess Leucothea surfaces to offer him her scarf, a saving talisman. But Odysseus is
wary of further help from immortals and reverts to the first rule
of seamanship: Stick with your ship as long as it floats:

The goddess Leucothea surfacing to aid Odysseus after his final shipwreck.
From a drawing by Flaxman in an 1853 edition of the *Odyssey* published in
London.

> Oh no—
> I fear another immortal weaves a snare to trap me,
> urging me to abandon ship! I won't. Not yet.
> That shore's too far away—
> I glimpsed it myself—where *she* says refuge waits.
> No, here's what I'll do, it's what seems best to *me*.
> As long as the timbers cling and joints stand fast,
> I'll hold out aboard her and take a whipping—
> once the breakers smash my craft to pieces,
> then I'll swim—no better plan for now.
>
> (5: 392–401)

Soon another wave breaks up Odysseus's boat and scatters her timbers. Now swimming, he struggles to get ashore on a rock-bound coast without being battered to death in breakers:

> a tremendous roller swept him toward the rocky coast
> where he'd have been flayed alive, his bones crushed,
> if the bright-eyed goddess Pallas had not inspired him now.
> He lunged for a reef, he seized it with both hands and clung
> for dear life, groaning until the giant wave surged past
> and so he escaped its force, but the breaker's backwash
> charged into him full fury and hurled him out to sea.
> Like pebbles stuck in the suckers of some octopus
> dragged from its lair—so strips of skin torn
> from his clawing hands stuck to the rock face.
> A heavy sea covered him over, then and there
> unlucky Odysseus would have met his death—
> against the will of Fate—
> but the bright-eyed one inspired him yet again.
> Fighting out from the breakers pounding toward the coast,
> out of danger he swam on, scanning the land, trying to find
> a seabeach shelving against the waves, a sheltered cove,
> and stroking hard he came abreast of a river's mouth,
> running calmly, the perfect spot, he thought . . .
> free of rocks, with a windbreak from the gales.
>
> (5: 468–88)

Thus, before he is allowed to approach home, the hero of the Trojan War has been reduced to a naked swimmer struggling to survive in a hostile sea. His adventures have stripped him of ships and men and led him first to an imminent death off an alien coast, then back to Ithaca alone, a stranger, about to face the fearsome struggle to regain his wife and kingdom. This isolation is one extreme in the larger rhythm of expanding and contracting groups around Odysseus throughout the epic, from the assembly of Agamemnon's huge fleet before the war through Odysseus's solitary return to Ithaca and his eventual reintegration with society as king.

The fullness of this chapter reflects the enormous influence of the *Odyssey* on subsequent sea voyage narratives, as well as Western literature as a whole. Complex in narrative structure and intricate in convincing detail, the epic captures the essence of voyage experience in an era when contact with wind and wave was direct and often fearful. It contains many recurrent themes of the genre—anxiety about the threat of unexpected hazards afloat and danger ashore in unknown places, conflict between the need for discipline and the temptation to escape it, the fusion of immediate physical experience with imagination and fantasy, and the linkage between geographical discovery and self-discovery. Balanced between the desire to return home and the urge to see more, Odysseus is by turns brash and prudent, perplexed and resourceful, a master of deceit and trickery, and enduring, while his story is full of ambiguities as he wanders beyond the margin of the known world.

Just as the word *odyssey* has become a common term for difficult and venturesome journeys of all kinds, Odysseus's wanderings served as the archetype for more than two millennia of sea voyage narratives in Western culture, with appropriate transformations for different times and places. The *Argonautica* of Apollonius of Rhodes repeats many episodes with variations—Circe, the Sirens, Scylla and Charybdis, the wandering rocks, even a visit to Phaeacia—during an improbable return route from the Black Sea. The first half of Virgil's *Aeneid* has been regarded as a Roman *Odyssey*, complete with storms and a visit to the underworld, and Canto 26 of Dante's *Inferno* takes Odysseus beyond the Pillars of Hercules and sinks him for breaking divine prohibitions in a Christian transmutation of the cattle-of-the-sun episode. Odysseus reappears as a character in the plays of Sophocles, Euripides, and Seneca, in Ovid's *Metamorphoses*, and in lyrics of a score of modern poets—Sefaris, Graves, d'Annunzio, Pascoli, Saba, Stevens, Brodsky, and others. An aging hero sets out for a second voyage in Tennyson's "Ulysses," and the wanderings are transported to the Caribbean in Derek Walcott's *Omeros*. They come ashore in two of the masterpieces of twentieth-century literature, Joyce's *Ulysses* and Kazantzakis's *The Odyssey: A Modern Sequel*. Such Protean transformations indicate the sustaining power of the first extended voyage narrative in the Western world.

Chapter 3

Voyages of Discovery: Columbus and Cook

In one of the many volumes spawned by the Columbus quincentenary in 1992, Eviatar Zerubavel makes an ostensibly radical declaration:

> It certainly cannot be claimed that Europe had indeed discovered America in 1492 when its actual image of it at that time was that of a few islands off the shores of China. Yet not until 1778, 286 years after Columbus's first encounter with the Bahamas, were Europeans fully convinced that what he had discovered beyond the Atlantic was a previously unknown fourth continent that was absolutely distinct and separate from the other three—a New World, so to speak.[1]

Claiming that it took 286 years to discover America puts a new twist on an interpretive tradition growing out of Edmundo O'Gorman's influential *The Invention of America*.[2] At the heart of the tradition is the notion that discovery entails preconception, that mental constructs of what is to be discovered are essential and fundamental. In recent years many scholars have argued persuasively that Columbus's internalized cosmography was more medieval than modern, and that it was thus perfectly natural for him to persist in the belief that he was skirting the islands and shores of Asia.[3]

Among many possibilities in his inherited Eurocentric world view, two were prominent and immediately relevant to the voyages he undertook: On the one hand, he might be encountering some of the islands and land masses postulated in ancient and medieval texts—the Antipodes, Antilia, St. Brendan's isles—that Ferdinand and Isabella's commission conglomerated as "islands and mainlands" he might come upon in the Ocean Sea; on the other, he might believe in the "narrow" Atlantic postulated by Paolo Toscanelli, a Florentine cosmographer, and a corresponding "wide" Asia that he could reach quickly and efficiently by sailing westward.[4] Columbus may have focused on the second alternative for political and economic reasons, but others in Europe were ready to believe that he had inadvertently confirmed ancient speculations about the existence of the Antipodes. Apart from the anomalies of finding and taking possession of land that had been inhabited for millennia, Columbus did not "discover" America so much as come upon it by chance; his cosmography included no possibility of a "new" continent unknown to Europeans.

Disparate strands of European thought in the fifteenth century, overlaid by five centuries of interpretation and reinterpretation, create a labyrinth for modern scholars to navigate. Zerubavel's three centuries of discovering America are not so outlandish as they may seem if we accept his premise that discovery involves not only physical landings on strange shores but also a corresponding concept of what is being discovered, in this case a continent "seen as a *single* as well as a *separate* geographical entity that is fully detached from Asia" (38). By such a criterion Columbus's landings in the Bahamas in 1492 and in Venezuela in 1498 were the mere beginning of a long process that he never completed, one that did not conclude until Bering sailed through the strait named after him in 1741 and Cook confirmed that Alaska was not an island lying off Asia in 1778. These are not new ideas among historians of European voyages, although they do challenge traditional categories that separate the age of discovery, roughly 1450 to 1580, stretching from Prince Henry's school of navigation at Sagres through Drake's circumnavigation, and the later exploration of the Pacific. Many historians recognize that discovery is not an instantaneous result of physical encounters so much as a series of adjustments between preconceptions and direct experience that does not match them. In a similar vein one might argue that the discovery of Australia was a long, fragmented process lasting centuries, just begun rather than concluded when Dutch voyagers heading for Java stumbled onto the west coast and when Tasman reached Tasmania in the early seventeenth century, to be continued when Cook followed the east coast from Botany Bay to the Torres Strait in the late eighteenth century. The geographical concepts that would connect such observations were lacking, leading many to argue that there was no genuine discovery until the idea of another new continent began to form.

If coming upon strange lands in unexpected places does not count, what, then, constitutes a voyage of discovery? The answer lies in appreciating the far narrower context of mariners, one that is less cognizant of cutting-edge geographical conceptions of the world than of immediate dangers to navigation, especially the hidden ones lurking below the surface. Columbus, after all, founded his first colony, La Navidad, because a sleepy helmsman turned the tiller over to a ship's boy who let the *Santa Maria* drift onto a reef in a flat calm, and a far more meticulous Cook discovered the Great Barrier Reef with the *Endeavour*'s bottom after he had left soundings and was sure of deep water. In both cases disaster was imminent, and seamanship, not geographical speculation, became the priority for survival. Mariners have always tended to be a practical lot, wanting to get from A to B and back with as little trouble as possible, especially if they were setting out on the open ocean. Apart from a yachtsman's day sail for pleasure, voyages without purpose or destination are unthinkable because one half of the navigator's technical calculation, the way to lay a course from the point of departure to an intended landfall, is missing. Thus it is not surprising that sailing directions have a long history, stretching from the periploi of the ancient world through medieval portolan charts to modern charts and coast pilots. At first they were secretive, to be passed on only to allies, commercial partners, and countrymen, and gradually through centuries they entered the public domain for all mariners who needed to plot their destinations worldwide. But this ecumenical era in world navigation did not arrive until long after competing Europeans had located all the destinations they wanted to monopolize for trade and colonization, and it is quickly suspended in wartime.

Conflating the desires of geographers with the purposes of mariners is easy to do as one reads certain passages in their journals aimed at sponsoring investors, or whole documents, like Columbus's 1493 "Letter to the Sovereigns on His First Voyage"; supposedly begun off the Azores on the return voyage and finished just before his arrival in Lisbon, it was addressed to the court official who had orchestrated the financing of the expedition, Luis de Santangel, Queen's Keeper of the Privy Purse.[5] From a mariner's point of view, what distinguishes the earlier voyages of discovery from later maritime errands of trade or war is not so much a difference of purpose as a lack of information. Heading out without charts or pilots that would set courses and measure distances, discomforting as that must have been, was not equivalent to sailing without an intended destination. For both Columbus and Cook, the objectives of their first voyages were clearly laid out in elaborate official documents, respectively the Capitulations of Santa Fe (1492) and instructions from the Royal Society and the Admiralty (1768). Both sets of documents authorize discovering and taking possession of islands and even continents previously unclaimed by Europeans, but by no means were Ferdinand and Isabella, much less the Royal Society and the Admiralty, investing in aimless ocean wandering. On his first voyage, Columbus was directed to claim all islands and mainlands he came upon for the sovereigns and allowed to keep a tenth of the treasure and other produce obtained as well an eighth of the profit from any ship's future trading voyages if he paid the same share of the ship's expenses. Amidst the complex legal arrangements and royal decrees preparing for the Columbus expedition, the prime purpose of the voyage—testing a shorter route to the riches of Asia—is never mentioned. Many scholars explain this startling omission as a shrewd stroke of political caution designed to ward off any claims that Spain was trespassing in oceanic domains ceded to Portugal in the agreements at Alcáçovas in 1479 and note that there is plenty of evidence about Columbus's main objective in other parts of the Capitulations, including specific mention of Oriental products and diplomatic letters greeting Asiatic potentates.[6]

A study of these elaborate contracts and accompanying royal decrees indicates that Columbus was not sailing into blank space as he voyaged along new ocean tracks to uncharted islands and coastlines. But he was entering regions of the globe constructed from the hypotheses of philosophers and geographers at best, and derived from ancient myth and irrepressible sailors' lore at worst. The speculation that shaped his mission was more fictional than scientific, confirmed, if at all, by vague and apocryphal reports of other voyagers, yet he was nevertheless enjoined to make discoveries and bring back hard evidence to establish them—especially the riches of Asia. In tracing these expectations in the fifteenth century, Valerie Flint tries "to reconstruct, and understand, not the New World Columbus found, but the Old World which he carried with him in his head" (Flint xi). She argues that the mix of "fact" and "fancy" cannot be separated into distinct elements and that "fantasy of a certain sort becomes proper, indeed vital, to the complete understanding of fact itself" (xii). Columbus's mental world was built from "practical experience, as are all mental worlds; but personal devotion fired by private reflection, reading, and, above all perhaps, dramatic storytelling, sacred and secular, contributed more to its makeup than has always been recognized" (xii).

Columbus's Atlantic had been filled for a long time with inhabited islands, and there was very little distinction between real islands like Thule (Iceland) or the Canaries and imaginary ones like Brasil (not to be confused with Brazil) or Perdita, the lost island. Many legendary islands are the heritage of antiquity, especially the *Odyssey*, the *Iliad*, the legend of the Isles of the Blest from Lucian's *True Histories*, of Atlantis from Plato's *Timaeus* and *Critias*, of Thule from Seneca's *Medea*, the seagoing labors of Heracles and the voyage of the Argonauts from Seneca's *Heroides* and Ovid's *Metamorphoses*.[7] The sea pilgrimage and story of exile across a sea flourished among Irish monks, and early medieval Christian sea stories like the legend of Antilia and the voyage of St. Brendan were particularly influential. The former, also called the Isle of the Seven Cities, describes an island in the Atlantic peopled by Spanish exiles escaping the Moors in 734; it has sources in Toscanelli's letter (1474) and Martin Behaim's globe (1492). The *Navigatio Sancti Brendani Abbatis* (ca. 800) describes the Abbot's sixth-century voyages westward to the Promised Land of the

Saints, discovering on the way a series of islands filled with flowering plants, fruit-laden trees, springs, fish, sheep, and, of course, an abundance of precious metals and stones; the discoveries are spread over a cycle of seven years and linked to the Holy Days of the liturgical year. During each annual cycle the voyaging monks encounter further perils and wonders until they finally reach the Island of Paradise and return home, where Saint Brendan dies and a messenger prophesies that his successors, also persecuted Christians, will rediscover the land.[8]

Five heavily annotated books that survived from Columbus's library provide further clues about his voyage expectations: Pierre d'Ailly's *Imago Mundi* (1480–1483), Pope Pius II's *Historia Rerum Ubique Gestarum* (1477), a version of Marco Polo's travels, *De Consuetudinibus et Conditionibus Orientalium Regionum* (1485–1486), a translation of Plutarch's *Lives* (1491), and another of Pliny's *Natural History* (1489). Columbus's annotations include his account of Diaz's voyage through the torrid zone to the Cape of Good Hope in 1488, arguments about the distance from Spain to the Indies, cannibalism, strange and sometimes fantastic inhabitants of distant regions, precious metals, jewels, and spices in these lands, the size of the Asian landmass and the islands lying off its eastern coast, the navigability of the northern ocean, Solomon's sea trade with Tarshish and his return from Ophir with gold, the riches of the Kublai Khan, the precious metals, gems, spices, cloths, woods, and other valuable products of the Indies, the closeness of Cipangu (Japan) and other islands to Spain, the length and difficulty of the sea voyage from Arabia east to India. With such an internalized seascape in mind, it is no wonder that Columbus persisted in believing that he was skirting the coasts of Asia, at least through his second voyage.[9] Like other ocean explorers of later ages, he projects his expectations on the islands and land masses that he encounters.

The maps available to Columbus reinforced the belief that he had reached Asia in a number of ways.[10] One type, the *mappamundi*, was based on the authority of the *Bible* more than the observations of fifteenth-century voyagers. With Jerusalem at the center on an axis running from Paradise in the east and the Gates of Hercules in the west, they displayed a triadic array of Europe, Africa, and Asia, all enclosed in the surrounding Ocean Sea. These *mappaemundi* assumed the shape of a *T* inside an *O*; in addition to Paradise, they represented many biblical places like Ophir, the lands of Gog and Magog, and the legendary Christian kingdom of Prester John. Mapmakers used supplementary treatises from the ancients and church fathers to fill in the blank spaces with subhuman races and monsters, blurring distinctions between natural history and legend in the service of biblical topography. Some maps drawn later than the thirteenth century, like the Catalan Atlas, reflect the geographical discoveries of Atlantic voyagers and Marco Polo but without abandoning either their penchant for the marvelous or their biblical roots.

Because such maps represented habitable land masses as surrounded by an encircling ocean, voyages of circumnavigation to reach the lands of the Great Khan were theoretically possible, and the biblical proportions of the Creation—Ezekiel's six parts of land to one of water—suggested that such voyages might be feasible. The rediscovery of Ptolemy's *Geography* early in the fifteenth century modified but did not replace the traditions of *mappaemundi*; for example, Columbus rejected Ptolemy's estimate of the size of the Asian land mass in favor of Marinus of Tyre's larger one and thereby erroneously foreshortened the distance of a westward sea voyage to reach the East.

A second type of cartography, the zone and climate map, tells a different story. Of the five zones in the world (two polar, two temperate, and one torrid) only two were thought to be habitable, and sea passages through the polar and torrid zones were deemed impossible, thereby encouraging the westward passage through the temperate zone that Columbus espoused. Traditions of the zone maps allowed for the possibility of a fourth land mass in the southern temperate zone, but biblical genealogy suggested that it could not be inhabited by human beings since the three sons of Noah each had their continents to populate. A third type of map, the portolan chart used by mariners, was filled with compass roses sprouting radial rhumb lines to help navigators set courses from place to place and was often detailed, especially along the coasts of the Mediterranean, Atlantic Europe, and Atlantic Africa as far south as the Portuguese had sailed; such portolans had no interest in the interior and usually left it blank. In known waters they were less subject to the influence of biblical typology, as one might expect, but still filled the Atlantic with hypothetical islands, a mix of the real and the mythical.

Portolan chart of the Atlantic by Zuane Pizzigano of Venice (1424), with a mixture of real islands and legendary islands like Antilia (the large blot with seven cities). Courtesy of the James Ford Bell Library, University of Minnesota.

We have to remember that islands once sighted were often "lost" again because it was impossible to determine their longitude precisely, not only in Columbus's era but also through most of Cook's; thus both the Atlantic and later the Pacific came to be filled with hypothetical islands that could be found again only by the crude method of sailing a latitude, a practice used by European navigators from the fifteenth through the eighteenth centuries. (In this respect the Polynesian navigators, who had voyaged over vast spaces of the empty Pacific to locate and relocate small islands for millennia—without instruments of any kind—were far more successful than their European counterparts.) Islands also figure in the mysterious "Columbus Chart" (ca. 1488–1492), an anomaly because it combines two of these very different cartographic forms, a *mappamundi* and a portolan chart.[11] The chart and map plot many very real islands, including the Azores, the Canaries, the Cape Verdes, the British Isles, Iceland, and perhaps the Faroes, but the Atlantic also contains Antilia, Brasil, and half a dozen of Saint Brendan's allegorical islands, including the Terrestrial Paradise. The real and the only imagined coexist, and sometimes they have equal weight in determining action or interpreting events. In "Geography and Some Explorers," a retrospective essay published in the year of his death, Conrad expresses a navigator's dismay at the intellectual baggage Columbus had to carry on his first voyage:

> Geography had its phase of circumstantially extravagant speculation which had nothing to do with the pursuit of truth, but has given us a curious glimpse of the medieval mind playing in its ponderous childish way with the problems of our earth's shape, its size, its character, its products, its inhabitants. Cartography was almost as pictorial then as are some modern newspapers. It crowded its maps with pictures of strange pageants, strange trees, strange beasts, drawn with amazing precision in the midst of theoretically conceived continents. It delineated imaginary kingdoms of Monomotapa and of Prester John, the regions infested by lions or haunted by unicorns, inhabited by men with reversed feet, or eyes in the middle of their breasts.[12]

There are many differences in the expectations that brought Columbus into the Atlantic and Cook into the Pacific centuries later. The canons of rationalization had changed, yet it would be a mistake to regard Columbus's journals as largely fanciful and Cook's as nothing more than scientific documents. Maritime historians now recognize a sharp distinction between ships' logs and voyage journals. Logs are legal documents precisely recording the ship's position, weather and sea conditions, and major events on board like punishment, death, or any endangerment of the ship; entries are written by the officer on watch, without expressions of attitude or opinion, and falsifying them is a crime. Journals, on the other hand, record personal impressions and have all the defining characteristics of narratives, including plot. We cannot impose such a distinction on either Columbus or Cook, whose journals performed both functions simultaneously and were indirectly influenced by the literary traditions of their day. For Columbus, one of those traditions, more literary than scientific, was cosmology. Valerie Flint feels that structures of expectation derived from his geographical preconceptions colored his observations deeply: "Scenes preenacted, as it were, behind his eyes, were reenacted before them, and were then reported to the admiral's sovereigns with all the imaginative and emotional intensity which drives the visionary" (xiii).

A second literary tradition was embellishment, represented by two influential medieval travel narratives. Marco Polo really went to China, but his descriptions of the Great Khan's empire were dated when it collapsed long before the manuscripts describing its wonders ceased circulating, and Sir John Mandeville's fantastic travel accounts may have been invented in a library rather than experienced anywhere. Columbus makes good use of embellishment in his "Letter to the Sovereigns on His First Voyage," first published in late March or early April 1493 in Barcelona by Pedro Poso; by 1500 another Spanish edition and fifteen translations had appeared. The letter reads like a travelogue and is devoted to the abundance of fine harbors, the richness and beauty of the land and its marvelous variety of trees, plants, and fruits in Cuba (Juana) and Hispaniola (La Spanola), as well as a description of the inhabitants. Like a skilled propagandist, Columbus concentrates on these lands of plenty, enlarges them (Cuba is bigger than Spain), mentions gold, refers to searching for but not finding cities, calls the tiny settlement of La Navidad a large town, and makes no direct reference to the circumstances of its founding or the embarrassing loss of the *Santa Maria*. Here, almost as if we were in the world of the *Odyssey*, we find exaggerated travel notes about real places, wishful thinking, convenient lacunae of memory about untoward events, and a pervading sense of wonder that any travel writer might do well to emulate.

Columbus: *Diario* of the First Voyage, 1492–1493

Writing about Columbus after 1992 requires wading through a morass of sometimes contentious scholarly print and largely irrelevant political attacks and defenses of the effects of the voyages. Anyone who tries to be comprehensive will become, ipso facto, a lifelong bibliographer in many languages, as well as face the confusion created by unwarranted hagiography and excessive vilification. The glorification began with Columbus's illegitimate son Ferdinand, who wrote his biography, *The Life of the*

"Cristoforo Columbo" by Leonardo Lasansky.
Courtesy of the James Ford Bell Library, University of Minnesota.

Admiral Christopher Columbus (first published posthumously in an Italian translation in 1569) to embellish his father's reputation and to substantiate his own claims as heir against those of his half-brother, Diego. In America, flattering portraits of Columbus became a sign of patriotism after Washington Irving's monumental *The Life and Voyages of Christopher Columbus* (1828) and James Fenimore Cooper's *Mercedes of Castile* (1840), a historical romance based on the first voyage. That euphoria lasted through the elaborate Columbian Exposition and other quadricentennial celebrations in 1892 but shattered as the next round approached a century later. Sources for excoriating what Columbus had done personally and the Spanish collectively can be found as an undercurrent throughout Bartolomé de Las Casas's *History of the Indies* (also published posthumously in 1575), which exposes the rapaciousness of the conquistadores and the decimation of the

Indian population. (Las Casas was also the abstractor of Columbus's log into the *Diario* we know.) As the 1992 commemorations arrived, a spate of published attacks materialized, including one anthology that announced its intention to "correct the historical record" and tell the "real story" of "subjugation and greed," including "the very specific crimes he [Columbus] committed."[13] Luckily, our task is nautical rather than political, so we can pass by this onslaught against the character of Columbus, as well as previous whitewashes, to focus on the experience of the first voyage.

Unfortunately, four other unremitting controversies are germane—in varying degrees—to our reading of the first-voyage narrative. The first has always generated political acrimony by challenging ethnic loyalties, particularly among Americans of Italian or Scandinavian descent and especially when it is phrased negatively: Columbus was not the first voyager to sight or set foot on American soil. Scholars no longer argue about this, in spite of hoaxes like the Kensington Rune Stone and the furor over the authenticity of the Vinland map—first published by Yale in 1965, discredited as a twentieth-century forgery after chemical analysis in 1972, and now republished in 1996 after x-ray emission tests have provided some support for the original conclusion.[14] Whatever the provenance of the map, there is significant literary evidence for Viking voyages to America from the Icelandic *Greenlander's Saga* (ca. 1200) and *Eric the Red's Saga* (ca. 1275), although, as with all oral compositions redacted to text several centuries later, such evidence has to be handled with care.[15] Yet, put in conjunction with the archaeological evidence from excavations at L'Anse aux Meadows in Newfoundland, the case is compelling: The Vikings reached North America at the turn of the eleventh century, if not before.[16]

For our purposes only one subordinate question is relevant: How much Atlantic ocean knowledge did Columbus have before he set out from Palos in 1492, and what were its sources, either from his own experience or from hearsay? Until questions about the Vinland map settle out, it is pointless to speculate about whether he knew of its existence or had seen it, but argument about a related question remains: Had he sailed as far north as Iceland? Scholars disagree about the answer because it is based primarily on a single shred of evidence, a note quoted in Ferdinand's biography, but most allow for the possibility. In the note Columbus claims to have sailed 100 leagues beyond Thule in February 1477 and also mentions traders from Bristol visiting the island, in the context of commenting on the navigability of all five zones of the world.[17] More important than any geographical knowledge that might have emerged from such a voyage is prolonged contact with the prevailing westerlies in the Atlantic north of latitude 35 degrees, and a voyage toward Iceland from Portugal would have established the breadth of that band. For Columbus, such experience would guarantee that he could return home downwind after sailing westward to the Indies. The mention of Bristol traders in the note Ferdinand quotes strengthens the probability that Columbus had some direct experience in the higher latitudes of the North Atlantic, perhaps even on a Bristol ship. A number of documents substantiate the activity of Bristol seamen in voyages northward and westward during the last two or three decades of the fifteenth century, and some believe that one of them, John Lloyd, undertook one or more voyages to "Brasil" and may have reached Newfoundland in the 1480s.[18] Regardless of whether that is true, it is likely that Columbus was aware of other North Atlantic voyages during the decades immediately prior to his own departure because of a strong trading connection between Bristol and Lisbon.

Far more certain is Columbus's familiarity with the lower latitudes of the North Atlantic from a much broader Portuguese context. Although very little is known about the details of Columbus's activities during the decade he spent in Portugal before leaving for Castile in 1485, the outlines are clear. He had help in establishing himself from the Genoese community in Lisbon and married Felipa Moniz, a woman from that community whose family had strong court connections and whose father had been granted the island of Porto Santo in the Madeiras. Columbus lived for a time on the island, learned Portuguese, Castilian, and Latin, the language he would need to develop his geographical conceptions, made a number of Atlantic voyages, including one down the West African coast to Guinea, and was associated in some way with the chart-making activities of his younger brother, Bartolomeu.

No situation could have been more opportune for tapping into the ocean knowledge that the Portuguese had been accumulating for more than a century before Columbus arrived. Three of the four Atlantic island groups so important to Columbus's voyages—the Canaries, the Madeiras, and the Azores—were known and partially charted before Prince Henry began his activities in the third decade of the fourteenth century. The notion that he established a formal "school" of navigation at Sagres on the spectacular tabletop cliffs overlooking the Atlantic is the invention of nineteenth-century historians, now abetted by modern tourist authorities, but he did collect navigational information and launch aggressive exploratory ventures in two directions—to the Atlantic islands and down the West African coast. In the 1420s and 1430s Prince Henry began the Portuguese colonization of the Madeiras and the Azores and tried, unsuccessfully, to wrest control of part of the Canaries from Castile. During the same decades he began sending expeditions southward to explore the African coast, a stage-by-stage process that continued with sporadic voyages until his death in 1460. While Columbus was in residence in Portugal, King John II energetically resumed that process of leapfrogging down the coast, cape by cape, with the ultimate objective of reaching the end of Africa and establishing an eastward sea route to India, a process later completed in the voyages of Bartolomeu Días and Vasco da Gama. Nowhere else could Columbus have learned so much about currents and winds in parts of the ocean he was soon to traverse, and he also had access to the lore of the port in Lisbon, a melange of rumors and sightings of land to the westward of the Azores, as well as whatever information his deceased father-in-law had collected in Porto Santo. In addition, he had the advantage of the navigational prowess that Portuguese seamen had acquired in this burst of Atlantic activity. David Waters of the National Maritime Museum in Greenwich assesses what he was able to assimilate: "Columbus had gleaned from the Portuguese pilots their empirical knowledge of the North Atlantic wind system, how to measure variation, and a smattering of their art of equal altitude navigation, but not yet enough to apply always correctly the Rule of the North Star, nor to observe always reliably with the instruments that they used, quadrant and astrolabe."[19]

A second nautical problem related to the first voyage is really a gap in knowledge that escalated into controversy only when the Columbian celebrations of 1892 and 1992 required replicas.

Although the generic types of the three vessels were known, two caravels and a nao, neither lines nor models for the specific ships were available for a variety of reasons succinctly summarized by Richard W. Unger as lack of documentation from builders and difficulty in interpreting what little there is, the unreliability of artistic representations, and the paucity of archaeological evidence. He outlines further difficulties in knowing precisely what Columbus's ships were like: "If difficulties with sources of information is not enough to make the task daunting, the history of ship design in the period compounds the problem. The fifteenth century, the end of the Middle Ages and early Renaissance in general, was a time of great change in the design, construction and even in the conception of ships. In such periods of change and novelty, a variety of technologies often exist side by side, the old remaining in place next to the new along with a number of intermediate forms vying for prominence."[20]

General characteristics of the two types are known: Caravels, the workhorses of Portuguese ocean exploration, were relatively small, narrow ships with low freeboard (height of deck above the water), two masts carrying lateen (triangular) sails, although sometimes mixed with at least one square sail (the rig *Pinta* originally carried and the one Columbus adopted when he rerigged *Niña* after experience on the first leg of the voyage to the Canaries); their size (usually 50 to 70 tons) was measured by the cargo of wine they could carry. Naos were larger, broader of beam in relation to their length, had greater freeboard and three masts, two of which were rigged with square sails, and could carry anywhere from 90 to 200 tons of cargo. Most scholars think the *Santa Maria*—whose sailing qualities at sea Columbus apparently disliked—was a nao. Beyond this any consensus on all three ships breaks down, largely because there is no reliable way of projecting the basic dimensions (length of keel, waterline length, overall length, beam, depth of hold, draft) that would define their basic hull shapes from tonnage. For example, estimates of overall length of the *Niña* range from 38 to 70 feet, of the *Pinta* from 41 to 74 feet, and of the *Santa Maria* from 46 to 86 feet.[21] Thus the "replicas" built for the Columbian quadricentenary in 1892 and destined for the Chicago Exposition a year later, like those built for the Seville Exposition in 1927, the New York World's Fair of 1964–1965, and the quincentenary of 1992 are all

The caravel *Pinta,* typical of the vessels used for exploration by Portugal and
Spain. Drawn by Joaquin Sorolla y Bastida (1863–1923).
Courtesy of the Hispanic Society of America, New York.

hypotheses fleshed out in wood and canvas. We know a bit more
about them than we do about the galleys Odysseus would have
used, but that increased knowledge is more a matter of informed
speculation rather than authenticated knowledge.

A third controversy—by far the most acrimonious—is the
scholarly dispute about the site of Columbus's landfall in the
Bahamas. Fueled by geographers' zeal for precision, abetted by
renavigations, both on the water and simulated by computers,
and encouraged by the need for identifying the "right" place for
1992 commemorations, it seems never ending, even after the
event. Attempts to identify the landfall site date back to 1731, and
renewed interest in the question emerged after Martín Fernández de Navarette published a version of the *Diario* in 1825;
Washington Irving's biography of 1828 included an appendix on

the topic written by Alexander Slidell Mackenzie (later the central figure in the *Somers* affair, another long-lasting naval and literary controversy).[22] By the end of the nineteenth century most of the 11 candidate islands had been identified, and the rest began appearing on the hustings in the middle of the twentieth century after the publication of Morison's biography, the result of an expedition that renavigated the voyage and elected Watling Island as the winning candidate. (Watling had been rechristened San Salvador in 1926 in deference to Columbus, who thus renamed Guanahaní, the island of his landfall.) In the decade before 1992, the landfall question boomed as a focus for conferences and publications of the Society for the History of Discoveries, and it exploded into a public dispute in 1986 after the *National Geographic* took an unequivocal position. The lead of its article reflects the new passion the argument would arouse: "Christopher Columbus first came to the New World at reef-girt, low, and leafy Samana Cay, a small outrider to the sea lying in haunting isolation in the far eastern Bahamas, at latitude 23 degrees 5 minutes north, longitude 73 degrees 45 minutes west. It has taken me five years to write that sentence."[23] The author, Joseph Judge, was only one of many to get into the fray, and the next year two oceanographers from the Woods Hole Oceanographic Institute ran a computer simulation based on Columbus's log that factored in winds and currents, reaching no firm conclusion but suggesting that San Salvador was a more likely landfall than Samana Cay; a renavigator later reached the same conclusion.[24] Many of the major players attended a landfall debate sponsored by the Phileas Society in November 1989, a meeting full of sound and fury that was filmed by WGBH for possible use in its then forthcoming Columbus documentary. By this time the field had narrowed to three major contenders—Watling's Island, Samana Cay, and Grand Turk—although some of the others were still mentioned. When someone questioned the significance of the landfall question in the summative session of the conference, the response was immediate: The Spanish reenactment fleet that would set out from Palos in 1992 should not sail to the wrong place.

Clearly, the issue had left the realm of scholarly journals and entered the domain of the media, where it would generate public attention for several years. Some of its fascination, apart from the imminence of 1992 commemorations throughout the world, reflected the interdisciplinary nature of the question, which could be addressed in different ways by historians, ocean navigators, mathematicians, oceanographers, geographers, textual scholars, and informed amateurs who had studied the Columbus voyage for many years. Some respected professional historians, like Felipe Fernandez-Armesto, opted out: "An enormous amount of time and effort has been wasted on attempts to identify the island where Columbus made his first landfall. The toponymy of the islands he visited on this first voyage has changed too much, and his surviving descriptions, except Cuba and Hispaniola, are too vague, inaccurate, and mutually contradictory, linked by sailing directions too corruptly transmitted, to reconstruct his route around them with any confidence."[25] David Henige, who has written the most comprehensive recent reviews of the controversy and its bibliography, agrees that the landfall question is unanswerable: "The lack of precise information in the sources, rather than discouraging these attempts, has invited students of the question to impose their own preconceptions on the data. There is no indication that this ever more intricate dancing with the evidence is about to cease."[26]

Even though the circumstances are different, the problem is comparable to that faced by retracers of Odysseus's voyage; as we have seen in chapter 2, those seeking specific identification of possible *Odyssey* sites in the Mediterranean must face the fact that many have a topography that matches the text neatly.[27] In addition to questions of Columbus's track across the Atlantic, much evidence analyzed by scholars deals with tracing his courses from island to island or reversing them from a confirmed and identifiable later landfall, noting, with either method, which islands seem best to fit the descriptions in the *Diario*. Unfortunately, the lack of many distinctive features in the low and reefbound islands of the Bahamas makes interpretation uncertain, and nearly every geographical identification must account for topographic and hydrographic anomalies that do not match the text.

Thus the fourth controversy—the reliability of the text— became a central issue for scholars, and it is disconcerting for general readers as well. To what extent are we reading what Columbus wrote or something else? The question is inescapable since the *Diario* text is Bartolomé de Las Casas's abstract of a copy of Columbus's log/journal; the original is not extant and the history of its scribal transmission is murky. David Henige has provided the most devastating analysis of this problem in his book, *In Search of Columbus: The Sources of the First Voyage* (1991). The argument is complex and intricate, but it boils down to an unsettling conclusion: "Whatever the log was, and the diario is, it is much more than a terse and disinterested nautical account of passing events. It also served as a subterfuge to beguile the Portuguese, as a propaganda device and apologia in the service of Columbus, as a paean to a new world discovered as well as a testimony to the monumental illusions that it was really just another part of the Old World, and as an instrument for Las Casas to buttress his own worldview of the Spanish discovery and conquest and pass it along to others" (Henige 122). Evidently we face some of the same questions that plague any study of the *Odyssey* as a text, but as skeptical readers we can distinguish between doubts about internal contradictions or external geographical references from broader questions about the events reported in the narrative. The doubts may keep the true identity of Guanahaní forever elusive, as Henige suggests, whereas the questions about incidents in the *Diario* must also be answered in rhetorical terms—appropriateness to the context of the narrative, to the beliefs of the writer, and to effects on the intended audience.

A case in point is the climactic moment of the voyage out, when an improbable light appears as a sign of landfall on the night of 11 October:

> A sailor named Rodrigo de Triana saw this land first, although the Admiral, at the tenth hour of the night, while he was on the sterncastle, saw a light, although it was something so faint that he did not wish to affirm that it was land. But he called Pero Gutierrez, the steward of the king's dais, and told him that there seemed to be a light, and for him to look: and thus he did and saw it. He also told Rodrigo Sanchez de Segovia, whom the king and queen were sending as *veedor* of the fleet, who saw nothing because he was not in a place where he could see it. After the Admiral said it, it was seen once or twice, and it was like a small wax candle that rose and lifted up, which to few seemed to be an indication of land.[28]

As one can imagine, this mysterious light has generated many pages of explanation and commentary, especially because it is seen when the *Santa Maria* is supposedly more than 40 miles from the landfall island, and no one can see over the horizon that far. Moreover, the Admiral's assertion robs Rodrigo de Triana of the substantial rewards offered by the sovereigns and by Columbus for the first sight of land, which Columbus claimed for himself. Was the passage inserted later to substantiate this reward or as preemptive insurance against anticipated controversy with the Pinzón family over Columbus's hereditary rights as Admiral of the Ocean Sea, claims that plagued his heirs through a protracted legal proceeding from 1513 to 1536?[29] Or could it simply be an illusion that the Admiral is unwilling either to confirm or disconfirm at first sighting? Anyone who has sailed at night knows how difficult it can be to distinguish an illusory light from a real one, so Columbus's caution could be simply the measured response of an experienced seaman.[30] And most important from our nautical perspective is the question of seamanship the sighting raises. Columbus ordered a good lookout but kept the *Santa Maria* on course booming ahead at an estimated eight knots (probably near her maximum hull speed) for four hours of the night, from the sighting of the light at 10 P.M. until confirmation of the landfall at 2 A.M., when she finally stood off until daylight. Even without knowledge of coral reefs, which Columbus had no way of acquiring, this is impetuous and foolish seamanship and a direct contradiction of his own standing orders against night sailing at this stage of the voyage.

In such ways does the shaky provenance and textual history of the *Diario* raise questions that cannot be answered easily, if at all. If the questions are debilitating to those who try to settle the landfall dispute once and for all, they have no comparable effect on readers interested in the voyage narrative for its own sake. The text we have, now finally in more authentic transcription and translation, may be part history and part fiction, a point that Henige grants somewhat obliquely: "In reasserting the primacy of the text, the analysis of real voyages cannot be separated entirely from the overwhelming demonstration of the ability of imaginary voyages to fascinate and beguile both in their own time and after" (164). Put more directly, that is the central thesis of this study: Whether they intend to produce accurate accounts or fictional representations, writers of voyage narratives characteristically drink from both wells—experience and imagination.

Much of the abstract of Columbus's log of the outward voyage from Gomera in the Canaries to Gauanahaní in the Bahamas, wherever that may be, records the course sailed, speed, distance covered (although that is problematic, as we shall see), wind and sea conditions, and observations of clouds, weeds, or birds that may signal the presence of land. Like most logs it has little intrinsic narrative structure beyond the progression of the ship and would be rather dull reading in ordinary circumstances. But the circumstances are not ordinary here for one poignant reason: There are two unknowns: where the ship is and what is out there. In the years since the oceans of the world have been charted, sailors contend with only one—where they are in relation to known coasts, islands, reefs, currents, and even wind patterns. Voyagers who sailed into uncharted seas had no such advantage, and they often paid dearly for it, as Cook did when he "found" the Great Barrier Reef off Australia, previously an unimaginable structure rising out of ocean depths well offshore. Columbus could have had a similar disastrous experience with the reefs surrounding most islands in the Bahamas and disappeared forever if he had not stood off the land sighted on the night of 11 October 1492 until daylight. As noted earlier, Columbus is by turns brash and prudent during this most important night of the outward voyage, first sailing downwind at full speed during the darkest hours and then tacking back and forth under reduced sail in the predawn hours. Like Cook, he acts in a mariner's void, lacking any knowledge or experience of coral reef systems in the new sea world he had blundered into. So the stark narrative of partly guessed positions on an unknown ocean is loaded with intrinsic tension in an era long before a ship's position could be determined with some certainty.

Scholars are still not sure whether Columbus relied on sailing a latitude or dead (deduced) reckoning, or a combination of the two methods. Those who sailed latitudes measured the angle of the polestar to maintain their position on a specific parallel that would lead to a desired landfall; those who used dead reckoning plotted their course made good by combining compass bearing, speed through the water, and time on course. Either method was fraught with potential errors. Columbus seems to have had trouble getting accurate altitudes of Polaris with a quadrant; his estimates of speed were based on observation without any measuring instruments; his corrections for magnetic variation of the compass were erratic and excessive; and he had no way of calculating leeway or drift in ocean currents. Adding up all these uncertainties, sailing westward out into the Atlantic in Columbus's time was like playing blindman's buff without having anything to identify.

Buried within the navigational material are some other compelling narrative elements. Like much else in the *Diario*, the distances made good are suspect. No attentive reader can avoid noticing Las Casas's intrusions to justify a puzzling aberration from sound nautical practice: double logging of the distance sailed each day, once in Columbus's figures, which are greater, and once in the pilot's, which are lesser and available for public consumption on board. Such discrepancies would astound any Admiralty court, but they are explained here as a means of placating the men's anxiety about how far they had come without sighting land, in addition to fears about how they could ever get home against the prevailing winds that had pushed them this far. As might be expected, the double distances have confounded the landfall scholars and produced a debate within a debate: Which are the more accurate figures, and what was the length of the Columbian "league" and the "mile" in various parts of the text? Estimates of the league vary from 2.67 to 3.18 nautical miles (in the current standard measure of 6,080 feet per mile), and since the higher figure inconveniently places Columbus's landfall west of Miami many interpreters of the *Diario* have applied corrections to get him to whichever Bahamian destination they favor.[31] But even if we get the mathematics straightened out, the more interesting question of Columbus's motive remains. Why would he have embraced such an unseamanlike practice, or alternatively, why would Las Casas have inserted something into the *Diario* that was bound to raise eyebrows and create the need for an apologetic strategy?

The *Diario* provides a direct but slim answer in the entry for 9 September, when the fleet was just a few days out of Gomera: "He made 15 leagues that day and he decided to report less than those actually traveled so in case the voyage were long the men would not be frightened and lose courage" (29). The search for a more elaborate rationale has provided a field day for speculation among biographers and translators. Morison accepts the "phony" reckoning as a ploy to calm the crew without questioning it, Taviani sees it as a precalculated policy, and Fernando-Armesto asserts that Columbus "revelled in his role of lone manipulator with evident relish and feigned unease"; more soberly, William and Carla Phillips favor James Kelley's explanation that Columbus's private log was calculated in the shorter Genoese leagues he was familiar with and then converted into the longer Portuguese leagues used in Iberian navigation.[32] The *Diario* itself (in a later passage) suggests yet another possibility in this mix of motives, a kind of long-range protection policy for the Admiral's control of the Ocean Sea: "And he says that he pretended to have gone a greater distance to confuse the pilots and sailors who were charting their course so that he would remain the master of the route to the Indies, as in fact he does, since none of them showed on their charts his true route, because of which no one could be sure of his route to the Indies" (375).

The double logging is also related to another important narrative element in the voyage out, the restiveness of the crew that may have led to "incipient mutiny" (Morison 1942, 208). Again, the *Diario* is sparse and the interpretive embellishments profuse. The discontent openly appears in only two brief entries, the first on 10 October, just two days before landfall:

> Here the men could no longer stand it; they complained of the long voyage. But the Admiral encouraged them as best he could, giving them good hope of the benefits that they would be able to secure. And he added that it was useless to complain since he had come to find the Indies and thus had to continue the voyage until he found them, with the help of Our Lord. (*Diario*, 57)

This language has the tone of a quarterdeck conference more than a tense and potentially explosive confrontation, but there is a second, much stronger entry written in retrospect during the great storm on the voyage home. In that moment of stress the prospect that his life's great enterprise might founder at sea and be forgotten leads Columbus to admit to a "loss of confidence in Divine Providence" and to recollect the earlier crisis that could have destroyed the project:

> [He writes here] that, since earlier he had entrusted his destiny and dedicated all of his enterprise to God, Who had heard him and given

him all he had asked for, he ought to believe that God would grant him the completion of what he had begun and would take him to safety. And more so since He had delivered him on the outward voyage, when he had greater reason to fear from his troubles with the sailors and people that he took with him, who all, with one voice, were determined to go back and to rise against him in protest. And the eternal God gave him strength and resolution against all of them. (*Diario*, 369)

From these bare bones rises the tale of a disastrous mutiny that nearly was.[33] Las Casas adds marginal notes indicating the men's discontent to the *Diario* entries for 22 and 23 September; his *History of the Indies* follows up by describing increasing disquiet as the ship reaches the weed of the Sargasso Sea (variously believed in sailor's lore to cover rocks or to immobilize ships), then encounters erratic gyrations in the position of Polaris, which was used to check the reliability of the compass. Frequent signs of land and false sightings provide a roller coaster of expectation and disappointment. The story soon bulges with new material, both in Las Casas's *History* and in Ferdinand's *Life*:

> As these signs [of land] proved fruitless, the men grew ever more restless and fearful. They met together in the holds of ships, saying that the Admiral in his mad fantasy proposed to make himself a lord at the cost of their lives or die in the attempt; that they had already tempted fortune as much as their duty required and had sailed farther from land than any others had done. Why, then, should they work their own ruin by continuing that voyage, since they were already running short of provisions and the ships had so many leaks and faults that even now they were hardly fit to retrace the great distance they had traveled? . . . Others said they had heard enough gab. If the Admiral would not turn back, they should heave him overboard and report in Spain that he had fallen in accidentally while observing the stars; and none would question their story. That, said they, was the best means of assuring their safe return. (Ferdinand 52–53)

In other accounts Columbus is forced to quell the mutiny on 10 October by agreeing to turn back if land is not found in three days. From his own seafaring experience, Morison adds an anatomy of shipboard discontent that can lead to mutiny, then analyzes the final stages of the story's growth, variations, and contradictions (Morison 1942, 207–10, 215–21). In the papers of the endless lawsuit between the Pinzóns' interests and those of Columbus's heirs during the sixteenth century, heroes and villains reverse, with a faltering Columbus bolstered by Martín Alonzo Pinzón's exhortation: " 'Come sir, we have hardly left the town of Palos and your honor is already discouraged; onward sir, that God give us victory that we may discover land, that in no wise doth God wish that shamefully we turn back' " (Morison 1963, 190). At this point the story has political and literary overtones that overwhelm any canons of historical accuracy or logbook reporting. Like folktales, historical legends, or sensational crimes (e.g., the Lindberg kidnapping, President Kennedy's assassination, the O. J. Simpson murder story), the potential

The nao *Santa Maria,* shipwrecked on the coast of Hispaniola on Christmas Eve, 1492. Drawn by Joaquin Sorolla y Bastida (1863–1923).
Courtesy of the Hispanic Society of America, New York.

mutiny can assume various shapes with Protean ease. At its core is an archetype that has many earlier and later manifestations in voyage narratives, ranging from the Aeolus and cattle-of-the-sun episodes in the *Odyssey* to the mutiny on the *Bounty* and the aborted mutiny on board Conrad's *Narcissus*.

While Columbus was poking through the shallow and reef-strewn waters of the Bahamas he exercised a great deal of cautious seamanship, reducing sail and holding offshore for the night if he could not reach a potential anchorage near an island in good light. Along the coast of Cuba and Hispaniola he was almost as assiduous as Cook would later be in surveying every bay and river mouth he came upon, describing the entrance, measuring the depth of water in various parts, and suggesting good anchorages and even possible docking sites for ships. Thus it is with some surprise—on a first reading of the *Diario* at least—that we come upon the untoward loss of the *Santa Maria* a few miles east of Cape Haitien on Christmas Eve, 1492. Apart from the ironic juxtaposition of the ship's name and the date—a symbolism that would not be lost on either Columbus or his crew—this incident epitomizes the fears of any mariner navigating in unknown waters. The conditions were anything but threatening, with a calm sea and enough light wind for steerage way, but discipline on board was slack and the improbable disaster struck. The *Diario* is the only primary source for the shipwreck:

> It pleased Our Lord that at the twelfth hour of night when they had seen the Admiral lie down and rest and saw that it was dead calm and the sea as smooth as water in a bowl, all lay down to sleep and left the tiller in the hands of that boy; and the currents of water carried the ship upon one of those banks, which even though it was at night, could be seen, and which made a sound that from a full league off could be heard; and the ship went upon it so gently that it was hardly felt. The boy who felt the rudder and heard the sound of the sea cried out, at which the Admiral came out, and it was so quick that still no one had sensed that they were aground. Then the master of the ship, whose watch it was, came out, and the Admiral told him and the others to haul in the boat that they were pulling astern and to take an anchor and throw it astern. And he with many others jumped into the boat, and the Admiral thought that they would do what he had ordered. But they cared for nothing but to flee to the caravel, which was upwind half a league. The caravel, dutifully, did not want

to receive them, and for this reason they returned to the ship, but the caravel's launch got there first. When the Admiral saw that it was his men who were fleeing, that the waters were diminishing, and that the ship already lay crosswise to the seas, seeing no other remedy, he ordered the mast cut and the ship lightened of as much as they could to see if they could get her off; and as the waters still continued to diminish they could not remedy matters; and she listed toward the cross sea, although there was little or no sea running. And then the planking opened up, but not the ship. (*Diario*, 278–79)

On the surface, this account seems straightforward enough, but it raises more questions than it answers. Earlier we are told that no one had slept much during the previous two days of meetings and ceremonies with friendly local Indians to explain why the Admiral, the master on watch (Juan de la Cosa, part owner of the ship), and the crew are so exhausted. Also, somewhat ironically, this was one of the few coastal regions not entirely unknown on board because a boat's crew had traversed it two days earlier. Yet with no lookout in the bow and no one on deck to check courses (the boy at the tiller could not see where the ship was heading), the *Santa Maria* was sailing blind in an area infested with known reefs. Had there been a watch on deck, even if the wind died totally and the ship was being carried slowly toward the reef, it would have been relatively easy to use the boat to tow her clear. The unseamanlike and cowardly defection of the master (roughly equivalent to a captain or executive officer in our terms) is both insubordinate and ridiculous in a calm sea within several miles of shore, and it suggests continued resonance of the discontents that had earlier fed mutinous sentiments. Although Columbus orders precisely the right steps to get the ship off the coral reef, he later abandons these efforts rather abruptly, which is puzzling because we are never quite sure how bad the damage is, especially in a negligible swell.[34] At one point we are given the contradictory line quoted above—"the planking opened up, but not the ship"—yet later we are told "that of everything that was in the ship not even a lace-end was lost, neither plank nor nail, because she remained in as good condition as when she left [Spain], except that she was cut and opened up somewhat to get out the storage jars and all the merchandise" (*Diario*, 291).

Columbus rationalizes the loss of the ship as if it were a biblical fortunate fall: It made him found the colony of La Navidad, building the fort with timbers from the wreck, and gave him time ashore to find out more about where the gold was (*Diario*, 289–91). Never mind that the wreck had reduced his fleet by a third and that he had to put some men ashore because there was no room for them on the *Niña*, the only ship at hand, since Martín Alonzo Pinzón had sailed off on his own with the *Pinta* a month earlier. Such sophistry carries Columbus on to a final complaint: "[T]he ship, he says, was very sluggish and not suited for the work of exploration; and in taking such a ship, he says, the men of Palos failed to comply with their promise to the king and queen to provide suitable vessels for that trip, and they did not do it" (*Diario*, 291). Apart from the tone of exculpatory whining and the blatant non sequitur, this final charge is simply false: Palos had provided the two caravels as required by the order of the sovereigns, and Columbus himself had arranged the charter of the *Santa María*. These passages of apologia, whether written at the time or inserted later, do not show the Admiral at his best, and they would not have helped him much in a court of inquiry about the loss of his ship.

Eleven days after the wreck, Columbus continued sailing eastward along the coast of Hispaniola in the *Niña*, now his flagship, met the *Pinta* two days later, and heard the excuses of the returning prodigal. In mid-January 1493 the two caravels began the final leg of the voyage home, making good a course roughly northeast against the trade winds that had carried them westward to the Bahamas. Some scholars feel that Columbus's attempt to sail eastward undermines any assumption that he understood the circulatory wind patterns of the North Atlantic, arguing that such knowledge would have guided him in sailing north until he hit the westerlies that would bring him home downwind.[35] Had the benefits of great circle sailing been known to Columbus, the argument would be more convincing. An expanding and shrinking band of variable winds separates the northeast trades from prevailing westerlies at various seasons of the year, with the full force of the latter uncertain below 35 degrees north latitude. Under such circumstances, why should Columbus not try to make as much easting as he could through a variable zone whose width he could have no way of predicting? In fact, the course he did sail home was quite efficient because he reached the edge of the westerlies in the first days of February at about 33 degrees north, roughly the latitude of Bermuda, and carried them eastward with few interruptions until he was overwhelmed by a great southwesterly gale off the Azores in mid-February.

That gale is the centerpiece in the narrative of the voyage home, and in many ways the caravels were ill prepared to deal with a storm of such intensity. As Columbus takes his departure from Hispaniola, seeking to call at the island of the Caribs before heading toward Spain, "he noticed that the men began to get gloomy because of deviating from the direct route" and, more

The caravel *Niña*, Columbus's minuscule flagship for his return voyage. Drawn by Joaquin Sorolla y Bastida (1863–1923).
Courtesy of the Hispanic Society of America, New York.

curiously, that "he was unable to delay because of the water that the caravels were taking in" (*Diario*, 343). Two days earlier he had complained about leaks near the keel and the bad job the caulkers at Palos had done (*Diario*, 337). What better reason not to put to sea can one imagine, especially at the beginning of an ocean crossing of unknown duration? Later, in the midst of the storm, we learn that the *Niña* is severely underballasted because the Admiral had forgotten to give reballasting high priority, distracted first by his search for gold and then for the island of the Caribs: "[A] lack of ballast helped to increase the danger, her cargo having been lightened by the consumption of provisions and the drinking of water and wine: which [ballast], because of their greediness during the prosperous time they had in the islands, the Admiral did not provide, intending to order the ship ballasted on the Isla de las Mugeres where he had proposed to go" (*Diario*, 367).

Leaking and half ballasted with seawater poured into empty wine and water pipes (casks), the *Niña* meets one of the very severe storms that do occur in the waters west of the Azores. By studying meteorological data on storms that match Columbus's description closely, Morison estimates its strength at force 9 or 10 on the Beaufort scale, that is, with winds from 41 to 55 knots and waves from 23 to 41 feet high (Morrison 1942, 324–26). A storm of similar ferocity produced steep waves as high as 50 feet and sank yachts not much smaller than the caravels off the Irish coast during the 1979 Fastnet Race, with a loss of 15 lives. The comparison is anachronistic but apt since both storms involved the convergence of separate systems that mounted the enormous, irregular seas that Columbus described: "Tonight the wind increased and the waves were frightful, one contrary to the other, so they crossed and held back the vessel which could neither go forward nor get out from between them, and the waves broke on her" (*Diario*, 363–65). In such extreme conditions the caravels would have been especially vulnerable to battering and swamping because of their low freeboard (distance from the waterline to the deck), so Columbus took the only possible action: "The seas and wind were increasing greatly, and seeing the great danger, he began to run before the wind wherever it would carry him, for there was nothing else to do" (*Diario*, 365). Even that recourse was fraught with extreme danger, as anyone who has tried to steer a sailing vessel downwind in big seas knows. The slightest inattention on the part of the helmsman—who is always tempted to look over his shoulder to see what foaming monster might be coming—can lead to a "broach": A wave catches and pushes the stern in one direction, rotates the ship and slams her down on her side to wallow in the trough and take the full force of waves coming in from abeam. Or just plain bad luck in being over-whelmed by a rogue wave from astern can lead to swift and sure disaster.

Under such desperate circumstances, Columbus's next move as a Christian mariner is not unexpected or irrational: He orders everyone on board to draw lots for three pilgrimages should they be saved from death at sea. In so doing he was continuing a sailors' tradition that filled the churches, cathedrals, and shrines of Europe with votive ship models and paintings from Columbus's era through the nineteenth century. (Not far south of his native Genoa, I once visited a shrine perched on a mountain above Rapallo that was filled with votive ships of all kinds; among them was a painting of Conrad's *Narcissus*.) Columbus draws the chickpea marked with a cross two times out of three, and once again when there is another drawing in a later storm.[36] As an added expression of thankfulness for delivery from the storm, "the Admiral and all the men made a vow that, as soon as they reached the first land, all would go in their shirt-sleeves in procession to pray in a church dedicated to Our Lady" (*Diario*, 367). That land happens to be Santa Maria in the Portuguese Azores, and the vow becomes the immediate cause of the capture of half of the ship's crew who were sent ashore to fulfill it.

In narrative terms, the very name of the island echoes that of the wrecked former flagship, and the incident links the storm with the political troubles that mark the end of the voyage. In this instance what Morison calls the "Azorean agony" turns out to be a tempest in a teapot filled with inflated language and military posturing, but when Columbus is driven into Lisbon after another sequence of severe storms he is indeed in serious politi-cal straits (Morison 1942, 324). Not much detail about these later storms creeps into the *Diario*, apart from another drawing of lots, shredding of sails, and the ultimate peril of being driven onto an unfriendly lee shore (the cliffs of Sintra just north of Lisbon) at night in a storm; luckily, he is able to claw off the land with a remaining untorn sail until daybreak. Each major leg of the voyage has had its crisis—potential mutiny near the end of the westward crossing, unexpected shipwreck during the island hopping in the Caribbean, and two major storms on the way home. Whatever the source of its more questionable passages and details, the *Diario* has status as a full-blown voyage narrative that reflects both the realities of adventurous seafaring and human responses to them.

Cook: Journal of the First Voyage, 1768–1771

Nothing comparable to the controversies swirling around almost everything related to Columbus's Enterprise of the Indies attached itself to Cook's exploration of the Pacific. Cook scholarship is generally uncluttered by books claiming that he is either a saint or a demon, although he has been extolled as a heroic figure and his death exalted to tragic proportions. To be sure, Cook shares some of the obloquy aimed at the whole cast of explorers who created a European presence in the Pacific, which some regard as having a "fatal impact" on native peoples.[37] Yet most recent scholars of Cook's voyages, like Lynne Withey, espouse a more moderate view: "[W]hile the force of what Alan Moorhead called 'the fatal impact' is undeniable, the indictment of Europeans' impulse to explore the world ignores both the certainty that no group could remain undiscovered forever and the extent to which at least some of the Pacific islanders welcomed their involvement with Europeans. Discovery was a two-way business, although certainly the advantages in the exchange were heaped on the side of Europeans with their greater technological sophistication."[38] Cook's own actions, as recorded in his journals, help sustain the view that it is a mistake to blame the discoverer for the subsequent misuse of the world he opened up. In journal entries on the first voyage alone, we note how careful he was in laying down rules for fair trade with the often belligerent Maoris in New Zealand and how disturbed he was to think his men had introduced venereal diseases in Tahiti until he learned otherwise.

Most of the uncertainties that obscured a clear view of Columbus's first voyage had evaporated by the late eighteenth

Replica of Cook's ship on the first voyage, owned and operated by the HM Bark
Endeavour Foundation.
Photo by Rick Yoerg, Milktoast Productions.

century. Cook's ship for the first voyage, *HM Bark Endeavour,* was a well-known type, a Whitby collier, with bluff bows, a flattish bottom, and a capacious hold well suited to provisioning for a long voyage. Because she was extensively refitted by the Admiralty in 1768, only four years after she had been built, detailed plans are in the archives of the National Maritime Museum in Greenwich, and they provided a solid basis for the replica launched in Freemantle, Australia, in 1993.[39] Just as there are no unanswered questions about the dimensions, rig, or capabilities of Cook's ship, so too are his landfalls crystal clear, meticulously described and recorded in the journals, and backed up by the excellent charts he made.[40] His accomplishments as a hydrographer had recommended him to the Admiralty as a suitable captain for an exploratory voyage, so it is not surprising that he was a practiced and skilled navigator, using all the methods then available—dead reckoning, finding latitude with a sextant, and even learning to use Nevil Maskelyne's complicated new method of determining longitude by lunar observation.[41] (On his second voyage, Cook tested Kendal's version of the Harrison chronometer and found it far more accurate—and easier—than lunar observation.)

One problem similar to those confronting readers of Columbus's *Diario* did remain until the middle of the twentieth century: There was no fully reliable text of Cook's journals until J. C. Beaglehole produced his massive scholarly edition under the aegis of the Hakluyt Society.[42] The first official version of the journal to appear produced a publishing imbroglio of the first order. Dr. John Hawkesworth, one of the literati in Dr. Johnson's circle, had been commissioned by the Admiralty to adapt and transform captains' journals (as well as that of Joseph Banks) from a splurge of recent Pacific explorations—the voyages of Byron, Wallis, Carteret, and Cook—into a coherent narrative. In doing so he used his own canons of literary taste for travel narratives, some of which he shared with Johnson. The result was a disaster, offending the captains with nautical inaccuracies and superfluous classical and literary allusions that had never entered their heads; also the geographers, like Alexander Dalrymple, whose theories were questioned; and Christian leaders like John Wesley, who was scandalized at the description of Tahitian sexual mores. Cook received a copy while homeward bound from his second voyage and was "mortified" by its style and inaccuracies, especially because Hawkesworth had adopted the first person singular as a rhetorical strategy to close the gap between the captains and their audience (Beaglehole 1974, 439). Cook determined to insist on his own style in the published volume of the second voyage; Beaglehole restored that style in his scholarly edition of the first voyage but was generous in recognizing Hawkesworth as "a sort of classic unacknowledged by the historians of literature, the indispensable introduction to 'Cook's Voyages', whether laid out in full, or pillaged and abridged"; Hawkesworth died in chagrin six months after the publication of his magnum opus.[43]

No more than Columbus was Cook setting out into blank space on his first voyage. Nearly three centuries after the early Iberian ventures in ocean navigation, the Pacific had been traversed many times.[44] Magellan began the first circumnavigation (1519–1522) less than 30 years after Columbus's first voyage to America, although he did not survive it; he was succeeded by Drake (1577–1559) and Cavendish (1586–1588). In the late sixteenth century and first half of the seventeenth a number of Spanish and Dutch explorers—Mendaña, Quiros, Schouten and Le Maire, Tasman—undertook transpacific voyages, mostly in the tropical belt. At the end of the century Dampier's *New Voyage Round the World* (1697) again fanned a literary and practical interest in Pacific voyages that would last through the eighteenth century, with the chief players now from France, Russia, and especially England. English efforts to establish a trading empire in the South Seas, directed by the Admiralty, produced a remarkable series of circumnavigations with growing scientific as well as geopolitical objectives.[45] The disasters attending the first (1740–1744) under the command of Anson, whose crews were decimated by scurvy and squadron of six ships reduced to one before he returned, did not deter the Admiralty from mounting further circumnavigations led by Byron (1764–1766) and by Wallis and Carteret (1766–1769); meanwhile the French were at the same task with an expedition (1766–1769) under the command of Bougainville.

As one might expect in this context, Cook had even more detailed instructions about the purposes of his first voyage than Columbus. But most of the Pacific had not yet been sailed or charted, and, like Columbus, Cook was enjoined to make "Discovereys of Countries hitherto unknown, and the Attaining a Knowledge of distant Parts which though formerly discover'd have yet been but imperfectly explored"; he was given carefully qualified instructions about taking possession:

> You are also with the Consent of the Natives to take possession of Convenient Situations in the Country in the Name of the King of Great Britain; or, if you find the Country uninhabited take Possession for His Majesty by setting up Proper Marks and Inscriptions, as first discoverers and possessors.[46]

Such instructions requiring circumspection and even consideration of native populations were designed to prevent difficulties and Cook followed them meticulously, even though he did manage to get himself killed by native Hawaiians on his third voyage, largely through a combination of bad luck and a flawed policy for dealing with theft.[47]

The greater part of the instructions for the first voyage deal with a matter of geography that was thought to have great military and commercial importance for the expanding world empires of European nations: confirming or disconfirming the existence of a great southern continent, generally called *Terra Australis* (not to be confused with Australia). Its existence had been postulated as the Antipodes, a necessary balance to northern continental land masses, by Greek philosophers and geographers since Aristotle, and the circumnavigations of the sixteenth century whetted an appetite for its discovery. Alexander Dalrymple, the geographer who expected to lead the expedition that Cook was chosen to command, thought the presumed continent to be larger than Asia.[48] "Mighty is the power of a theory," writes Conrad, "especially if based on such a common-sense notion as the balance of continents":

> What is surprising to me is that the seamen of the time should have really believed that the large continents to the north of the Equator demanded, as a matter of good art or else of sound science, to be balanced by corresponding masses of land in the southern hemisphere. They were simple souls. The chorus of armchair people all singing the same tune made them blind to the many plain signs of a great open sea. Every bit of coast-line discovered, every mountain-top

glimpsed in the distance, had to be dragged loyally into the scheme of the Terra Australis Incognita. (Geography, 6–7)

The British circumnavigations dispatched during the 1760s were in part an unsuccessful attempt to settle the still open question, and although Cook was given many other botanical and ethnographic tasks as well as the charting of New Zealand, he was to perform them "without Suffering yourself however to be thereby diverted from the Object which you are always to have in View, the Discovery of the Southern Continent so often Mentioned" (*Explorations*, 19). After observing the transit of Venus in Tahiti, the Royal Society project that precipitated this voyage, he was to sail southward until he fell in with the continent, then survey it. Here the Admiralty was counting on Cook's proven mastery of charting unknown coastlines to provide the very practical navigational information it wanted:

> If you discover the Continent above-mentioned either in your Run to the Southward or to the Westward as above directed, You are to employ yourself diligently in exploring as great an Extent of the Coast as you can; carefully observing the true situation thereof both in Latitude and Longitude, the Variation of the Needle, bearings of Head Lands, Height, direction and Course of the Tides and Currents, Depths and Soundings of the Sea, Shoals, Rocks, &c. and also surveying and making Charts, and taking Views of such Bays, Harbours and Parts of the Coast as may be useful to Navigation. (*Explorations*, 18)

Cook never got beyond the ice to discover the much smaller continent of Antarctica on this or succeeding voyages, but he did meticulously chart New Zealand—proving that there were two separate islands and that neither was connected to a great southern continent—and virtually the entire east coast of Australia. But he never would have surveyed the real continent without the Admiralty's persistent interest in finding the hypothetical one that had a pedigree in ancient myth and geographical speculation.

Assessing the relationship between cartographic and literary representation, David Fausett remarks that "the region's persistent unknownness was an object of interest that went beyond merely commercial considerations into the realms of epistemology, and beyond problems of geography to focus those of literature."[49] The melding of fact and fiction was no longer seamless by the time Cook set out in the latter half of the eighteenth century, yet there were frequent crossovers between voyage accounts and voyage fictions. Ever since Defoe had adopted the strategy of loading *Robinson Crusoe* (1719) with meticulous surface detail to convince his readers that the story was true, it had been hard to distinguish reportorial from novelistic modes in voyage narratives. Defoe's novel is partly based on published accounts of the adventures of Alexander Selkirk (who had been marooned on the uninhabited island of Juan Fernández in 1704) as well as his wide reading in Hakluyt and other voyage narratives. Such narratives were immensely popular and lucrative when Cook began his voyages, so much so that Hawkesworth received 6,000 pounds for his work as compared to the 1,000 Fielding got for his masterpiece, *Tom Jones* (Beaglehole 1974, 290). When a ship returned from a long voyage, pirated editions—often embellished with sensational adventures—were produced with a rapidity and regularity that anticipates the spate of books we see within a month or two of any modern scandal. To curb such aggressive if specious pursuit of best-sellers, standing orders routinely directed captains, including Cook, to collect all log books and journals from officers and crew at the end of the voyage and deliver them to the Admiralty. The speculations of geographers still had a fictional quality, too. Alexander Dalrymple claimed that the hypothetical *Terra Australis* that Cook was to look for stretched more than five thousand miles through the South Pacific from a west coast in New Zealand to an east coast in the vicinity of Easter Island (Beaglehole 1974, 121). One of Cook's greatest accomplishments was the meticulous cartography of the coasts he surveyed, a process that replaced rampant geographical speculation with fragments of precise knowledge that gradually congealed into an accurate representation of the Pacific basin.

In an era when fictions struggled to put on the face of true accounts, the literary qualities of Cook's journals are more subtle than they are in Columbus's *Diario*. Reading Cook's journals requires selection, not interpretation, since many entries have navigational and scientific rather than narrative interest. But Cook's descriptive powers, spare rather than ornate, are considerable even in this first journal, and much of the narrative advance grows from the shape and pacing of unforeseen events in unknown places. Perhaps it is difficult for us to appreciate the surprises that jumped off many pages for readers in the eighteenth century. Such pages, in plain and direct style, represented outlandish customs and behaviors as well as unanticipated dangers to the ship or her men in strange waters or in encounters with natives ashore, where both groups had to invent their reactions on the spot. Relations with the Polynesians in Tahiti, the Maoris in New Zealand, and the Aborigines in Australia were not cut from the same piece of cloth, and ways of coping with each had to be learned through trial and error. By the time Cook's journals began appearing, the canons of verisimilitude were well established—if not always followed—for the novel and its near relatives, especially the burgeoning genre of travel narratives. The connection is not accidental, and many major literary figures of the day, including Defoe, Swift, Johnson, Boswell, Fielding, Smollett, and Sterne, wrote travel narratives.[50] Because such narratives often involved voyages in the eighteenth century, the substance of nautical experience in travel narratives and the forms developed in voyage fiction often commingled.

Voyage fiction itself assimilated elements from other literary genres; the picaresque journey goes to sea in Defoe's *Captain Singleton* and Smollett's *Roderick Random*, and Swift inverts the imaginary voyage to utopia/dystopia as a strategy for discovering strange and outlandish customs at home in *Gulliver's Travels*. The surprises encountered on unknown shores and the potential disasters endemic to seafaring appear in journals and novels alike, requiring arrangement more than invention. The subsequent story of one of Cook's lieutenants, Captain William Bligh, is a case in point: The central narrative of the mutiny on the *Bounty*, of Bligh's 3,600-mile boat voyage across the Pacific to Timor, and of the fate of the mutineers in Tahiti and on Pitcairn Island remains substantially intact—in spite of discrepancies—whether told in the journals of Bligh, those attributed to Fletcher Christian, reconstructions of events by many others, or the novel by Charles Nordhoff and Norman Hall. Voyage narratives seldom lack for events, and in response to the huge market for such accounts, whether genuine or fabricated, generic conventions had developed. Although not identical to those used by Columbus, these ways of structuring events at sea are a mix of patterns going back to the *Odyssey* and those more narrowly descended from Defoe. From Cook's running encounter with the Great Barrier Reef to the sequence of events leading to his death in Kealakekua Bay (narrated by James King), portions of the journals extrude dramatic action that is almost indistinguishable from the plots and incidents of contemporary voyage fiction.

Like most voyage narratives, the journal of Cook's first voyage has a dramatic shape dictated by events rather than the invention of imaginary crises and resolutions; "plot" rarely has to be imposed upon such narratives. The first phase of the voyage took the ship to Tahiti, where the scientists prepared to observe the transit of Venus. After an annoying encounter with a suspicious Portuguese viceroy in Rio de Janeiro, the *Endeavour* headed for the Straits of Le Maire; there Joseph Banks, the prominent scientist who had replaced Dalrymple, went ashore and was caught in a freak summer snowstorm in which two of his men froze to death. The rounding of Cape Horn and the passage to Tahiti were largely uneventful, a situation much desired by most long-distance voyagers. There Cook found the Tahitians peaceable and friendly but expert thieves with no European inhibitions about what was mine and thine. After the theft of the quadrant they had brought for observations of the transit of Venus, Cook began to develop the policy of taking native chiefs hostage until stolen goods were returned, a policy that was generally effective throughout his voyages but one that helped precipitate his death in Hawaii 10 years later. He also used it to recover two deserters on the day before sailing, when it backfired and nearly led to a serious altercation; in retaliation for the capture of their chief, the Tahitians held Cook's search party hostage in turn. The long stay in this island paradise, combined with the free sexual mores of the attractive women, created a situation as old as voyaging and as young as the dreams that lead our contemporaries to drop out of the rat race and sail to the south seas. Jason faced it on the island of Lesbos, as did Odysseus on Circe's island, and Melville himself deserted from the whaleship *Acushnet* at Nukahiva in the Marquesas. Every captain knew how the harsh discipline and danger of seafaring stood against a soft life ashore, and Cook was lucky that only two men succumbed to the lure of staying in Tahiti.

In the second phase of the voyage, Cook sailed southward for a month and a half in search of *Terra Australis* as he was directed by Admiralty instructions; he reached the edge of the notorious roaring forties where severe gales and the possibility of damage to rigging and sails made him reverse his course into milder latitudes before heading west again for New Zealand, his next objective. Cook was not averse to taking risks, but in this case—with a long voyage ahead—prudence overcame curiosity about a hypothetical, vast continent that might be found in a number of places. One of them was New Zealand, thought by Dalrymple and others to be a spur of the continent, so when Cook arrived he began surveying what turned out to be 2,400 miles of coastline in an extended circumnavigation. His careful work finally dispelled any notion that New Zealand was part of a larger land mass. At one point during the circumnavigation, some of the officers continued to favor the continental hypothesis because one small section of the northeast coast had been missed; Cook then sailed north a second time to Cape Turnagain and had them witness the fact that the North Island had no continental attachments to the east. Earlier, while anchored in Queen Charlotte Sound, Cook had climbed a hill and discovered the likelihood of what others had suspected—that New Zealand consisted of two major islands—and set out to navigate the channel between them (now called Cook Strait). The result was a foretaste of the near disasters that were later to be all too frequent along the Australian coast: In a calm with four to five knots of current, "we narrowly escaped being dashed against the rocks by bringing the Ship to an Anchor in 75 fathom water with 150 fathoms of Cable out; even this would not have save'd us had not the tide, which first set SBE, by meeting with the Island changed its dire[c]tion to SE and carried us past the first point" (*Explorations*, 51).

Anyone who has tried to sail through Woods Hole in Southern Massachusetts or some of the narrow tidal passages along the coast of British Columbia will appreciate what is happening to the *Endeavour* and marvel that the anchor did not drag with minimal scope (i.e., too steep an angle on the anchor cable) in such deep water and strong current. Ashore, Cook almost always met initial resistance from warlike Maoris but managed to set up trade with some. At sea, he was often blown offshore and encountered one "gale of wind . . . which for its strength and continuence was such as I hardly was ever in before" (Beaglehole 1966, 242–43). When he had finished his survey after six months in New Zealand waters, Cook had a choice to make since the Admiralty had left it in his judgment whether to sail east toward Cape Horn or west toward the Cape of Good Hope on his return to England. After deliberations with his officers, he chose the latter and headed west to the unexplored eastern coast of Australia, then named New Holland.

The story of finding and coping with the most massive living thing in the world, the Great Barrier Reef, is the focal point in this third and climactic phase of the first voyage. Before this unwanted discovery, Cook had hoped to sight Van Diemen's Land (Tasmania) and determine whether it was connected to New Holland, but southwesterly gales drove him farther north before he closed with the coast. As he headed northward he put into Botany Bay, so named for the plenitude of exotic botanical specimens Banks and his associate Solander found there, but sailed by Sydney Heads without entering one of the best natural harbors in the world. The trouble began when he reached the Queensland coast, where the 1,250-mile-long reef blockades any easy approach to the continent from the ocean; at its southern end, the reef lies as much as 150 miles offshore and gradually approaches the coast until it is roughly 30 miles offshore near Cape Tribulation, Weary Bay, and the Endeavour River, all names suggesting what happened next. Cook had become familiar with much smaller atolls surrounding Pacific islands and was a cautious seaman, so when he saw islands and reefs ahead at sundown while following the trend of the coast three to four leagues (approximately 9 to 12 miles) offshore on 11 June 1770, he ordered the appropriate actions—shortening sail, taking soundings, and standing away from the coast for the night. What he did not know—and could not have known—was the very existence of a reef unlike any other in the world, rising precipitously out of deep water, off soundings, where all seamen feel safest; he had been inside it for weeks. Thus at about 11 P.M. he discovered the reef that might have ended the *Endeavour*'s voyage and his career: "Before 10 oClock we has 20 and 21 fathom and continued in that depth untill a few Minutes before a 11 when we had 17 and before the man at the lead could heave another cast the Ship Struck and stuck fast" (*Explorations*, 70–71).

What happens during the next 23 hours is a tale of some luck, much sound seamanship, and extraordinary cool-headed discipline in a crisis. The crew immediately takes soundings all around the ship, carries anchors out in the direction of the deepest water to kedge her off, then when that effort fails, lightens the ship by 40 or 50 tons, mans the pumps, and waits for the next high tide:

> By this time it was 5 oClock in the pm, the tide we observed now begun to rise and the leak increased upon us which obliged us to set the 3rd Pump to work as we should have done the 4th also, but could not make it work. At 9 oClock the Ship righted and the leak gaind upon the Pumps considerably. This was an alarming and I may say terrible Circumstance and threatened immidiate destruction to us as soon as the Ship was afloat. However I resolved to resk all and heave her off in case it was practical and accordingly turned as many hands to the Capstan & windlass as could be spared from the Pumps and about 20N past 10 oClock the Ship floated and we hove her off into deep water having at this time 3 feet 9 Inches water in the hold. (*Explorations*, 71)

The risk was worth taking since Cook could not count on the lucky calm of the past 24 hours continuing, and large waves or swells would have ground the ship to pieces in short order. The crew gains on the leak, fothers the ship (that is, hauls a sail filled with oakum, wool, and dung under the hole), sets sail and heads for the nearest place to get her bow ashore and inspect the damage at low tide. There they discover their second bit of luck: a large piece of coral jammed into one hole between close-set timbers. Only later in Batavia will they learn that the thick planking had been reduced to one-eighth of an inch in one place (Beaglehole 1966, 256).

After nearly two months of repairs in the Endeavour River, Cook put to sea again and encountered a maze of minor reefs inside the great one. With a short supply of provisions and an endless task of beating against the prevailing wind if he reversed his course or the danger of getting embayed (that is, trapped on a lee shore by a following wind) if he continued northward between the coast and the reef, on 13 August Cook decided to seek a channel through the Barrier Reef and continue the voyage in open ocean. Sending the ship's pinnace ahead to check channels, he got through one the next day and found himself instantly off soundings, unable to reach bottom at 150 fathoms

The *Endeavour* careened for repairs in the Endeavour River, Queensland, Australia.
Courtesy of the National Maritime Museum, London.

(900 feet). But he was far from done with the reef, and that steep outer face would prove more terrifying than the inner side he had grounded on before. The trauma begins on 16 August in a calm with the unobstructed swells of the open Pacific setting the *Endeavour* toward the reef:

> [W]e were not above 80 or 100 Yards from the breakers, the same Sea that washed the sides of the Ship rose in a breaker prodigiously high the very next time it did rise so that between us and distruction was only a dismal Vally the breadth of one wave and even now no ground could be felt with 120 fathoms. The Pinnace by this time was patched up and hoisted out and sent ahead to tow; still we had hardly any hopes of saving the Ship and full as little our lives as we were full 10 Leagues [approximately 30 miles] from the nearest land and the boats not sufficient to carry the whole of us, yet in this truly terrible situation not one man ceased to do his utmost and that with as much calmness as if no danger had been near. All the dangers we had escaped were little in comparison of being thrown upon this Reef where the Ship must be dashed to pieces in a Moment. A Reef such as is here spoke of is scarcely known in Europe, it is a wall of Coral Rock

109

rising all most perpendicular out of the unfathomable Ocean, always overflown at high-water generally 7 or 8 feet and dry in places at low-water; the large waves of the vast Ocean meeting with so sudden a resistance make a most terrible surf breaking mountains high especially as in our case when the general trade wind blowes directly upon it. (*Explorations* 77 – 78)

The literary qualities of passages such as this are self-evident, conveying both the tension of a stark moment and the descriptive powers of a writer who can simultaneously portray the nature of the reef. Cook now sends a boat out to look for a channel that will take the ship and its crew inside the reef again, finds one, and cannot enter it because the ebb tide surges against them. Not until the next day will they find a suitable opening and a flood tide to carry them through it, and they stay inside until they reach Cape York and navigate a tricky channel westward to confirm what only Torres had known before—that New Guinea and New Holland were not joined together. This experience with the reef produced one of Cook's most reflective journal entries, which begins, characteristically, with the bedrock reality of their specific deliverance:

[W]e had got quite within the Reef where we anchor'd in 19 fathom a Corally & Shelly bottom happy once more to incounter those shoals which but two days ago our utmost wishes were crowned by getting clear of, such are the Vicissitudes attending this kind of service and must always attend an unknown Navigation: Was it not for the pleasure which naturly results to a Man from being the first discoverer, even was it nothing more than sands and Shoals, this service would be insuportable especialy in far distant parts, like this, short of Provisions and almost every other necessary. The world will hardly admit of an excuse for a man leaving a Coast unexplored he has once discover'd, if dangers are his excuse he is than charged with Timorousness and want of Perseverance and at once pronounced the unfitest man in the world to be employ'd as a discoverer; if on the other hand he boldly incounters all the dangers and obstacles he meets and is unfortunate enough not to succeed he is than charged with Temerity and want of conduct. The former of these aspersins cannot with Justice be laid to my charge and if I am fortunate enough to surmount all the dangers and obstacles we may meet the latter will never be brought in question. I must own I have ingaged more among the Islands and shoals upon this coast than may be thought with prudence I ought to have done with a single Ship and every other thing considered, but if I had not we should not have been able to give any better account of the one half of it than if we had never seen it, that is we should not have been able to say whether it consisted of main land or Islands and as to its produce, we must have been totally ignorant of as being inseparable with the other. (*Explorations*, 78–79)

Apart from the element of getting it into the record—an impulse familiar to naval officers of all eras—this eloquent analysis of the dilemmas Cook had faced throughout the first voyage is both an apologia and a manifesto for further action.

The final phase of the first voyage is both a denouement and an anticlimax. Cook reached Dutch Batavia, found his ship in worse shape than he had imagined, and persuaded very competent shipwrights there to make the necessary repairs. The long stay in a land notorious for its fevers, from 22 August to 26 December, wreaked havoc with his enviable health record. Alone among circumnavigators, his rigid food regimen that had been specifically designed to prevent scurvy among the crew had succeeded, and he had lost no man to the disease through two years of ocean voyaging.[51] Sadly, the long stay in Batavia brought other plagues, malaria and dysentery, that killed a third of his complement before he reached England, including key officers and scientists. On this first voyage he had partially laid the ghost of the phantom southern continent, charted the most difficult coast of the real one, Australia, as well as those of New Zealand, proved that Torres was right in separating New Guinea from Australia, and established a scientific pattern for exploring the Pacific. Among many other accomplishments on his second and third voyages, he succeeded in surveying the northwest coast of America, disconfirmed the existence of a passage between the North Pacific and the North Atlantic, discovered the Hawaiian Islands, and proved the value of the chronometer in solving the longitude problem that had dogged European mariners through three centuries of ocean navigation. Perhaps an unpretentious hero and certainly unfortunate in his premature death—if any death can be such for an explorer—Cook's practical intelligence and common sense brought a distillation of eighteenth-century rationalism to the exploration of the Pacific.

Chapter 4

THE SEA QUEST: MOBY-DICK AND
THE OLD MAN AND THE SEA

The sea quest is easily the oldest voyage pattern in Western literature, deriving from the *Odyssey* and the *Argonautica* and continuing in a few revealing episodes in Canto 26 of Dante's *Inferno,* where Ulysses violates the restraints imposed by God when he sails beyond the Pillars of Hercules into the open Atlantic. In all three cases the voyagers go beyond the bounds of the world known in their day, not so much to discover what is there as to seek something, to fulfill a mission. Odysseus sails home to regain his kingdom in Ithaca, Jason must return to Iolcus with the golden fleece, and Dante's Ulysses, like Tennyson's six centuries later, seeks experience for its own sake by sailing into the setting sun. The quest came ashore during the medieval era, especially in the chivalric romances of France and England, but there were important exceptions like St. Brendan's cycle of voyages to seek the Promised Land of the Saints and Paradise itself, as well as voyages to the Holy Land during the Crusades. In the sixteenth century Vasco da Gama's voyage to India appeared as both a historical voyage and a mythic quest in Camões's epic, the

Lusiads, and Cervantes's *Don Quixote,* written at the beginning of the next century, produced a double vision of the quest that would reverberate in its sea versions throughout succeeding centuries down to Conrad, Monserrat, and Golding. The quest put to sea again in modified form during the eighteenth century, when it combined with the realistic canons of the burgeoning picaresque novel to reproduce the characteristic tests of a hero in works like Defoe's *Robinson Crusoe;* it reentered the world of the surreal in the early nineteenth century with Coleridge's "Rime of the Ancient Mariner."

In an era when the original American colonies still clung to the sea for profit and sustenance, it is not surprising that sea literature was prolific and popular through the first half of the nineteenth century, when the sea quest flourished. Following Coleridge's lead, many of Poe's short stories and *The Narrative of Arthur Gordon Pym* exploit the external setting of a mysterious

"In the very heart of the Leviathanic life," drawn by Henri Durand-Brager for *Baleinier Francais en Peche* (ca. 1844–1845); Melville admired the accuracy of this representation.
Courtesy of the Kendall Whaling Museum, Sharon, Massachusetts, USA.

ocean as a metaphor for the interior worlds of consciousness. The sense of mission at the heart of the quest marked Cooper's sea romances, especially the earliest three—*The Pilot, The Red Rover,* and *The Water-Witch*—written in the 1820s. Cooper's later sea novels, eight in all, became more realistic, a tendency reinforced by Dana's *Two Years Before the Mast* (1840), but his last and most complex novel, *The Sea Lions* (1849), is built around an overt quest.[1] While the conventions of romance flourished ashore in the work of Hawthorne, they also permeated the work of many sea writers, including Melville, who adopted them in *Typee, Omoo,* and especially *Mardi.* His monumental *Moby-Dick* (1851) and Hemingway's slender *The Old Man and the Sea* (1952), separated by an almost formulaic century and a year, attest to the persistence of the sea quest as a central pattern in voyage narratives, and the gap between them is filled with many other examples, including works by Stephen Crane, Jack London, and a host of writers less well known today.[2] Their successors, Peter Matthiessen's *Far Tortuga* (1975) and Derek Walcott's *Omeros* (1990), reveal the continuing power of the archetype.

Like most terms long used in literary criticism, *quest* and especially *romance* have accumulated layers of often contradictory definition. It is particularly important to be clear about the meanings attached to each in the context of voyage narratives, which are often larded with sentimental romanticism—either through the nostalgia of retired seaman-writers reliving their past adventures or the blue-water fantasies of men and women who ride ferries or sail yachts alongshore. One can scent it in vast quantities of unsophisticated writing about voyages, and it is also represented in minor classics of the story of growing up at sea, like Melville's *Redburn*, Conrad's "Youth," and Kipling's *Captains Courageous*. Such naive romanticism, an attitude toward sea experience that often dissipates with the first nasty gale offshore, has very little to do with the more sophisticated versions of romance. W. H. Auden succinctly describes four tenets of the attitude as it applied to literary voyaging in the nineteenth century:

1. To leave the land and the city is the desire of every man of sensibility and honor.
2. The sea is the real situation and the voyage is the true condition of man.

3. The sea is where the decisive events, the moments of eternal choice, of temptation, fall, and redemption occur. The shore life is always trivial.

4. An abiding destination is unknown even if it may exist: a lasting relationship is not possible nor even to be desired.[3]

Such an attitude, a desire for the physical and mental freedom of open ocean experience—what Ishmael calls "landlessness"—projects the literary form of the sea quest; that form is illuminated by the attitude but should not be confused with it. The sea quest is one variant of the larger, more inclusive, pattern of romance, perhaps the most persistent narrative structure in literature. Several decades ago, Paul Smith and I formulated a description of romance that still seems useful and pertinent in this context:

There are historical reasons for thinking of the romance as a primary form. The romance narrative most often dominates the earliest period in the literary history of a culture. It is the dominant form in Anglo-Saxon and medieval English literature. The same is true in American literary history. From the late eighteenth century when Joel Barlow wrote his ponderous epic about Columbus to the early nineteenth when Cooper wrote his Leatherstocking saga, poets and novelists turned to the romance pattern to fashion heroes and articulate ideals commensurate with the American adventure. . . .

In the romance pattern everything leads to or follows from its primary action, the quest; the hero's advent and initiation mark its prologue, his descent and recognition its epilogue. The most common form of the quest is the journey, often a sequence of three adventures, leading to a climactic struggle between the hero and a dragon or some dark human opponent for the prize of a beautiful maiden, wealth, or power. The journey often describes a movement into the realm of the unknown and back: Odysseus, and Leopold Bloom for that matter, trace paths that circle from the familiar to the mysterious and back to the familiar. . . .

The evolution of the helper figure in the history of the romance pattern deserves comment. As the romance pattern became more sophisticated, this sometimes simple character tended to assume the features of the hero or to become his reincarnation. *Moby-Dick*— which for all its apparatus of tragedy may well be read as a romance—is one culmination of this tradition. It is almost as if the romance writers, becoming restive with the form's "two-party" moral system, trained their imaginative and analytic powers on the quality of evil in the antagonist and found it not all that bad, or at best of some utilitarian value. Then reconsidering the quality of virtue in the protagonist they seem to have found it not all that good, or at worst hell-bent for heaven. In the light of this analysis, the secondary figure gradually assumed a new, more subtle, and often chastened capacity for heroism that his superior lacked. We see something of this capacity in Beowulf's Wiglaf, perhaps even in Arthur's Sir Bedivere; it is developed in Huck Finn's Jim with his simple moral grandeur and in Ahab's Ishmael and Gatsby's Nick Carraway, both of whom serve as witnesses and narrators of quests that fail. . . .

The antagonists in romance—like Milton's Satan—may sometimes command our interest more than the heroes they oppose. Once the antagonist is associated with nature and is freed from the Christian moral system, his ambiguous qualities often make him the most memorable feature of the narrative. Gawain's character can be explained, but the Green Knight remains an enigma, even when he appears in the cultivated figure of Lord Bercilak. The ambiguous white whale in *Moby-Dick* is the most familiar example, and from the Green Knight to Old Ben, the bear in Faulkner's story, these "natural" antagonists do not admit to the same sort of moral explanation that poets use for Grendel or the Blatant Beast or even Satan. As the antagonist becomes less purely evil, the protagonist set against him becomes less purely good. Their conflict is no longer a matter of one or the other's victory—who finally wins the contest between Gawain and the Green Knight?—but a mystical confrontation in which neither is defeated. . . . These observations suggest that as the moral system of the romance shifts from the rigid dialectic of the religious quest, and as the antagonist is associated with natural, more neutral forces, the quest takes on the character of a second initiation.[4]

Of course, one rarely finds a pure example of any narrative pattern in the work of an accomplished writer, and this is particularly true of forms that were dominant in earlier literature. In various ways Cooper, Hawthorne, Melville, and, later, Hemingway tap into the power of romance without submitting to any formulaic representation of it. In some cases its structure is modified by the perceived need for surface verisimilitude and submerges just out of sight; in others it is amalgamated with complementary structures to widen the reach of the narrative; always it is accommodated to the style and sense of pacing of the writer. Northrop Frye explains the massive scope of *Moby-Dick* by suggesting that it combines romance with another narrative structure, the "anatomy," resulting in a hybrid "where the romantic theme of the wild hunt expands into an encyclopaedic anatomy of the whale" (Frye 313). With characteristic Rabelaisian gusto, Melville is playfully explicit about the nature of that expansion:

> One often hears of writers that rise and swell with their subject, though it may seem but an ordinary one. How, then, with me, writing of this Leviathan? Unconsciously my chirography expands into placard capitals. Give me a condor's quill! Give me Vesuvius' crater for an inkstand! Friends, hold my arms! For in the mere act of penning my thoughts of this Leviathan, they weary me, and make me faint with their outreaching comprehensiveness of sweep, as if to include the whole circle of the sciences, and all the generations of whales, and men, and mastodons, past, present, and to come, with all the revolving panoramas of empire on earth, and throughout the whole universe, not excluding its suburbs. Such, and so magnifying, is the virtue of a large and liberal theme! We expand to its bulk. To produce a mighty book, you must choose a mighty theme. No great and enduring volume can ever be written on the flea, though many there be who have tried it.[5]

In the anatomy, the encyclopedic impulse is given free reign to amass enormous quantities of erudition, to digress, to satirize characters and ideas, and to indulge in rhetorical flourishes; as the preceding passage demonstrates, the impulse is closely related to irony, the antithesis of romance. Frye traces the ancestry of the anatomy back to Menippean satire and finds it the favored form of writers like Erasmus, Rabelais, and Robert Burton, as well as Swift, who combined it with the structure of voyage narratives. Explaining the frequency of hybrid forms in literature, Frye continues: "I deliberately make this sound schematic in order to suggest the advantage of having a simple and logical explanation for the form of, say, *Moby-Dick* or *Tristram Shandy*. The usual critical approach to the form of such works resembles that of the doctors in Brobdingnag, who after great wrangling finally pronounced Gulliver a *lusus naturae"* (Frye 313).

Moby-Dick fairly bulges with whaling materials of all kinds, as well as digressions aplenty, and with an understanding of the anatomy as a literary form we can appreciate how their entwinement into the fabric of the hunt enriches the romance. The book swallows as much of the world as it can, reaching out from cetology and the history of whaling to theology, philosophy, literature, art, and the farthest reaches of human history in meteoric flashes of analogy and metaphor. Like many anatomies, it displays and sports with erudition in nearly every chapter, often with a rhetoric reminiscent of Shakespeare, whom Melville had been reading while the book was gestating in his imagination. But Melville, like Cooper before him and Conrad after, was not romancing out of tune with the reality of voyaging. Every one of his novels prior to *Moby-Dick—Typee, Omoo,* even *Mardi, Redburn,*

"Cutting in," removing the blubber of the whale for rendering into oil. Photo by John Miller. Courtesy of the Kendall Whaling Museum, Sharon, Massachusetts, USA.

White-Jacket—had sprouted from his experience at sea, and the leviathan was no exception. Melville gathered much of his whaling lore during an eighteen-month voyage on the New Bedford whaler *Acushnet,* lasting from 3 January 1841 until 9 July 1842, when he deserted at Nukaheva in the Marquesas. In the writing process, Melville had access to many written sources, including five major ones: Thomas Beale's *Natural History of the Sperm Whale* (1839); Frederick Bennet's *Whaling Voyage Round the Globe, from the Year 1833 to 1836* (1840); J. Ross Browne's *Etchings of a Whaling Cruise* (1846); the Rev. Henry T. Cheever's *The Whale and His Captors* (1850); and William Scoresby Jr.'s *Account of the Arctic Regions with a History and Description of the Northern Whale Fishery* (1820).[6] Melville also had access to artistic representations of whales and whaling scenes in galleries, museums, libraries, and bookstalls in London, Paris, and Boston, especially in the years immediately preceding publication of *Moby-Dick,* although exactly what he saw cannot be tracked.[7]

The ferocious white whale that propels the quest also had two sources in whaling history and legend. The first was a documented incident in which an 85-foot sperm whale (not white) rammed and sank the Nantucket whaler *Essex* in 1819, leading to disastrous, long whaleboat voyages in the Pacific by her captain and two mates.[8] The second was the reputation of an extraordinary massive, white sperm whale about 100 feet in length with distinctive markings and a long record of destructive attacks on whaleboats, ships, and men all over the ocean world: Between a possible first sighting in 1810 and his death in 1859, Mocha Dick is credited with attacks on 14 boats, six ships, three of which sank, and the death of 30 men; he carried 19 harpoons at his death (Vincent 168–77). Of such stuff are legends made, and Mocha Dick's notoriety persisted within the whaling community as well as the larger world after J. N. Reynolds wrote a story about him in *The Knickerbocker, New York Monthly Magazine* for May 1839, although Reynolds killed Mocha Dick off in fiction before he had got properly started on his greatest outrages in the real world.[9] Historical, legendary, and fictional all at once, after the publication of *Moby-Dick* the great white whale would become a permanent fixture in literary consciousness. Northrop Frye notes that, like other powerful symbols, "it is bound to expand over many works into an archetypal symbol of literature as a whole. Moby-Dick cannot remain in Melville's novel: he is absorbed into our imaginative experience of leviathans and dragons of the deep from the Old Testament onward" (Frye 100).

Moby-Dick; or, The Whale

From the opening words of Moby-Dick—"Call me Ishmael"—and the incessant strings of Biblical and mythological names throughout the novel, we know we have entered a narrative with ambitions far beyond recording the realities of whaleship life, although it does that too in a highly stylized manner. In terms of pure information, the novel is encyclopedic, providing not only anatomical and taxonomic information about whales but also detailed descriptions of every phase of the practice of whaling, from equipment to technique; indeed, many readers have used this material in the book as a manual on whaling. But this is only one dimension of Moby-Dick. "He who would follow Ishmael must exert the symbolic imagination, for Ishmael's 'pursuit' of the whale is the evolution of an image" writes Charles Feidelson Jr., yet we are neither voyaging in the world of Coleridge's Ancient Mariner nor trapped between the parallel lines of real events and allegorical signification.[10] Warner Berthoff distinguishes four substantive contexts or "worlds" in the novel: 1) "dry land, or at least the thronged edges of it"; 2) "the quaint, rare, old, noble, trophy-garnished, battle-worn, cannibalistic, melancholy Pequod ... a fit instrument for Ahab and his purpose"; 3) "the non-human world of the sea and the indifferent elements"; and 4) "the 'world' of the unknown and inscrutable" as conceived in sailors' folklore.[11] Symbolic yet substantive, dramatic yet detailed, and constantly linking unseen with seen worlds, Moby-Dick has always remained an enigma for those who try to capture meanings that never hold still. The elements of romance and anatomy described above are pointers, not containers; no more than Moby-Dick can the book itself be caught, cut up, and rendered for interpretive consumption.

In Moby-Dick the cues to the progress of the quest lie quite near the surface of the text, sometimes leaping out of it, and they are enhanced by an archaic and exuberant rhetoric. But, as often happens when the encyclopedic impulse is loosed in big books like Sterne's *Tristram Shandy* or Joyce's *Ulysses,* narrative elements rarely appear in stark isolation. Here they are surrounded and mixed not only with erudition but also with generous doses of meditation, a way of interrupting the chronological sequence of events that is almost inescapable in voyage narratives. At sea other fictional devices like flashbacks or juxtaposed scenes that create unexpressed implications are often artificial or awkward; ships do crawl along time lines, plotted day by day on their charts, and the scene is always locked on board or at least confined within the visible horizon. As we have seen in chapter 1, expanding the implications of events through meditation is highly developed in many voyage narratives, including Dana's *Two Years before the Mast.* Thus it is not surprising that in "Loomings" *Moby-Dick* begins with Ishmael's invocation not to the muse but to meditation:

> Let the most absent-minded of men be plunged in his deepest reveries—stand that man on his legs, set his feet a-going, and he will infallibly lead you to water, if water there be in all that region. Should you ever be athirst in the great American desert, try this experiment, if your caravan happen to be supplied with a metaphysical professor. Yes, as everyone knows, meditation and water are wedded forever. (ch. 1, 13)

By the end of the chapter this invocation reaches its ebullient rhapsody: "[T]he great flood-gates of the wonder-world swung open, and in the wild conceits that swayed me to my purpose, two and two there floated into my inmost soul, endless processions of the whale, and, midmost of them all, one grand hooded phantom, like a snow hill in the air" (ch. 1, 16). Later in "The Mast-head," meditation swells to "thought-engendering altitude" with "the problem of the universe revolving in me" until the context includes both immediate and ultimate risks:

> There is no life in thee now, except that rocking life imparted by a gently rolling ship; by her, borrowed from the sea; by the sea, from the inscrutable tides of God. But while this sleep, this dream is on ye, move your foot or hand an inch; slip your hold at all; and your identity comes back in horror. Over Descartian vortices you hover. And

perhaps, at mid-day, in the fairest weather, with one half-throttled shriek you drop through that transparent air into the summer sea, no more to rise forever. Heed it well, ye Pantheists! (ch. 35, 140)

This passage adds metaphysical dimensions to a common accident on board sailing ships (long before anyone thought of using safety harnesses for work aloft), and later in the voyage an unnamed seaman plunges into the sea from the masthead and is seen no more (ch. 126, 429). It also anticipates one half of the diving motif that recurs throughout this book, linking Ishmael's admiration for "thought-divers" with Moby-Dick's sounding to the depths. Unlike a similar fall by the protagonist near the end of *White Jacket*, which is followed by his rise to the surface, diving in *Moby-Dick* often has ambiguous or demonic associations. After taking fright at a vision of the flaming *Pequod* as "the material counterpart of her monomaniac commander's soul" in "The Try-Works," Ishmael struggles to find an analogy that can temper what he has seen:

> There is a wisdom that is a woe; but there is a woe that is madness. And there is a Catskill eagle in some souls that can alike dive down into the blackest gorges, and soar out of them again and become invisible in the sunny spaces. And even if he for ever flies within the gorge, that gorge is in the mountains; so that even in his lowest swoop the mountain eagle is still higher than other birds upon the plain, even though they soar. (ch. 96, 355)

Some are ill prepared even to glimpse what a fall into the ocean can reveal. When Pip leaps from a whaleboat the second time and is temporarily abandoned "in the middle of such a heartless immensity . . . [h]e saw God's foot upon the treadle of the loom, and spoke it; and therefore his shipmates called him mad" (ch. 93, 347). In "The Sphynx," "Ahab meditates on a severed whale head sinking to "this world's foundations . . . where in her murderous hold this frigate earth is ballasted with bones of millions of the drowned" and concludes with a grim apostrophe: "O head! thou hast seen enough to split the planets and make an infidel of Abraham, and not one syllable is thine!" (ch. 70, 264). This association of diving with knowledge reconfigures an archetype as old as Jonah's descent in the maw of a whale and Odysseus's visit to Hades, both downward movements toward

"The crow's nest," scene of watchfulness and meditation.
Courtesy of the Kendall Whaling Museum, Sharon, Massachusetts, USA.

death that reverse themselves in resurrections to the world of the living. But here images of descent mark the final stages of the quest in the hawks that dive on the masthead to snatch Ahab's hat and the flag that Tashtego guards. At the end we see a sinking ship and a sounding whale with drowned Ahab attached. The apotheosis of the protagonist one expects in romance has given way to a more sinister consummation that terminates the quest begun by the loss of a limb. Only the coffin rises to float the sole survivor who, transformed like the Ancient Mariner, must tell the tale and continue the elusive search for its meaning.

Many meditations also involve landlessness, which Melville exploits both as a condition of whaling and as an emblem of the quest. Whaling voyages, unlike most others, have no destinations except the open ocean and are quite properly called "cruises." When laid out on a chart, the courses of whale ships meander from one whaling ground to another, and their structure, if any is visible, is bound to be circular rather than linear. Such ships depart with empty oil casks and full water casks and return to the same place they left only when the ratio of those fluids has been reversed. "Hence it is, that, while other ships may have gone to China from New York, and back again, touching at a score of ports, the whale-ship, in all that interval, may not have sighted one grain of soil; her crew having seen no man but floating seamen like themselves. So that did you carry them the news that another flood had come; they would only answer—'Well, boys, here's the ark' " (ch. 87, 319).

Elaborate land versus sea dichotomies are endemic to voyage narratives, and they often involve a polarity between the corruption of the land and the purity of life at sea, as they do in Conrad. Characteristically, Melville complicates such polarities with a series of waverings and ambiguities throughout *Moby-Dick*. Earlier, in *Mardi*, in a chapter entitled "Sailing On," he had affirmed the sea quest without any qualifications as he established a metaphoric parallel between Columbus sailing toward the Indies and those seeking the new "world of mind": "So, if after all these fearful, fainting trances, the verdict be, the golden haven was not gained;- -yet, in bold quest thereof, better to sink in boundless deeps, than float on vulgar shoals; and give me, ye gods, an utter wreck, if wreck I do."[12] In *Moby-Dick* the wreck becomes more ominous and the shore a double-edged value as

Melville elaborates a familiar nautical metaphor into a miniature elegy for Bulkington, a seaman who has shipped on board the *Pequod* immediately after returning from a four-year voyage and is later lost at sea. In "The Lee Shore" both vehicle and tenor of the metaphor become explicit:

> Let me only say that it fared with him as with the storm-tossed ship, that miserably drives along the leeward land. The port would fain give succor; the port is pitiful; in the port is safety, comfort, hearth-stone, supper, warm blankets, friends, all that's kind to our mortalities. But in that gale, the port, the land, is that ship's direst jeopardy; she must fly all hospitality; one touch of land though it but graze the keel, would make her shudder through and through. With all her might she crowds all sail off shore; in so doing, fights 'gainst the very winds that fain would blow her homeward; seeks all the lashed sea's landlessness again; for refuge's sake forlornly rushing into peril; her only friend her bitterest foe!
>
> Know ye, now, Bulkington? Glimpses do ye seem to see of that mortally intolerable truth; that all deep, earnest thinking is but the intrepid effort of the soul to keep the open independence of her sea; while the wildest winds of heaven and earth conspire to cast her on the treacherous, slavish shore?
>
> But as in landlessness alone resides the highest truth, shoreless, indefinite as God—so, better is it to perish in that howling infinite, than be ingloriously dashed upon the lee, even if that were safety! (ch. 23, 97)

Although the chapter ends in an elegiac "apotheosis" of Bulkington, the dangers of seafaring have been subsumed into the subtler perils of a bold intellectual quest, and the focus is on Ishmael more than Bulkington.

The values attached to land and sea shift again in "Brit," where "however baby man may brag of his science and skill, and however much, in a flattering future, that science and skill may augment; yet for ever and for ever, to the crack of doom, the sea will insult and murder him, and pulverize the stateliest, stiffest frigate he can make" (ch. 58, 235). (That sentence should have been recommended reading for the builders and owners of the *Titanic*.) On the same page the underlying archetype of landlessness appears explicitly: "Yea, foolish mortals, Noah's flood is not yet subsided; two thirds of the fair world it yet covers." After a disquisition on sharks and "the universal cannibalism of the sea," the chapter concludes with an admonition that reverses the polarity of the Bulkington passage:

> Consider all this; and then turn to this green, gentle, and most docile earth; consider them both, the sea and the land; and do you not find a strange analogy to something in yourself? For as this appalling ocean surrounds the verdant land, so in the soul of man there lies one insular Tahiti, full of peace and joy, but encompassed by all the horrors of the half known life. God keep thee! Push not off from that isle, thou canst never return! (ch. 58, 236)

Four more times Melville evokes the peace of the land, now serving as an antithesis to the menace of the ocean and a deterrent to the quest. "The Grand Armada" provides the first variant in the quiet center of a vast gathering of whales, described in the imagery of a lake, sheepfold, bridal chamber, and nursery. "[A]mid the tornadoed Atlantic of my being," asserts Ishmael, "deep down and deep inland there I still bathe me in eternal mildness of joy" (ch. 87, 326). In "A Squeeze of the Hand" (ch. 94), while squeezing spermaceti, Ishmael has a more conventional vision of home, hearth, and universal brotherhood. Once again imagery of prairies, hills, vales, woods, and flowers represents the calm sea as if it were the land in "The Gilder," making Ishmael momentarily forget "the tiger heart that pants beneath it" (ch. 114, 405–6). And in "The Symphony," the chapter just preceding the three days of the final chase, Ahab begins a review of his life in the pastoral mode, while Starbuck listens and once more urges him to abandon the quest; the scene ends abruptly when Ahab crosses the deck, looks down at the water, and sees the eyes of his mysterious harpooner, Fedallah, reflected there. The very next time he looks down into the ocean, he sees Moby-Dick rising to meet him and enters the final phase of his quest.

Thus by following just one theme of meditation—landlessness—through the book, we see how volatile and inconclusive it is, leading to a bundle of contradictions rather than belief. All of this indefiniteness may seem out of place in romance, which usually delineates characters and events in bold, clear strokes that separate good from evil and success from failure, all within a framework of inevitability. Yet the most sophisticated of medieval romances, like *Sir Gawain and the Green Knight*, are clothed in just as much ambiguity as the pursuit of the white whale. The fluidity of reverie, where unbounded imagination plays freely, propels or impedes the intellectual quest of the book just as the wind favors or opposes the surface voyage of the *Pequod*. Near the end of the voyage, the twin strands of action and thought often merge, as when the shift of wind after the typhoon appears to allow Ahab to resume his pursuit of Moby-Dick, whereas in fact just the opposite has happened since lightning has reversed the polarity of the compasses. Also, the surface paraphernalia of romance— prophecies, omens, riddles, oaths, superstitions, rituals, and encounters with strangers (ships in this case)—frequently generate meditations that meld with the action. In one sense the erudition and meditation form the flesh that fills out the bare bones of the romance narrative in a leviathanic book; in another, they are its internal organs of comprehension.

No matter which metaphors we apply to the substance of the book as a whole, the stages of the quest are marked unmistakably. As in all romances, the journey begins with a setting out, a call to action, and then proceeds through the stages of Ishmael's preliminary initiation in New Bedford, which requires a bonding with Queequeg. Next we are introduced to the ancient *Pequod*, a curious but appropriate vehicle for the quest, and her absent captain, whose stature is magnified. Before sailing there are dire prophecies from Elijah, and soon afterward the supporting characters appear, ranged in a perfect symmetry that could be easily borrowed and amplified from the practices of manning whalers: three mates, each representing specific ways of relating to the external world; three harpooners, drawn from different races and religions; three crews that would man the whaleboats in the hunt; and the supernumeraries, a carpenter and a blacksmith, who would fashion the tools needed for the hunt. Outside of this pattern stand "hair-turbaned" Fedallah and his phantom boat crew, to be revealed later only at the first lowering, and Pip, the cabin boy who succumbs to visions after being abandoned in the sea; both will bond with Ahab later in the voyage. The whaling voyage has begun, but the overt revelation of the quest to destroy Moby-Dick appears only in chapter 36, and it is confirmed by sworn oaths in an elaborate and eclectic ritual with harpoons and lances in hand. Other chapters provide epic descriptions of the tools used to kill whales.

As the voyage continues, further private and corporate rituals emerge: Ahab throws his contemplative pipe overboard and nails the enigmatic Ecuadorian doubloon to the mast, 'with a symbolism variously interpreted by all who gaze at it. Later he stamps on the quadrant (a tool for celestial navigation), declares himself "lord of the level loadstone," and creates a new compass to replace the one lightning had reversed; at the height of the typhoon, he dares the lightning to strike him and embraces the glowing corposants. His creation of the special harpoon to subdue Moby-Dick requires the blood of the harpooners in a ceremony inverting baptism, not in the name of the father but of the devil. All on board the *Pequod* read events as omens, and when Ishmael finds himself looking astern while steering, he converts his sleepy helmsmanship into a parable. Each encounter with another ship—and there are nine of them—has a special significance, including the last, in which Ahab refuses to obey the Golden Rule and help a fellow captain search the sea for his miss-

"Garneray's Sperm Whaling Scene," by Ambrose Louis Garneray, published in *Peche du Cachalot* (1834).
Courtesy of the Kendall Whaling Museum, Sharon, Massachusetts, USA.

ing son.[13] Finally, both quest and narrative end in three days of fatal combat. These are the filaments of romance, and they all come together in the Protean story that we, like Menelaus, must wrestle with.

Such an array of symbolic and ritual elements might indeed swamp our sense of reality, as it does in Melville's earlier *Mardi*, were it not for the quotidian details of a whaling voyage that undergird nearly every chapter in *Moby-Dick*. The plenitude of information about whales, the ship, its men and their work may annoy some readers, but it tells others that Ishmael's metaphoric leaps and bounds are grounded in human experience at sea. In this sense Ishmael is both narrator and coprotagonist with Ahab, with a double vision that can see clearly both the voyage of a real whaling ship and the disturbing macrocosmic images it engenders. Like Conrad's Marlow, he finds the ocean conducive to meditation, and that impulse reminds us of the strong links between fictional and historical voyage narratives: Columbus and Cook, too, felt the need to meditate on the vicissitudes and uncertainties suggested by their immeasurable surroundings.

Of course, no structural analysis of *Moby-Dick* can do justice to its richness of metaphorical texture and soaring rhetoric or even skirmish with its metaphysical implications. Those have proved endlessly enticing for readers and critics alike, and they never seem to settle out, no matter how hard one tries to separate the gold from the dross. Casting himself as a rereader who needs to embark on Ishmael's voyage from time to time, novelist Emilio De Grazia is lured by "the majesty of its inscrutability" and finds that "with each new reading, more comes indistinctly into view, the book always growing beyond a reader seeking to become its equal."[14] Critics are more likely to fall into positions along a wide spectrum of interpretation. At one end stand those who assert Melville's ultimate if troubled affirmation of a Christian God lying somewhere behind the pasteboard facade of surface reality. Among them is Auden: "When we have finished the book, we realise why Father Mapple's sermon was put in where it was: in order that we might know the moral presuppositions by which we are to judge the speeches and actions of Ahab and the rest" (Auden 122). In the middle of the spectrum we find those who separate Melville from Ahab, as Willard Thorp does: "It is not merely for the purpose of saving the narrator that Ishmael-Melville survives the White Whale's assault. However much he sympathized with Ahab's Promethean determination to stare down the inscrutableness of the universe, Melville hurled, not himself, but Ahab, his creature, at the injurious gods."[15] At the other end of the spectrum are those who believe the book is thoroughly subversive, pretending to affirm Christian values while undermining them at every turn. They are likely to cite Melville's letter to Hawthorne after he had finished the book and was leaving for New York to see it through the press: "What I feel most moved to write, that is banned,—it will not pay. Yet, altogether, write the other way I cannot. So the product is a final hash, and all my books are botches."[16] In a chapter entitled "Wicked Book" in *Melville's Quarrel with God,* Lawrance Thompson summarizes the "sophomoric attitude" that Melville took, insinuating it by a method of veiled indirection:

> Baldly stated, then, Melville's underlying theme in *Moby-Dick* correlates the notions that the world was put together wrong and that God is to blame; that God in his infinite malice asserts a sovereign tyranny over man and that most men are seduced into the mistaken view that this divine tyranny is benevolent and therefore acceptable; but that the freethinking and enlightened and heroic man will assert the rights of man and will rebel against God's tyranny by defying God in thought, word, deed, even in the face of God's ultimate indignity, death.[17]

At Princeton in 1951, a year-long critical disagreement between Willard Thorp and Lawrance Thompson culminated in the stellar campus event of the year, a debate about the meaning of *Moby-Dick,* then and now an elaborate puzzle that has never been fully assembled.[18] Like the book, the debate was indeterminate, with all particles of meaning suspended for a fresh encounter in yet another rereading—and that long before poststructuralism was on the horizon. Although the underlying structure of the quest is linear in the sense that the sinking of the *Pequod,* the death of Ahab, and the survival of Ishmael resolves it, our experience as readers is perpetually just as circular as the motion of waves or the track of the whaling voyage itself, and we encompass beginnings and endings simultaneously, sleeping with Ishmael in Peter Coffin's inn and riding with him on his floating coffin.

The Old Man and the Sea

If *Moby-Dick* is the Brobdingnag of the sea quest, so *The Old Man and the Sea* is its Lilliput. Despite the difference in size, both follow protagonists through assertions of power in the ocean world, various degrees of pride and obsession as they undertake quests that seem necessary to them, and ultimate failure partially redeemed by a survivor or successor. Both books take the quest to the open sea and maintain the heroic disproportion between hunted and hunter—whale and whaleboat, marlin and skiff—that romance requires; both insist on the essential determination of will and isolation of the hunter, whether walled up in his own obsession, as in Ahab's case, or in the waning strength of a single old man, as in Santiago's. But in some other respects the two are polar opposites. *Moby-Dick*'s encyclopedic scope swallows anything and everything in the intellectual world, whereas *The Old Man and the Sea,* apart from a few analogues, focuses narrowly on the physical world of the village, the shack, and most of all the skiff in a surrounding sea. Again, the big book deliberately espouses elaboration of scenes and rhetorical energy, whereas the little one just as deliberately commits itself to spareness of incident and flatness of style. Hemingway never could have written a gargantuan "Brother Marlin" any more than Melville could have written a minuscule "Old Man and the Whale." However, Hemingway did begin with ambitious intentions for his slim classic, as indicated by its working titles, first "The Sea in Being" and then "The Dignity of Man," both of which he wisely rejected for their pretentiousness; originally the novella was to be part of his tripartite Caribbean novel, *Islands in the Stream.*

Like Melville, Hemingway had direct knowledge of the context in which his story would unfold; he was an avid and experienced deep-sea fisherman in Cuban waters. Also, he described one specific anecdote in an article written in 1936:

> Another time an old man fishing alone in a skiff out of Cabanas hooked a great marlin that, on the heavy sashcord handline, pulled the skiff far out to sea. Two days later the old man was picked up by fishermen sixty miles to the eastward, the head and forward part of the marlin lashed alongside. What was left of the fish, less than half, weighed eight hundred pounds. The old man had stayed with him a day, a night, a day and another night while the fish swam deep and

pulled the boat. When he had come up the old man had pulled the boat up on him and harpooned him. Lashed alongside the sharks had hit him and the old man had fought them out alone in the Gulf Stream in a skiff, clubbing them, stabbing at them, lunging at them with an oar until he was exhausted and the sharks had eaten all that they could hold. He was crying in the boat when the fishermen picked him up, half crazy from his loss, and the sharks were circling the boat.[19]

The anecdote mixes some true grit with pathetic helplessness in the old fisherman, but it could easily be molded into a sea quest by changing the ending and bolstering the stature of the old man, and Hemingway was able to reshape it into the story of Santiago's ordeal with uncharacteristic speed in January of 1951.[20] He needed to frame it and did so by adding the helper figure of romance, in this case Manolin, who merges into the archetypal "boy" to counterbalance and complement the "old man." Individuality dims as the story assumes some of the qualities of parable and fable but never fades entirely, primarily because of digressions—the dream of lions on an African beach, identification with Joe DiMaggio, the arm-wrestling episode—all building images associated with heroic power. Unlike Melville, who blazons emblems in nearly every chapter heading, Hemingway buries tags to the quest in descriptive text and repeats them as motifs. One is the notion that he was predestined to be a fisherman:

That which I was born for.

Perhaps I should not have been a fisherman, he thought. But that was the thing that I was born for.

You were born to be a fisherman as the fish was born to be a fish.[21]

Another is "I wish the boy was here," which becomes a refrain as the struggle with the marlin stretches both the line and his endurance to the breaking point. Yet a third is both an explanation of his predicament and the prideful motivation for his quest:

His [the marlin's] choice had been to stay in the deep dark water far out beyond all snares and traps and treacheries. My choice was to go there to find him beyond all people. Beyond all people in the world. Now we are joined together and have been since noon. And no one to help either one of us. (*Old Man,* 50)

Unlike Melville's landlessness, this theme is compressed into an unchanging, formulaic "I went out too far" and repeated almost as a mantra throughout the later stages of Santiago's ordeal. Like Melville, Hemingway also shapes the quest with some of the traditional structures of romance, including the magic overtones of the number three: The great marlin makes three lurches to get free in the later stages of his entrapment, and the whole action takes place in three days. During the final test of strength between the combatants, the fish circles the man many times as he is hauled closer to his imminent death in concentric circles until he is within striking range of the harpoon, reversing the role played by Moby-Dick as he circles Ahab and the *Pequod* to destroy them.

More overtly, in the struggle between the old man and the marauding sharks, we encounter unmistakable symbols. Unlike Melville, who flaunts Christian symbols throughout *Moby-Dick,* Hemingway slips them in sideways, often as an analogy that juts out of descriptions: "'Ay,' he said aloud. There is no translation for this word and perhaps it is just a noise such as a man might make, involuntarily, feeling the nail go through his hands and into the wood" (*Old Man,* 107). Ironically, whereas Melville invites and sometimes demands symbolic interpretation on nearly every page, Hemingway does not, yet receives it almost in inverse proportion to the few cues in the text. Anyone who has taught *The Old Man and the Sea* will have met the reductive Christ allegory many times. As soon as attentive students have noticed a few allusions, like the one quoted above, they think they have the keys to the kingdom, including a high grade on the final exam. Unfortunately, some critical commentary adds fuel to the reductive fire:

The Christian symbolism which Hemingway uses throughout his story is subtle and suggestive. The lines which cut into Santiago's palms draw blood; the cry of "Ay" when he sees the first of the sharks is "just such a noise as a man might make, involuntarily, feeling the nail go through his hands and into the wood"; and as he climbs the hill to his hut Santiago stumbles under the weight of the mast and cross-tree he is carrying, to collapse finally on his bed with his arms out straight and the palms of his lacerated hands upwards.[22]

But no more than *Moby-Dick* is *The Old Man and the Sea* locked into allegory. Gerry Brenner summarizes the case:

> A skeptical reader finds problems in all of these religious allusions and analogues. Santiago shares too few traits in common with Christ: Christ is a fisher of men, but Santiago is merely a fisherman; Christ is a figure with a divine mission, Santiago one with a secular mission (to bring back an oversized fish); Christ is a martyr who willingly but reluctantly dies for his convictions, Santiago is a persevering champion who is willing to die only to win a battle with a fish; Christ is a teacher of spiritual and ethical wisdom, Santiago is a professional with skill and slogans to impart. A skeptical reader, in short, balks at the comparison, however well intentioned: correspondences between two characters must be deeper than a few generalized traits and strained analogues.[23]

The character of Santiago has variously been interpreted as noble or flawed, or both, depending upon how one reads his relationship with the "brother" fish he is so bent on killing. Some critics cast him as a maritime Saint Francis, picking up clues from the text that suggest his harmonious appreciation of all finned and flying creatures; others point out that he is in fact a professional fish killer, dedicated to mortal combat with his "brothers" to eke out a meager living. A more difficult problem is assessing his state of consciousness, since he is the sole narrator, source of both inner, unvoiced thoughts and the human voice of a man who talks to himself in the void of a silent ocean. Tony Tanner doubts Santiago's capacity for thought in any Melvillian sense of that word:

> Thought has a way of spiralling up and away from our concrete surroundings. That is why at various key points in *The Old Man and the Sea* the fisherman fights against the onset of thought. . . . A basic distinction must be made between the ordinary intelligence which interprets difficulties, formulates intentions, and modifies actions, etc.; and the sort of vague speculation, metaphysical or theological, etc., which the fisherman is countering. It is, of course, only this latter form of thought which the Hemingway hero tries to avoid. . . . The point is that for the Hemingway hero only concrete things are "true"

and only practical tasks efficiently undertaken and rigorously seen through offer any meaning and salvation: salvation from the crippling and undermining sense of nothingness which is his perpetual nightmare.[24]

Such limitations would suggest that Santiago is in a false position because he cannot interpret the meaning of his own story, and Hemingway has no other mouthpiece. Conrad faced the same dilemma in *The Nigger of the "Narcissus"* with Singleton, an old man similarly incapable of abstract thought. But in the years before he had found Marlow or subscribed to the Jamesian rigors of a consistent point of view, he solved the problem by simply reverting to an authorial omniscience in which he described the old seaman's sudden recognition of his own mortality: "He had panted in the sunshine, shivered in the cold; suffered hunger, thirst, debauch; passed through many trials—known all the furies. . . . He had to take up at once the burden of all his existence, and found it almost too heavy for his strength."[25] Hemingway's technique in presenting Santiago does not allow him the same solution; whatever metaphysical implications may attach to the story must emerge from his limited interpretation of the events of the voyage.

The real problem in both *Moby-Dick* and *The Old Man and the Sea* is a confrontation with sharkishness in the ocean world. That unveiled malignancy in the foundations of the universe transfixes Ahab and drives him into an obsessive quest. Without the same capacity for abstract comprehension, Santiago differentiates the more powerful sharks from those who simply grovel for leftovers without any impulse to generalize the implications of their voraciousness. As a result he is more effective in killing them—until his tools are exhausted—than Ahab can ever be in seeking revenge on the unknown presence, or absence, behind the furrowed brow of the white whale. Bert Bender makes that confrontation moot for Santiago by reading it in Darwinian rather than Christian terms:

> This cycle of the hunt is the necessary driving force in life—"that which I was born for," as Santiago understands. Had Melville written in the twentieth century, he might have seen it as the "fate" that ordered life as he could grasp it in "The Mat-Maker," rather than the biblical fate suggested as that scene ends with Tashtego's prophetic

cry, "Thar she blows!" ... Certainly, Hemingway's emphasis on Santiago's fated birth, his emphasis on "chance" ... and his emphasis on Santiago's and his marlin's "choice" constitute his own effort to weave from the same three forces that Melville interwove in "The Mat-Maker"—"chance, free will, and necessity"—a twentieth-century reality that might represent our existence more truthfully than Melville could in 1851. (Bender 193–94)

Whether those shifts in understanding the perpetual and unavoidable voraciousness of nature can justify sharkishness to human sensibilities is unclear. Yet both *Moby-Dick* and *The Old Man and the Sea,* separated as they are by a century and a year, struggle to bring sharkishness within human comprehension even as their protagonists fail in quests to destroy it. The monsters that Odysseus encountered and Columbus expected to see no longer stalk the land but their shadows still lurk below the surface of the sea around us.

Chapter 5

VOYAGES OF ENDURANCE: THE NIGGER OF THE "NARCISSUS"

Throughout the history of Western voyaging, from the earliest Greek forays in the Mediterranean through the latest news reports, tales of extraordinary human endurance at sea emerge. Whenever Odysseus draws near his goal of reaching Ithaca, Poseidon throws a fierce mountain squall or wild meltemi gale at him. In January of 1995 the French single-handed sailor Isabel Autissier appeared on television screens from Sydney after a dramatic helicopter rescue; on the second leg of a race around the world, her yacht was rolled over 360 degrees and dismasted by a giant wave in the southern Indian Ocean, leaving her drifting helplessly for four days, alone. From their own experience, Conrad and other seafarers often describe the ocean in anthropomorphic terms, regarding it as a fickle and perfidious foe whose moods are never totally predictable by the laws of meteorology; a sailor on a long voyage who is unable to dodge clear of gales or hurricanes has no choice but to endure them. And overwhelming storms are only the beginning of troubles at sea—prolonged calm for sailing vessels or engine failure for motorized ships, fire, collision, losing crew overboard, sickness, scurvy and starvation, sink-ing, struggles for survival in lifeboats or rafts, and stranding on reefs or shoals along unfriendly coasts. Thus it is not surprising that contests of human endurance furnish dramatic action in many voyage narratives and serve as the structural backbone of some.

Of course, many voyages are uneventful "if the sea is behav-ing, as it frequently is," according to seaman-writer William McFee,[1] but the possibility of an extraordinary adventure or dis-aster lurked beyond the horizon of every departure, especially on long sailing-ship voyages. Such voyages were the primary vehicle of geographical discovery, colonization, and world com-merce until the brink of the twentieth century. Throughout much of the nineteenth century, sailing ships were both the passenger liners and tramp steamers of ocean trade in spite of increased competition from steamships. As early as the 1820s companies like the Black Ball Line established a regular, scheduled passen-ger and mail service between America and England in sailing ships, allowing three to four weeks eastbound with the prevail-ing westerlies and five to six weeks for the upwind westbound voyage. The capacious but slow British merchant ships of the previous century had been challenged by smaller, faster American privateers during the war of 1812, and the Tonnage Law of 1836 revised the measurement system to eliminate tax advantages for deep, clumsy ships. In America, the Baltimore clippers gradually began to take over trades where speed in get-ting cargo to markets brought higher prices. A signal instance of this new economic demand was the China tea trade, which bur-geoned in the 1840s after Chinese ports were opened; new clip-pers built for this trade made spectacular voyages home from Hong Kong to New York—84 days for *Rainbow* in 1845 and a record 74 days for *Sea Witch* in 1849. The discovery of gold in California the year before and in Australia two years later pro-vided further impetus for fast passages, and the clipper boom was on. It lasted two decades at best, spreading to other market-sensitive commodities like wool and grain from Australia, but the quest for speed prefigured the sailing ship's obsolescence as the steamship became more technologically advanced. In an unfin-ished essay written just before his death in 1924, Conrad summa-rizes the last era of the sailing ship with typical nostalgia:

The last days of sailing ships were short if one thinks of the countless ages since the first sail of leather or rudely woven rushes was displayed to the wind. Stretching the period both ways to the utmost, it lasted from 1850 to 1910. Just sixty years. Two generations. The winking of an eye. Hardly the time to drop a prophetic tear. For the pathos of that era lies in the fact that when the sailing ships and the art of sailing them reached their perfection, they were already doomed. It was a swift doom, but it is consoling to know that there was no decadence.[2]

Had the transition from sail to steam been dramatically abrupt, there might be some grounds for accepting this romantic eulogy of the last era of commercial sail at face value, but the changes in the pattern of sea commerce were gradual and irregular. No year served as a decisive turning point, and no single development was the prime cause of the sailing ship's demise; the technological perfection of sailing ships and the development of steamships occurred more or less simultaneously. If the extremely fast clippers of the 1850s and 1860s provided the "golden" age of sail in the long-distance trades, steamships were significant enough to justify the founding of major companies like Cunard, the Pacific Steam Navigation Company, the Royal Mail Line, and the P & O as early as 1840. The opening of the Suez Canal in 1869, by decreasing the gap between coaling stations, made the long-distance trades to India and the Far East practicable for steamers. Sailing ships suffered a depression after the Canal opened, but in the late 1870s they still proved more economical for bulk trades (coal, grain, wool, rice, and jute) that demanded neither great speed nor regularity. The eventual supremacy of steamships depended upon a slow process of technological improvement, particularly the development of strong iron hulls, screw propellers, and high-pressure steam engines. Not until the 1880s were steamers able to depress sailing-ship freights permanently, and bulk cargoes were carried under sail in the long-distance trades until the German submarines of World War I finally dispatched all but a few relics of the diminished fleet.

The disappearance of commercial sail in the late nineteenth century was neither sudden nor complete, and the sailing ships that held on were not refined or improved clippers. The most important change was a marked increase in size, which would have been impossible without a technology based upon iron and steel rather than wood. The new sailing ship of the 1870s and 1880s, designed for cargo capacity rather than speed, had greater length, less beam, less freeboard (height of the deck above water) and a fuller bottom. Larger, heavier and clumsier than the clippers, they were not thoroughbreds in the lineage of sailing ships. They were often overmasted to make up for increased weight; their length sometimes made them cranky to maneuver and unmanageable when running before heavy seas; and their low freeboard made work on decks that were almost constantly awash exceedingly dangerous. Moreover, as the economics of the slow, bulk trades made profits marginal, these ships were often poorly maintained and undermanned, increasing the risks of injury and even disaster at sea. They simply do not represent what Conrad calls "the best period of sailing-ship practice and service."[3] Ironically, the last years of commercial sail were more dangerous for seamen than preceding eras, so it is not surprising that voyaging continued to produce tales of endurance. One of Conrad's early stories, "Youth," is filled with nostalgia but simultaneously reflects most of these deteriorating conditions within the British Merchant Service; although the ship is small rather than oversized, it is old, unseaworthy, undermanned, and filled with a mishandled and dangerous cargo.

Like most of Conrad's voyage tales, "Youth" is built around his own interrupted voyage of endurance on board the *Palestine* from 21 September 1881, until her cargo of coal exploded; she sank on 15 March 1883. That coal was destined to fuel steamships that were taking over many sailing-ship trades, and many of Conrad's other ships in the 1880s—the *Tilkhurst*, the *Riversdale*, even his beloved *Narcissus*[4]—were carrying coal to India and Indonesia so that steamships could return from the Far East through the Suez Canal. Conrad's years at sea bracketed the era of major changes in the conditions of seafaring, and he personally experienced and witnessed both the gradual decadence of the sailing ship and the inevitable shift to steam, which he disliked intensely. In his second novel, *An Outcast of the Islands* (1896), published just two years after he came ashore, he castigates the transition in exaggerated romantic contrasts:

> The hand of the engineer tore down the veil of the terrible beauty [of sailing ships] in order that greedy and faithless landlubbers might

pocket dividends. The mystery was destroyed. Like all mysteries, it lived only in the hearts of its worshippers. The hearts changed; the men changed. The once loving and devoted servants went out armed with fire and iron, and conquering the fear of their own hearts became a calculating crowd of cold and exacting masters. The sea of the past was an incomparable beautiful mistress, with inscrutable face, with cruel and promising eyes. The sea of today is a used-up drudge, wrinkled and defaced by the churned-up wakes of brutal propellers, robbed of the enslaving charm of its vastness, stripped of its beauty, of its mystery and of its promise.[5]

Those bred in sail could never forget that their paragon was being replaced by a tramp. Conrad again expresses the characteristic attitude, more moderately, in a later essay:

Cargo steam vessels have reached by this time a height of utilitarian ugliness which, when one reflects that it is the product of human ingenuity, strikes hopeless awe into one. These dismal creations look still uglier at sea than in port, and with an added touch of the ridiculous. Their rolling waddle when seen at a certain angle, their abrupt clockwork nodding in a sea-way, so unlike the soaring lift and swing of a craft under sail, have in them something caricatural, a suggestion of a low parody directed at noble predecessors by an impoverished generation of dull, mechanical toilers, conceited and without grace.[6]

In spite of these attitudes, Conrad did serve briefly in a number of steamships as officer's berths in sail became scarce, and he drew upon this experience in writing some of his finest voyage tales, including *Lord Jim, Typhoon*, and "The End of the Tether."

The details of Conrad's "three lives"—in Poland, at sea, and as a writer ashore in England—are too complex to be summarized here, but a few facts bear directly on the substance and themes of his voyage fiction. His seafaring career was in part an accident of politics. Born in the Ukraine, then the Russian sector of partitioned Poland, Józef Teodor Konrad Korzeniowski endured an early childhood that would now be considered traumatic: His father, a Polish patriot of the landowning class, was first imprisoned for political activity and then exiled to Vologda in northern Russia, where Conrad's mother died when he was seven. Four years later, after a reprieve that brought the exile back to Warsaw, Conrad's father died. As Conrad was emerging from adolescence, it was unsafe for him to return to the Ukraine; when his attempt to get citizenship in the Austrian sector of Poland failed, his uncle and guardian, Thaddeus Bobrowski, acceded to Conrad's wish to go to sea and established connections for him in Marseilles. There in 1874 the 17-year-old began sailing in French ships and between Mediterranean and West Indian voyages sowed his wild oats with a vengeance—amassing debt, attempting suicide, and perhaps engaging in a gun-running voyage to Spain.

Four years later he arrived in Lowestoft and joined his first British ship to begin a career in the British Merchant Service. During the years between 1878 and 1894 he rose through the ranks, passed mates' and master's examinations, became a British citizen, served as second mate a number of times, chief mate twice, and obtained a command once. In 1894 he came ashore for good, partly because commands and even mates' berths were scarce, partly to finish a novel he had begun between voyages five years earlier. During his years as a writer, fraught with unmet deadlines, debt, anxiety, and nervous breakdowns, he drew upon his sea experience for 21 of his short stories, novellas, and novels as well as many essays and *The Mirror of the Sea*, maintaining a lifelong attachment to the British Merchant Service. The ideals of that service, which matched those of his Polish heritage, came to represent what Wallace Stevens would later call a "rage for order" amidst Conrad's persistent themes of uncertainty, illusion, exile, and alienation.

Several years after coming ashore, Conrad began writing his first voyage narrative, *The Nigger of the "Narcissus,"* based on a voyage from Bombay to Dunkirk from 3 June to 16 October 1884. During this voyage Conrad served as second mate of the *Narcissus*, an elegant full-rigged iron ship of 1,300 tons (not oversized), launched in 1876. This first voyage tale is a bit of an autobiographical spree for a writer not yet concerned about using 20 years of sea experience economically and saving some for future work. The fictional voyage follows the actual voyage track quite precisely, with the exception of docking in London rather than Dunkirk. Apparently the real *Narcissus* did run into "an awful gale in the vicinity of the Needles, south of the cape [of Good Hope]," but there is no record of the ship being knocked down on her beam-ends during this gale.[7] Conrad did have the experience described in the novel's central storm scene while on board

The full-rigged ship *Narcissus*, 1,300 tons, built by Duncan of Glasgow in 1876. Courtesy of the National Maritime Museum, London.

the *Palestine* during an earlier voyage from London to Newcastle in 1881:

> There had been a troublesome week of it, including one hateful night—or a night of hate (it isn't for nothing that the North Sea is also called the German Ocean)—when all the fury stored in its heart seemed concentrated on one ship which could do no better than float on her side in an unnatural, disagreeable, precarious, and altogether intolerable manner. (*Notes*, 158)

The remarkable mustering scene comes from Conrad's experience on the *Duke of Sutherland*; there was no near mutiny on this voyage but apparently there had been a good bit of trouble with the crew on the ship's voyage out from Wales. A death at sea did occur when the *Narcissus* was near the Azores on 24 September 1884, but it is not clear that this seaman, James Barron, was a model for James Wait, since Conrad had sailed with a black man of that name, or a similar one, on the *Duke of Sutherland*. Sources for the rest of the fictional crew are eclectic, gathered from a number of Conrad's ships: Archie, Belfast, and Donkin come from the *Narcissus* herself, and perhaps Podmore as well, since a mad cook had been on board during a previous voyage; Conrad sailed with Baker, Knowles, and Davis on the *Duke of Sutherland*; the model for Singleton was Daniel Sullivan of the *Tilkhurst*; Captain Allistoun may be a composite of two Scottish captains, Duncan of the *Narcissus* and Stuart of the *Loch Etive*; and Creighton, although a recessive character, is an alter ego for Conrad himself, at least in his role on board ship if not in the novel.

Clearly, Conrad had no need to invent much of the story or its characters, but he did very carefully structure the narrative events without violating the inherent linear order of the voyage. Although there is plenty of dramatic action in many real voyages, it is not always distributed in ways that contribute to good story-telling. With a precision and sense of balance remarkable in a writer so near the beginning of his literary career, Conrad weights each part of the narrative with just the right kind of action. In the first chapter, the new crew gathers amiably in the forecastle until Donkin's arrival provides a foretaste of dissension to come, then moves to the quarterdeck for mustering in and the second, more dramatic, arrival of James Wait, whose interruption foretells the disharmony he will bring to the ship. Bracketing these two gatherings is Singleton, seen at the beginning reading a novel about the shore life he will never know and wrenching an extra half turn on the brake of the anchor windlass at the end. Balancing this opening, the fifth and final chapter begins in "a heavy atmosphere of oppressive quietude" in which "Jimmy bobbed up on the surface, compelling attention,"[8] a dying man who refuses to recognize his own mortality and enervates the crew with sentimentality and self-pity. The chapter then advances to the dramatic climax of Jimmy's death, with Donkin in attendance, and his burial at sea; it closes with the metaphoric death of the *Narcissus* herself in a grimy London dock and the dispersal of the crew that had been gathered at the outset.

In between the opening and closing chapters, the second and fourth also balance. In the second chapter, Wait, an accomplished malingerer, and Donkin, an equally accomplished rabble-rouser, use the specter of Jimmy's illness and doubt about his approaching death to corrupt crew members, who cannot deal with incertitude, and to destroy discipline; the chapter closes with Jimmy's removal from the forecastle to the deckhouse. The fourth chapter opens with the recovery of the ship after a fierce gale, focuses on the collapse of an exhausted Singleton, and rekindles the dissension created by Donkin's grievances and Wait's presence in the deckhouse. When Podmore inflames Wait with the fear of death and Captain Allistoun forces Jimmy to remain in the deckhouse rather than returning to duty, the chapter comes to a climax in an aborted mutiny. In the third chapter, at the very center of the narrative and at the geographical turning point of the voyage, stands the great storm scene, when the *Narcissus* is knocked down on her beam-ends and lies nearly capsized and powerless for almost 30 hours. At the very center of that conflict between ship and gale-torn ocean lies the core of emblematic and dramatic action—the rescue of James Wait from the deckhouse in which he is trapped, a rescue that preserves the source of past and future dissension on board the ship. The chapter ends with the most dangerous moment of the whole narrative, the righting of the nearly capsized ship. Taken as a whole, this sophisticated narrative structure superimposed upon a purely linear voyage is not only elegant but necessary. If the mutiny had occurred before the storm, the tension between forces unifying and fragmenting the crew would disappear, and without Wait's rescue during the storm the focus on the dissension he causes would be lost.

For many readers, visualizing exactly what is happening on board the *Narcissus* is not as simple as the famous preface to the story suggests. There Conrad declares his central artistic credo: "My task which I am trying to achieve is, by the power of the written word to make you hear, to make you feel—it is, before all, to make you see. That—and no more, and it is everything" (*Nigger*, x). Conrad evokes the great storm scene through heavily imagistic and metaphorical language and—for those with some knowledge of seamanship—a meticulous attention to nautical detail. Here the need for some technical information about sailing-ship maneuvers is essential if we are truly to "see" what is happening to the *Narcissus* and what her officers and crew are doing to regain control of the ship as the fierce gale abates.

The righting of the ship, for example, is unquestionably precise. The *Narcissus* has been drifting on her port side, lying nearly broadside to the huge seas. When Captain Allistoun thinks he has a chance to right her, he must swing the bow downwind about 120 degrees until the ship has crossed the wind axis. Since the ship is wallowing without headway and the rudder is mostly out of the water anyway, she cannot be brought around by steering. Allistoun orders the setting of the fore-

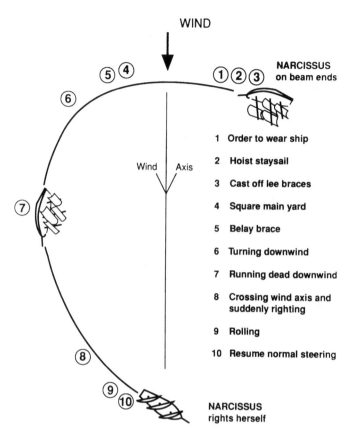

WIND

⑤④   ①②③ **NARCISSUS**
        on beam ends

⑥

Wind | Axis

1 **Order to wear ship**

2 **Hoist staysail**

3 **Cast off lee braces**

4 **Square main yard**

5 **Belay brace**

⑦

6 **Turning downwind**

7 **Running dead downwind**

8 **Crossing wind axis and
     suddenly righting**

9 **Rolling**

10 **Resume normal steering**

⑧

⑨
⑩

**NARCISSUS
rights herself**

Righting the *Narcissus.*
Diagram by Hunt Conard, Skidmore College.

topmast staysail (a triangular sail near the bow) in order to pivot
the ship by wind force; he then squares the yards (brings them
perpendicular to the centerline of the ship) so they will catch the
full force of the wind behind them when the bow has swung off
downwind. Only at that heading can the ship be relieved of the
wind pressure that holds her masts down and begin to move forward with wind and wave force. At this stage in the maneuver
the *Narcissus* is still lying on her side and in a more precarious
position than before with the forward motion—"at every slight
lurch we expected her to slip to the bottom sideways from under
our backs" (*Nigger*, 87)—but has partial steering control. She can

be righted only by wearing (letting the swing continue until the stern crosses the wind axis), at which point the wind will begin to angle over the low side and push upward on the inclined masts: "The ship trembled, trying to lift her side, lurched back, seemed to give up with a nerveless dip, and suddenly with an unexpected jerk swung violently to windward, as though she had torn herself out from a deadly grasp" (*Nigger*, 88). After a series of violent rolls with tons of water cascading back and forth on deck, she begins her flight northward with an exhausted Singleton at the wheel. His long vigil at the wheel while the ship had been lying on her beam-ends was pointless in practical terms, though useful symbolically, but now the skill of an experienced helmsman is crucial in a confused and heavy following sea.

Apart from the inherent drama of a scene in which a burst hatch could sink the *Narcissus* at any moment, it clearly demonstrates Captain Allistoun's competence as a seaman, and that knowledge has an important bearing on our judgment of his other acts. The success of the righting maneuver cannot cancel his responsibility for the plight of the *Narcissus*; it is his error of judgment that causes the knockdown and his refusal to act when she is first thrown on her beam-ends that needlessly endangers both ship and crew for nearly 30 hours. In the first instance he succumbs to the common temptation for sailing-ship captains— lugging sail in a rising wind long after it ceases to add any significant increment to the ship's speed. In the second instance he violates standard practice at a moment of crisis by refusing to cut away some topgallant masts and even topmasts, if necessary, to relieve the wind pressure and let the ship right herself immediately, thus forestalling a long and dangerous vigil as the crew clings to a half-overturned ship that may sink within minutes if the seas break open her main hatch. Both decisions involve taking risks, yet there is an enormous difference between the two cases: In the second instance Captain Allistoun lacks the sense of proportion that is essential for making sound decisions in seamanship—a sense that can distinguish between the options and necessities of action.

One of the standard manuals of seamanship throughout the late nineteenth century, written by Captain Alston (perhaps one source of Captain Allistoun's name), makes the distinction between the two cases quite clear in offering advice to captains.

Lugging too much sail—or hard driving—even though it can be costly in terms of torn sails, broken spars, and even injuries to men working aloft, is described as an avoidable but not fatal error of judgment:

> As a general rule . . . the moment a spar complains, in with the sail; and thus, knowing the futility of pressing a ship, you will be relieved from those unpleasant moments of hesitation, when, tempted to hold on against your half-formed convictions to the contrary, you stand, with anxious glance aloft at every lurch and bound, the image of hapless indecision.[9]

On the other hand, in discussing the critical situation of a ship being thrown on her beam-ends, Captain Alston is quite imperative:

> Let fly everything; when, if she does not right, but continues to go over, there is no resource left but to cut the lanyards of the weather rigging, if you have time, and let the masts go over the side. (Alston 199)

In *Seamanship in the Age of Sail,* John Harland describes one extreme peril for ships during storms just as succinctly: "The vessel could be knocked down 'on her beam ends', and if not recovered, be in immediate danger of foundering."[10] In testimony before the Committee on the Manning of Merchant Ships in 1894, just two years before Conrad began writing *The Nigger of the "Narcissus,"* he was asked similar questions about the relationship between carrying too much sail and avoiding potential disaster in a knockdown, and his answers indicate that he was fully aware of the difference between pushing a bit too hard to make a fast passage and risking the entire ship and crew.[11]

Conrad's sense of proportion is evident in the text of the novel itself. An anonymous fo'c'sle hand serving as narrator expresses the crew's ambivalence toward Captain Allistoun's hard driving. They admire his ability to get the most out of the ship: "Our hearts went out to the old man when he pressed her hard so as to make her hold her own, hold every inch gained to windward; when he made her, under reefed sails, leap obliquely at enormous waves" (*Nigger,* 27). Yet they are also aware of the risks the captain is taking with their lives when he refuses to put a full complement of men on a yard to take in a sail: "As at any moment the masts were likely to be jumped out or blown overboard, we concluded that the captain didn't want to see all his crowd go over the side at once. That was reasonable" (*Nigger*, 28). But there is no room for irony in the response of an anonymous crew member when the captain refuses to right the ship by cutting away the upper spars: " 'If the blamed sticks had been cut out of her she would be running along on her bottom now like any decent ship, an' giv' us all a chance' " (*Nigger*, 29). At the time of the knockdown itself, the carpenter, an experienced seaman who knows precisely what has to be done, "began to crawl to the cabin entrance, where a big axe was kept ready for just such an emergency" (*Nigger*, 30).

In interpreting this scene, it is easy to fall into the fundamental mistake of assuming that cutting away the masts will reduce the *Narcissus* to a derelict hulk at the mercy of the sea. Because often only a few sections of the three masts needed to be cut away to right the ship, this is simply not true. For a variety of reasons, originally including the height of trees and the need for a workable system of reducing windage aloft as ships neared the stormy southern ocean capes, the three masts of a full-rigged ship rose in three sections that could be dismantled. Model examination answers in *The New Handbook for the Board of Trade Examinations* of 1893 make action in even the worst cases abundantly clear:

Q: What do you do if thrown on beam ends?

A: Let fly everything—halyards and sheets; if she did not righten, but kept going over, I would call all hands to cut away the masts and clear away the boats.

Q: Which mast first?

A: The mizzenmast; cut the lee lanyards first, if possible; then the weather lanyards, beginning aft and working forward, cutting the stay and foremost shrouds last; and then the mainmast in the same way.

Q: Why?

A: Because with the foremast I could run for some port where I could get new masts.[12]

Thus the call to "cut," anticipated by the boatswain who goes for the axe kept ready for just such an emergency, is not so much an

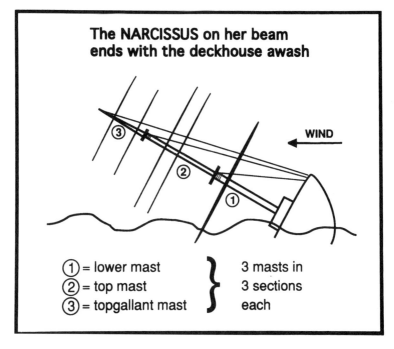

The *Narcissus* on her beam ends with the deckhouse awash.
Diagram by Hunt Conard, Skidmore College.

abandonment of hope as a sensible precaution for surviving the crisis and completing the voyage successfully. After the storm, the missing masts could be partially replaced by spare spars, and the ship, although slower, might even be seaworthy enough to continue the voyage without an extended refitting in port.

Such information about normal practices in handling square-rigged sailing vessels casts new light on the central and crucial storm scene in *The Nigger of the "Narcissus."* To suggest that the story needs the knockdown and subsequent drama of rescue and righting is to miss the point, both in historical and literary terms. Indeed, many ships were thrown on their beam-ends by carrying too much sail too long, and without this central chapter the narrative would lose much of its power. But neither the historical fact nor the literary judgment can reduce the scene to a simple tale of heroic action in a battle against the elements. Its meaning is far more complicated than the pronouncements of an overriding narrative voice, which excuses and even celebrates the captain's error in seamanship. Clues that undercut such pronouncements are clearly there, for those who know how to read them, but they are submerged in a rhetoric of praise for the unflinching captain and images that show him holding the ship up from final disaster by sheer force of will. And in a master stroke of narrative strategy, calls for the proper action are repeated again and again by the despicable Donkin, whose yells of "cut! cut!," opposed by the captain's "no! no!," are finally silenced by a blow from a crew member who cannot stand the doubt. All of the evidence, both inside and outside of the text, suggests that Captain Allistoun violates fundamental principles of seamanship in this instance, that he is either incapable of balancing risks against gains in the ship's battle with the gale or is unwilling to do so. If we ask why, we are given the central clue in a single sentence introducing the captain to the reader: "He loved his ship, and drove her unmercifully; for his secret ambition was to make her accomplish some day a brilliantly quick passage which would be mentioned in nautical papers" (*Nigger*, 31).

Captain Allistoun's egoism belongs to the *Narcissus* just as much as the other manifestations of self-interest that threaten the success of the voyage—Wait's overweening fear of death, Donkin's wheedling manipulation of everyone around him, the crew's submission to a "sentimental lie" that obscures the connection between pity and self-pity. In their attitudes toward Wait, the crew members fluctuate between the extremes of attraction and repulsion. Both are egoistic, the former as a self-pitying inversion of the Golden Rule, the latter as fear of being abused by an impostor. The feelings of the rescue party illustrate this polarity: "We could not scorn him safely—neither could we pity him without risk to our dignity. So we hated him, and passed him carefully from hand to hand" (*Nigger*, 73). Wait's symbolic blackness, emptiness, and remarkable voice—the images associated with Kurtz in *Heart of Darkness*—may obscure the humbler sources of his power over the men of the *Narcissus*. The man who can answer the mate's scolding with "'I must live till I die— mustn't I?'" (*Nigger*, 44) is both a pretender and a presence. He appears to be the successful malingerer Donkin admires, while the possibility of his impending death arouses natural awe in superstitious shipmates. By not working he escapes the drudgery imposed upon his fellows and leaves them shorthanded, magnifying the danger of their work aloft in bad weather; they envy his freedom and resent the imposition. But his blackness also automatically casts him in the role of a Jonah who could be crossed only with peril. West Indian Blacks often died of "consumption" (tuberculosis) on long-distance voyages that passed through many climatic zones, and fo'c'sle lore easily expanded that communal memory into superstition. When the crew first sees Wait, "a surprised hum—a faint hum that sounded like the suppressed mutter of the word 'Nigger'—ran along the deck and escaped out into the night" (*Nigger*, 17). With that recognition they have already granted him special power over their lives. Like most deepwater sailors who believed that a sole "nigger" could jinx the voyage, they are predisposed to treat him with the strange mixture of deference and exasperation that destroys morale on board the *Narcissus*. In the context of unsophisticated beliefs, Conrad did not have to invent the crew's obsessive interest in Wait, for a "nigger" on board ship was a "natural" symbol of death and disaster at sea. It is thus easy for the crew to identify their fortunes with those of Wait, just as his panic is an extreme form of their own unacknowledged fear of death. And it is this compact of egoism that makes pity corrupting in the novel.

Disguised forms of pity spread beyond the absurd sentimentality of Belfast and the wavering attitudes of other crew members to Captain Allistoun, Podmore, and even Donkin, all of whom have brief moments of identification with Wait's plight. Their gestures of pity are egoistic because they involve tampering with Wait in ways not justified by ordinary shipboard discipline or simple fellow feeling. Allistoun's pity takes the form of an impulsive lie that precipitates an incipient mutiny. If we juxtapose the captain's speech ordering Wait into confinement with his later explanation to the mates, the lie becomes apparent:

> "I've been sick ... now—better," mumbled Wait, glaring in the light.—"You have been shamming sick," retorted Captain Allistoun with severity; "Why ..." he hesitated for less than half a second. "Why, anybody can see that. There's nothing the matter with you, but you choose to lie-up to please yourself—and now you shall lie-up to please me. Mr. Baker, my orders are that this man is not to be allowed on deck to the end of the passage." (*Nigger*, 120)

"Did you think I had gone wrong there, Mr. Baker?" He tapped his forehead, laughed short. "When I saw him standing there, three parts dead and so scared—black amongst that gaping lot—no grit to face what's coming to us all—the notion came to me all at once, before I could think. Sorry for him—like you would be for a sick brute. If ever creature was in a mortal funk to die! . . . I thought I would let him go out in his own way. Kind of impulse." (*Nigger*, 126–27)

Presumably the half second of hesitation in the first passage is equated with the moment of impulse in the second. The repetition of the colloquial phrase "lie-up" calls attention to the other meaning of "lie" only when we have read the later passage since we are unsure of the captain's mind about Wait before. The phrase also calls attention to a central theme of the narrative— "the latent egoism of tenderness to suffering" (*Nigger*, 138)—by the parallel structure of its complements, "to please yourself" and "to please me." When we read the first passage, the captain seems to be using the occasion to reinforce discipline. The second passage reveals his true motive: "I thought I would let him go out in his own way." This is simple equivocation because Allistoun knows what Wait wants and needs after his scare with Podmore—the daily reassurance that he is part of the community of the living. In this "impulse" he has stepped out of his role as commander; a captain's prerogative does not include choosing another man's way of dying unless such choice is demanded by the needs of working the ship. And readers of later Conrad novels and stories will also remember Marlow's abhorrence of lies, a theme that emerges repeatedly in *Lord Jim* and *Heart of Darkness*.

This encroachment upon Wait's dying links Allistoun with Podmore, who a few pages earlier had tortured Jimmy to confirm the "addled vision" of himself as a savior of souls. When the captain intervenes and orders him to quit badgering Wait in the deckhouse, there is an interesting parody of his own egoistic pity in Podmore's response:

"Never," he stammered, "I . . . he . . . I."—"What—do—you—say?" pronounced Captain Allistoun. "Come out at once—or . . ."—"I am going," said the cook, with a hasty and sombre resignation. He strode over the doorstep firmly—hesitated—made a few steps. They looked at him in silence.—"I make you responsible!" he cried, desperately, turning half round. (*Nigger*, 118)

Podmore confuses his own ego with Wait's ("I . . . he . . . I") and his own role with the captain's ("I make you responsible"). Podmore's scene with Wait begins with a puzzling opposition between pity and conceit: "A spark of human pity glimmered yet through the infernal fog of his supreme conceit" (*Nigger*, 116). Allistoun's speech to the mates closes with the fusion of the same two qualities as he passes from sympathetic identification to manipulation:

> "Did you see the eyes of that sick nigger, Mr. Baker? I fancied he begged me for something. What? Past all help. One lone black beggar amongst the lot of us, and he seemed to look through me into the very hell. Fancy, this wretched Podmore! Well, let him die in peace. I am master here after all." (*Nigger*, 127)

The repetition of *begged* and *beggar* here—with all its sentimental humanitarian associations—is probably not accidental. And the same connection between pity and egoism is clinched by its more despicable exponent, Donkin, after he has precipitated Wait's death:

> And Donkin, watching the end of that hateful nigger, felt the anguishing grasp of a great sorrow on his heart at the thought that he himself, some day, would have to go through it all—just like this— perhaps! His eyes became moist. "Poor beggar," he murmured. (*Nigger*, 153–54)

Donkin's "poor beggar" echoes Allistoun's "one lone black beggar amongst the lot of us," and the corruption of self-pity is here made explicit.

Only Singleton seems to escape the unrestfulness of egoism because he lives "untouched by human emotions" (*Nigger*, 41). Yet even he, who "had never given a thought to his mortal self" is given a vision of his own death on a "black and foaming" sea: "He heard its impatient voice calling for him out of a pitiless vastness full of unrest, of turmoil, and of terror" (*Nigger*, 99). If Donkin represents all that the narrating voice despises, Singleton is his natural foil. In striking images throughout the narrative, he is cast in mythic proportions and given oracular functions. But if we are tempted to use Singleton's aphorisms as marks of meaning, we must remember that his "wisdom" is not a general explanatory system. The traditional superstition of sailors was largely a reaction to the ever-present peril of the unknown, and the certainty with which Singleton declares that a fair wind will not come until the "nigger" leaves the *Narcissus* was by no means rare. It can be reduced to a series of simple associations: Jimmy is the cause of head winds, and the cause can be removed only by the sight of an island (much more effective than a continent, we are told) that will kill Jimmy and free the ship of her "unfair burden"; then fair winds will return. And so it turns out. "But he couldn't explain why" (*Nigger*, 156). Such undercutting sentences remind us of Donkin's reaction to the crew's faith in Singleton's pronouncements: "When Nilsen came to him with the news: 'Singleton says he will die,' he answered him by a spiteful 'And so will you—you fatheaded Dutchman' " (*Nigger*, 43).

No more can we trust the narrating voice to give us the whole truth about the meaning of the voyage. To speak of the narrator of *The Nigger of the "Narcissus"* is to create a fiction within a fiction, for there are many as the point of view shifts. Spatially the narrating voice is as versatile as Proteus; just when we think we have its identity pinned down, it assumes a new guise and moves. Much of the time we hear the story from an unnamed seaman in the fo'c'sle or on deck; for several important conversations among the officers we are on the quarter-deck, out of hearing of the crew; in a number of passages we are high in the sky looking down on the ship as a whole; and at the very end, in a coda, we see the dispersal of the crew through a first-person narrator, also unnamed. As we hear this medley of voices, the American title for the novella, *The Children of the Sea: A Tale of the Forecastle*, seems just as appropriate as the English title we know it by.[13] Conrad had not yet found Marlow to tell his voyage stories, but even if he had, fixed first-person narration would not have worked in this narrative. The story of the *Narcissus* requires many perspectives, and the rigid social hierarchy of shipboard life prohibits the necessary freedom of movement for any individual character.

Yet in all these mutations of perspective, the reader's problem is clearly one of authority.[14] Is the narrating voice's placement an index of its reliability? Is it less fallible the higher it gets in the sky, the farther it is removed from the *we* who is presumably an ordinary, uneducated seaman yet serves as the conduit for sentences of extraordinary complexity and rhetorical polish? The easiest answer to these questions attaches greater authority to the withdrawn narrating voice, less to the one involved in specific scenes, but we cannot justify this weighting when we look closely at the generalizing passages in the text. They are charged with possible attitudes rather than simple truths. The narrating voice is just as susceptible to impulses and exaggerations in the third person as it is in the first person. In its attempts to allay the doubts and fears that trouble the crew, it sometimes intones and embellishes simplistic dichotomies between good and bad seamen, pure life at sea and sordid existence ashore, forgetting, for the moment, the more complex vision of life at sea that rings true for the reader: "[L]ike that earth which had given her up to the sea, she [the *Narcissus*] had an intolerable load of regrets and hopes. On her lived timid truth and audacious lies, and like the earth, she was unconscious, fair to see—and condemned by men to an ignoble fate" (*Nigger*, 29–30). And then there are passages like the one that opens the fourth chapter, just after the storm:

> On men reprieved by its disdainful mercy, the immortal sea confers in its justice the full privilege of desired unrest. Through the perfect wisdom of its grace they are not permitted to meditate at ease upon the complicated and acrid savour of existence. They must without pause justify their life to the eternal pity that commands toil to be hard and unceasing, from sunrise to sunset, from sunset to sunrise; till the weary succession of nights and days tainted by the obstinate clamour of sages, demanding bliss and an empty heaven, is redeemed at last by the vast silence of pain and labour, by the dumb fear and the dumb courage of men obscure, forgetful, and enduring. (*Nigger*, 90)

In such contexts the narrator's attempts to reach simple beliefs through polarities—black and white, good and evil, brave and cowardly, pure and tainted—are straws in the wind, as inadequate to Conrad's vision of the voyage as Singleton's pronouncements. When the narrating voice joins the rest of the crew in lying to Jimmy "with unshaken fidelity" (*Nigger*, 143), the dichotomy between truth and falsehood collapses. The poles coalesce as the voice questions the relevance of any belief to the structure of reality, if there is a structure. Its truths are partial, unstable, perhaps illusory, and always inadequate; its doubts, unlike Singleton's, cannot be allayed by the arrival of wind.

To be sure, the narrating voice has an important role in expressing attitudes with all the force of high rhetoric, and the novel ends in a celebratory tribute to the crew, "as good a crowd as ever fisted with wild cries the beating canvas of a heavy foresail; or tossing aloft, invisible in the night, gave back yell for yell to a westerly gale" (*Nigger*, 173). Yet in all of its pronouncements, the narrating voice gives us postures of belief, grasped hopes rather than absolute truths. If there is any guideline to reliability, it is this: We can believe what the person behind the voice sees and hears, in the fo'c'sle or on deck, but must judge what is said in generalizing passages against all the details of the text, many of which suggest anomalies or even contradictions. As a complex exploration of egoism, *The Nigger of the "Narcissus"* cannot be reduced to a comfortable vision of "hands busy about the work of the earth" (*Nigger*, xii) or to the narrating voice's hope that collectively the crew had "wrung out a meaning from our sinful lives" (*Nigger*, 173). Faced with the physical and moral tests of survival, the officers and men of the *Narcissus* are notably inconstant, fluctuating between public codes of conduct and private ambitions, sometimes shrouding hidden desires with the appearance of exemplary behavior or of humanitarian zeal, sometimes holding secret urges and overt restraints in unstable balance. No principle of fidelity to duty can encompass their varying impulses and motives; no momentary solidarity of communal effort can provide security for men "reprieved" by the "disdainful mercy" of a sea that offers them only "the full privilege of desired unrest."

His own voyage experience had given Conrad the ship, its men, the linear structure of the narrative, and many of its incidents to be shaped and amplified by a controlling vision. Unlike Columbus and Cook, he had no royal or official audience to please, but he shared with them a mariner's insistence on exactness of detail and a penchant for meditation. In rhetorical energy he falls somewhere between Melville's compulsive exuberance and Hemingway's severe restraint yet incorporates both modes, balancing the passionate beliefs of his narrating voices against a precise and direct rendering of what they see and hear. Like all of his predecessors in the genre, he had no need to import human conflict and potential disaster into his narrative because they belong to it naturally, just as Jimmy Wait "belongs" to the *Narcissus* and becomes the source and focal point for a full range of human fears, hopes, doubts, and illusions. In this sense Conrad and others who write voyage fiction do not have to invent their narratives any more than Columbus and Cook did, but they do orchestrate them, counterpointing attitudes against facts, setting the strident noise of a dense human community against the recurrent ground bass of ocean isolation, searching, sometimes in vain, for the harmonies and overtones that enrich human experience.

Chapter 6

POSTSCRIPT: VOYAGE NARRATIVES IN THE TWENTIETH CENTURY

A century that has seen transatlantic liners replaced by jet aircraft and ocean experience for many people reduced to the floating entertainment palaces of the cruise trade is not likely to rival the age of discovery or the era of clipper ships in voyage narratives. Now the word *voyage* itself is just as likely to evoke images of undersea or space exploration as trips on the surface of the sea. Thomas Philbrick begins his excellent book on American sea fiction by asserting that the sea fired the American imagination during the first half of the nineteenth century because "it represented the arena of past glories, the training ground of the national character, and the field on which wealth and power were to be won for the country" (Philbrick 1). Accepting the essence of the Turner thesis that attention turned from the sea to the frontier, Philbrick finds interest in voyage narratives waning at mid-century: "Melville's work, like the great clipper ships which were its contemporaries, was something of a historical anomaly, the last, magnificent flowering of a plant that was dying at its roots" (Philbrick 262). In another good book on the genre, Bert Bender challenges Philbrick's assessment: "This conclusion mistakenly assumes a parallel between the intensity of American maritime industry and the production of sea literature; it distorts the significance of a single element among the three that are featured in traditional sea fiction, the sea, the sailor, and the ship; it suggests that only sailing ships can excite the writer's imagination; and it does not account for the very impressive quantity and quality of American sea fiction that has appeared during the last century and a quarter" (Bender 6). *America and the Sea: A Literary History*, edited by Haskell Springer, buttresses the point: Its range stretches from the colonial era through the last decades of the twentieth century, and it also contains corollary chapters on sea music and art.

In spite of a marked decrease in public consciousness of ocean commerce and the undermining of any sense of romance associated with it—container ships cannot match clipper ships—people still gravitate to the edges of continents in Melvillean fashion, dream of islands, undertake long and arduous sailing voyages for no gain whatsoever, and, most of all, continue to read voyage narratives of many kinds. The flurry of publications in the last half of the twentieth century may even suggest that interest in voyaging is inversely proportional to its role in daily life. In an underappreciated voyage narrative, *N by E*, artist Rockwell Kent epitomizes the tension between the routines and daydreams of a commuter who tries to leap from his drab reality into an adventurous voyage. Such readers are clearly out there, and recent decades have seen the publication of works like John Barth's *Sabbatical,* Peter Matthiessen's *Far Tortuga,* Nicholas Monsarrat's *The Master Mariner Running Proud,* William Golding's trilogy (*Rites of Passage, Close Quarters,* and *Fire Down Below*), Derek Walcott's *Omeros,* John McPhee's *Looking for a Ship,* Charles Johnson's *Middle Passage,* Robert Stone's *Outerbridge Reach,* and a spate of novels in Patrick O'Brian's Aubrey/Maturin series. One can only conclude that Philbrick's obituary notice was premature. This brief postscript cannot comprehend extensive publications in a flourishing genre throughout an entire century, but it does suggest some principal lines of development.

Like the voyage narratives of previous centuries, whether overtly fictional, autobiographical, or documentary, most in the twentieth century fuse description, action, recollection, and meditation within a particular realm of sea experience, much as *Moby-*

Dick and *Two Years Before the Mast* had done earlier. Many of them refurbish old subgenres with variations, others invent new ones. One of the most flourishing of the new subgenres is the yacht voyage, appearing in both fictional and nonfictional modes and often, like most voyage narratives, assimilating elements of the other mode to its primary one. Coastal yachting had been around for a long time, especially in England and Holland, but the notion of putting to sea on an extended offshore voyage for *pleasure* would have seemed incomprehensible to the shellbacks of the nineteenth century who had to endure the rigors of the ocean to make their meager living. Yet the subgenre was not invented in the twentieth century. Lord and Lady Brassey sailed around the world in the auxiliary brigantine yacht *Sunbeam* with their family from July, 1876, to May, 1877. Brassey was a captain in his own right, a prominent authority on maritime affairs, and the Member of Parliament who introduced many of the bills designed to improve conditions in the British Merchant Service. Anne Brassey kept a journal that grew into the readable and immensely popular *Around the World in the Yacht Sunbeam: Our Home on the Ocean for Eleven Months* (1878). E. F. Knight had thrown up his shore profession as a barrister in London and sailed to South America in 1880–1881, recording his adventures in *The Cruise of the Falcon* (1884). But certainly the yacht voyage gained its first mass reading public in America with the publication of Joshua Slocum's *Sailing Alone around the World* (1900), a book so popular that it was taught in schools for generations.

Slocum's solo circumnavigation from 21 April 1895, to 27 June 1898 (accidentally replicating the usual three years for world-circling voyages ever since Drake), was a "first" and attracted the attention of newspapers all over the world, preparing the way for the success of the book. Slocum, by then an involuntarily retired captain in the depressed world of sailing ships, had written before about a voyage in some ways more remarkable: *The Voyage of the Liberdade* (1890) recounts the 5,500 mile voyage he made in a 35-foot boat of his own construction—with his wife and two children on board—to get home after a shipwreck on the Brazilian coast. The resourcefulness of the sailor was matched by the craft of the largely untutored but extremely effective writer, who developed a laconic, self-deprecating style laced with subtle humor and well-turned anecdotes. *Sailing Alone around the World* is deservedly the archetype of the subgenre that has flour-

161

ished throughout this century. Not only was it the first such account to be published, but it also remains among the most literary in quality, balancing just the right amount of quotidian detail against more dramatic episodes like Slocum's encounter with North African pirates, his stranding on the coast of Brazil, and his prolonged struggles with Indians and williwaws before he finally clears the Strait of Magellan.

Slocum's book motivated J. C. Voss to set out from Victoria, British Columbia, in 1901 on a voyage spanning three oceans in a 38-foot log canoe, later recorded in *The Venturesome Voyages of Captain Voss* (1913). That urge has never ceased, leading to many single-handed ocean crossings in all parts of the world, with exaggerated downsizing for the record books (*Tinker Belle* was only 13 feet long) and upsizing to more than 70 feet to get the speed necessary for winning single-handed races around the world. Clearly, just as the desire for fame had motivated many nineteenth-century captains to drive their ships to the limit—and sometimes beyond—so would twentieth-century solo sailors struggle for recognition by undertaking hazardous passages in small boats or racing for prizes in large ones that sacrificed seaworthiness to speed. These are voyages of endurance in new contexts, for new rewards, but the narratives that record them continue the patterns of previous centuries, pitting the vessel and her single crew against storm, calm, solitude, and the disintegration of will.

Just as various as the real voyages behind the books are the interests that their published narratives include. Two world wars dampened everyone's ardor for adventurous yacht voyages, but solo circumnavigations returned in new contexts, record breaking and then racing, especially in Great Britain in the 1960s. Perhaps these new maritime ventures resonated with echoes of Britain's centuries as ruler of the seas. So great was national interest in Francis Chichester's attempt to break the old records of clipper ships that when he returned from his circumnavigation in 1967 he was met by a vast flotilla of dignitaries at Plymouth. He was later visited by Queen Elizabeth II at Greenwich, where he was knighted (reminiscent of the first Queen Elizabeth and Sir Francis Drake) and given a huge welcome. His boat, the 54-foot *Gypsy Moth IV,* now sits next to the clipper *Cutty Sark* at the National Maritime Museum in Greenwich, symbolically connecting recent ventures with former maritime supremacy; his book, *Gypsy Moth Circles the World* (1967), was a best seller on both sides of the Atlantic. Within a year the London *Sunday Times* had announced a nonstop race around the world for solo navigators, which drew nine entrants. Hal Roth's *The Longest Race* (1983) describes what happened to them, and it is quite a story: One boat sank; another was found without its skipper on board; six withdrew for various reasons, including one whose skipper turned back to Polynesia and stayed there 11 years; one finished. Since then round-the-world races, either with full crews or single-handed, have proliferated and inevitably produced a growing number of voyage narratives and videos to whet the public appetite for the ultimate adventure on the surface of the ocean, as if windsurfing around Cape Horn were not enough. Yet some of them are well worth serious attention. The most ambitious recent work based on single-handed races around the world is Robert Stone's novel *Outerbridge Reach* (1992), which deals with some of the anomalies and contradictions of solitude at sea—peace, fear, self-doubt, and above all the hallucinations that have beset every solo sailor since Slocum. After the male protagonist, Owen Browne, puts to sea in a flimsily built catamaran, the novel alternates scenes of his gradual slippage into fantasy with those from the equally bizarre shoreside world that has sponsored and hyped his entry. When Browne's suicide is discovered, his widow prepares to set out on her own solo race in expiation for the voyage her husband had failed to complete.

Apart from solo racing and circumnavigations, many narratives of yacht voyages record passages to unfriendly coasts like those of Labrador and Greenland, including R. D. Graham's *Rough Passage* (1936) and Rockwell Kent's *N by E* (1930), which ends in shipwreck. Others, like David Lewis, undertook voyages that replicated those of Polynesian navigators and European explorers in the Pacific; in *Ice Bird* (1975) he recounts a circumnavigation of Antarctica, the real continent that lay hidden within the larger one imagined in the geographical speculations about *Terra Australis* during the eighteenth century. Other yacht voyages in the Pacific reawaken the lure of Polynesia that the first explorers felt, including those recorded in W. A. Robinson's *To the Great Southern Sea* (1957) and Sterling Hayden's *Wanderer* (1963), the tale of his escape from the tinsel of Hollywood to the South Seas with four of his children on board a 98-foot schooner. Such accounts of sailing to the tropical islands of the Pacific often have the overtones of a quest, including departure from the writer's personal version of dystopia and succeeding search for a utopian destination. Yet just as frequently they are filled with the reality of boats ill suited and badly prepared for ocean sailing, difficult passages, and the loss of the vessel among the reefs of uncharted coral atolls. Such are the marks of Jack London's self-deprecating *The Cruise of the "Snark"* (1911), which began a long line of South-Sea cruise narratives in the twentieth century.

Some narratives of yacht voyages have been inextricably entangled with politics. Erskine Childers's *The Riddle of the Sands* (1903) mixes a cruise in the tricky waters of the Dutch and German Frisian Islands with a spy story, and Hilaire Belloc's *The Cruise of the Nona* (1925) intersperses despair over the confused state of Britain and praise for Mussolini's vision with a cruise around England and Wales. John Barth's *Sabbatical: A Romance* (1982) is a complex novel built around a Chesapeake Bay cruise that encompasses a CIA spy drama, an exploration of the nature of writing, and a love story. Clearly and explicitly in the mode of metafiction, the novel asks us to hold both the action and the writing of the narrative in mind simultaneously, claiming that doing and telling are inseparable. Moreover, it reaches out to encompass all previous voyage narratives, with special reference to the *Odyssey* and *The Narrative of Arthur Gordon Pym,* and pulls them into itself. In form it is a nostos, the return from nine months of wandering in the Caribbean; it begins with a clash with Poseidon off the Virginia coast and ends with lovemaking in home port. Several of Barth's subsequent novels, *The Tidewater Tales: A Novel* (1987) and *The Last Voyage of Somebody the Sailor* (1991) continue to set voyaging and writing, love and politics, in metafictional parallels, gathering in the *Odyssey* and the *Arabian Nights;* the former is built around a two-week cruise in the Chesapeake, while the latter's protagonist resails seven of Sinbad's voyages in various reincarnations. Other cruise narratives, like William Buckley's informal symposia or floating conversations—*Airborne: A Sentimental Journey* (1976), *Atlantic High: A Celebration* (1982), and *Racing through Paradise: A Pacific Passage* (1987)—simply record the experiences and musings of literate friends who cross an ocean together, almost as if Dr. Johnson's circle had set out on a tour of the Atlantic or Pacific.

Early in the twentieth century the last age of commercial sail was moribund, but major writers continued to produce classic voyage narratives. Three of them—Jack London's *The Sea-Wolf*

(1904) and a pair by Joseph Conrad, "The Secret Sharer" (1910) and *The Shadow-Line* (1917)—perpetuate the sea Bildungsroman in darker biological or psychological contexts; in each case the initiation almost destroys the protagonist. Later in the century the world of sailing ships reappears in a familiar genre, the historical sea novel, first developed in America by James Fenimore Cooper. Beginning in the 1930s, it spawned a healthy and lasting subgenre dealing with British naval exploits during the Napoleonic Wars. Here the focus shifts from voyages of discovery or endurance to the internal conflicts on board men-of-war and the battles of naval expeditions. American interest in the Royal Navy during the last decades of the eighteenth century goes back to Melville's *Billy Budd* and Charles Nordhoff and Norman Hall's reconstruction of its most notorious event in *The Bounty Trilogy* (1932–1936); the bulk of the historical fiction dealing with naval action during the European wars between 1796 and 1815, however, has come from Britain and Ireland. If you are old enough, you will have encountered it first in the enormously popular novels of C. S. Forester, built around the naval career of Horatio Hornblower, who rises from captain to commodore and admiral in a sequence of novels, many of which are collected in *Captain Horatio Hornblower* (1944) and *The Indomitable Hornblower* (1958).

A direct descendent would seem to be Patrick O'Brian's Aubrey/Maturin novels, a series now numbering 18 volumes, which have been more enthusiastically reviewed as literary productions in recent years. In fact, interest in O'Brian's series of novels is a publishing phenomenon, stretching from the shelves of bookstore chains to the halls of academe; the novels have been reviewed in the *New York Times,* the *New Yorker,* and the *New York Review of Books.* A newsletter keeps his aficionados apprised of the latest events, including U.S. tours with O'Brian's appearances for interviews and panels at libraries and theaters in major cities. Why this passion for the intricate details of a remote era, an outmoded form of naval warfare, all in a genre that is seldom taken seriously late in the twentieth century? Many of his readers, perhaps most, know little or nothing about the Royal Navy beyond what he provides and even less about seafaring in general. The answer may lie in a combination of O'Brian's meticulous research and knowledge of his subject, his talent in forming complex characters and following them through stages of experience, his deft and pungent style, and his choice of an era during which world order seemed to be falling apart as a context. No matter what the explanation, it is clear that O'Brian has reinvigorated one subgenre of voyage narratives that many had written off for good.

Another major novelist has added further interest. William Golding's trilogy dealing with the same period but removed from any battle scenes—*Rites of Passage* (1980), *Close Quarters* (1987), and *Fire Down Below* (1989)—chronicles the voyage of an aging Royal Navy ship transporting passengers to Australia. It returns to both the sea Bildungsroman and the voyage of endurance for structure, following the education of a young and pompous protagonist, Edmund Talbot, through stages of his education in human nature during an interminable voyage on a slow and disintegrating vessel that never should have left port, much less carried passengers through the roaring forties to Australia. The portrait of the officers and men of the Royal Navy is complete and honest, from the role of patronage aft to buggery forward, and the full range of status among passengers creates a microcosm of British society within which the compression of shipboard life engenders conflicts that might be avoided ashore.

The historical sea novel has also focused on naval campaigns in twentieth-century wars, especially World War II in Herman Wouk's *The Caine Mutiny* (1951) and Nicholas Monsarrat's *The Cruel Sea* (1951). Both deal with voyages in relatively small warships, destroyer and corvette, respectively, that exacerbate the tensions among their crews, leading to mutiny in the first case. Perhaps taking a cue from Virginia Woolf's *Orlando*, Monsarrat also wrote a compendious novel surveying all of British naval history from the Armada to Trafalgar in *The Master Mariner Running Proud* (1978). Another famous mutiny that provided one source for Melville's *Billy Budd* is the subject of Henry Carlisle's *Voyage to the First of December* (1972), which retells the story of the nebulous *Somers* mutiny, court martial, and execution at sea in 1842. Carlisle also deals with the story of the whaleship *Essex*, battered by a whale, that lies behind the final chapters of *Moby-Dick* in *The Jonah Man* (1984). Charles Johnson's *Middle Passage* (1990) has its basis in another phase of maritime history: the infamous slave trade in the seventeenth and eighteenth centuries. Rooted in the genre of slave narratives and most particularly in the middle passage of the triangular trade between New England, West Africa, and Caribbean islands that brought slaves to

America, the novel also echoes voyage narratives from the *Odyssey* through Poe, Melville, and London. In spite of a lack of accurate nautical details, it tells a powerful story of the disintegration of order on board a ship devoted to a despicable trade. Another of the seamier eras in American maritime history is the subject of Sterling Hayden's *Voyage: A Novel of 1896,* which recounts a passage in an iron bark from the east coast around Cape Horn to California, the classic route for difficult voyages of endurance. In a chapter on *The Red Record,* which documented the incidents of barbaric treatment of seamen that made American merchant ships infamous throughout the world, Hayden sets up the model for the conflicts of shipboard life that propel the novel to its conclusion. Clearly, even this brief and incomplete survey of voyage narratives based on naval and maritime history indicates that the subgenre is alive and well.

In a related subgenre, scholar-adventurers reenact ancient voyages to validate their authenticity or to establish historical or anthropological theories, writing detailed accounts of their replicas, courses, and experience at sea. In *Kon-Tiki: Across the Pacific by Raft* (1950), Thor Heyerdahl sailed a raft made of balsa logs 4,300 miles from Peru to Tahiti to substantiate his theory that Polynesians had migrated westward from South America rather than eastward from Asia. His next venture in experimental anthropology was two tries at navigating a papyrus raft from Africa to the West Indies, reported in *The Ra Expeditions* (1971); in a third venture, documented in *The Tigris Expedition* (1981), Heyerdahl retraced ancient Near Eastern trade routes in the Indian Ocean and Arabian Sea, this time sailing a boat of reeds. At the same time others were plotting different routes for Polynesian migrations. David Lewis, in *We the Navigators* (1972), followed a legendary Maori route from Tahiti to New Zealand without any instruments, using the traditional methods of Polynesian navigators, and Herb Kane recreates an ancient voyage in *Voyage: The Discovery of Hawaii* (1976). It was based on a voyage from Hawaii to Tahiti in the 60-foot double-hulled canoe *Hokule'a,* undertaken to prove the possibility of two-way voyaging along this route. Tim Severin, an Irish sailor and geographer, has been more interested in retracing specific ancient voyages reported in myth and literature, with special attention to the performance of the vessels and the feasibility of routes. The first of his four ventures was crossing the

Atlantic in a leather boat, which produced *The Brendan Voyage* (1978); next he took on the Seven Voyages of Sinbad the Sailor from the *Arabian Nights* in an Arab *dhow* (the traditional trading vessel of the Red Sea, Persian gulf, and Indian Ocean), sailing from Oman to Canton in China, a voyage recorded in *The Sinbad Voyage* (1982). Then he turned to the *Argonautica* and the *Odyssey*, sailing the hypothetical tracks of their heroes and writing *The Jason Voyage: The Quest for the Golden Fleece* (1985) and *The Ulysses Voyage: Sea Search for the Odyssey* (1987). Retracing the route of Odysseus's wanderings by land, air, and sea (as documented in chapter 2) has produced a flock of travel and voyage narratives, among them Goran Schildt's *In the Wake of Odysseus* (1953), Ernle Bradford's *Ulysses Found* (1963), and Gilbert Pillot's *The Secret Code of the Odyssey: Did the Greeks Sail the Atlantic?* (1972).

Another subgenre deals not with sailing vessels but with voyages of cargo ships, a possibility richly explored at the turn of the century by Conrad in *Lord Jim* (1900), "The End of the Tether" (1902), and *Typhoon* (1903). Life in the engine room of steamships is the focus of many of Eugene O'Neill's short plays, like those in *Seven Plays of the Sea* (1919), and is also the core of B. Traven's *The Death Ship* (1934) and William McFee's *Watch Below* (1940). Perspectives from the deck control Noel Mostert's *Supership* (1974) and Christopher Buckley's *Steaming to Bamboola* (1982). Gabriel García Márquez's *Story of a Shipwrecked Sailor* (1986) reports the experience of a sailor washed overboard from a Columbian destroyer overloaded with contraband cargo. And two recent books spin stories around the deteriorating conditions in the U.S. Merchant Marine, a murder mystery in the case of Larry Reiner's *Minute of Silence* (1990) and a detailed account of a voyage along the western coast of South America in John McPhee's poignant character study, *Looking for a Ship* (1990).

Other major works continue the older traditions of the genre in new ways. Katherine Anne Porter's *Ship of Fools* (1945), the story of a voyage from Vera Cruz, Mexico, to Bremerhaven, Germany, in 1931 with German, Swiss, Spanish, Swedish, Cuban, Mexican, and American passengers on board, revives an archetype that goes back to Noah's ark—loading the whole world on board a vessel and putting to sea. Porter's remote source is a moral allegory by Sebastian Brant, *Das Narrenschiff*, first published in 1494, but her immediate subject is a human community heading toward the horrors of World War II. Another novel, Peter Matthiessen's *Far Tortuga* (1975), may be the twentieth century's *Moby-Dick*. Like Melville's big book, this less hefty one has equivalent ambitions to suck in the whole world, and it faces the sharkishness of that world without flinching. On the surface the story of a disastrous turtling voyage in a dying fishery, it comprehends everything from the Columbian discoveries to the biological world of the ocean to Zen Buddhism in an experimental form reminiscent of James Joyce. Cast as a voyage of endurance, like Conrad's "Youth," it has all the earmarks of failure from the outset: a partially converted and ill-equipped schooner, a crew filled out with drunks and drifters, and a competent but overbearing captain who makes a series of fatal mistakes—starting for the turtle banks too late in the season, unnecessarily alienating members of the crew, judging recovery of his father's knife more important than escaping a band of marauding Jamaicans, and presuming that he can navigate through uncharted coral reefs in the dark. After the ship founders, the small boat voyage that ensues is an inverted version of the one in Crane's "The Open Boat," with collective effort replaced by individual savagery in the sole survivor. Mathiessen, like Melville, had earned his direct knowledge as a commercial fisherman, and he later wrote eloquently of that world in *Men's Lives* (1988).

The long tradition of rewriting the *Odyssey* also continues through the twentieth century, often as an allusive context in voyage narratives, as we have seen. It was explicitly revived in small scale in the Tremolino episode of Conrad's *The Mirror of the Sea* (1906) and, of course, taken ashore in large scale in Joyce's *Ulysses*. Nikos Kazantzakis's massive narrative poem *The Odyssey: A Modern Sequel* (1938) started to recast the story in modern terms but soon plunged off into a quest for the ultimate meaning of life and death that went to the heart of Africa, far beyond what Tennyson had envisioned in the nineteenth century—"to sail beyond the sunset, and the baths / of all the western stars, until I die." In *Omeros* (1990), Derek Walcott continues the tradition in a Caribbean setting, but his narrative poem parallels both the *Odyssey* and the *Iliad* more closely as it revisits some of the figures and incidents of Homer's epics. Evidently, some 28 centuries later, no one has yet walked far enough inland for the oar over Odysseus's shoulder to be mistaken as a winnowing fan.

Notes and References

Chapter 1

1. John Masefield, "Sea Fever," in *Moods of the Sea: Masterworks of Sea Poetry,* ed. George C. Solley and Eric Steinbaugh (Annapolis, Md.: Naval Institute Press, 1981), 65; hereafter cited in text. The second passage is quoted in Constance Babington Smith, *John Masefield: A Life* (New York: Macmillan, ca. 1978), 28–29.

2. Joseph Conrad, "Initiation," in *The Mirror of the Sea* (London: J. M. Dent, 1946), 135–36; hereafter cited in text.

3. John McPhee, *Looking for a Ship* (New York: Noonday Press, 1990), 127.

4. Homer, *The Odyssey,* trans. Robert Fagles (New York: Penguin Books USA, 1996), 11: 138–49; hereafter cited in text as *Odyssey.*

5. Tom Lewis, "Marching Inland," from *A Taste of the Maritimes* (Scarborough, Ontario: Quality Special Products, 1991).

6. Alfred, Lord Tennyson, "Ulysses," in *An Anatomy of Literature,* ed. Robert Foulke and Paul Smith (New York: Harcourt Brace Jovanovich, 1972), 320.

7. Robert Stone, *Outerbridge Reach* (New York: Ticknor and Fields, 1992), 382; hereafter cited in text as *Outerbridge Reach.*

8. Richard Henry Dana, *Two Years Before the Mast: A Personal Narrative of Life at Sea* (New York: Penguin, 1981), 46–47; hereafter cited in text.

9. William Blackburn, ed., *Joseph Conrad: Letters to William Blackwood and David S. Meldrum* (Durham, N.C.: Duke University Press, 1958), 138, and G. Jean-Aubry, *Joseph Conrad: Life and Letters* (Garden City, N.Y.: Doubleday, Page, 1927), II, 34.

10. Tony Tanner, *The Oxford Book of Sea Stories* (Oxford and New York: Oxford University Press, 1994), xiv.

11. David Fausett, "Historical and Literary Parallels in the Early Mapping of Australia," *Terrae Incognitae* 26 (1994): 27; hereafter cited in text. Fausett refers to the voyage tale of Wenamon, an Egyptian priest at Thebes who sailed from Egypt to Syria ca. 1130 B.C.

12. Joseph Conrad, *Youth, Heart of Darkness, The End of the Tether* (London: J. M. Dent, 1946), 3.

13. Joseph Conrad, "Tales of the Sea," in *Notes on Life and Letters* (London: J. M. Dent, 1949), 55; hereafter cited in text.

Chapter 2

1. See the postscript to Homer, *The Odyssey,* trans. Robert Fitzgerald (Garden City, N.Y.: Anchor Books, 1963), 494.

2. For various perspectives on the complicated questions of composition and transmission of Homeric epics, see the introduction to Richmond Lattimore's translation of *The Iliad* (Chicago: University of Chicago Press, 1951), the translation hereafter cited in text for *Iliad* quotations; M. I. Finley, *The World of Odysseus,* 2d ed. (London: Chatto and Windus, 1978); Mark Edwards, *Homer, Poet of the "Iliad"* (Baltimore: Johns Hopkins University Press, 1987); and Jasper Griffin, *Homer: The "Odyssey"* (Cambridge: Cambridge University Press, 1987).

3. D. L. Page, *Folktales in Homer's "Odyssey"* (Cambridge, Mass.: Harvard University Press, 1973), 4; hereafter cited in text.

4. Erich Auerbach, "Odysseus' Scar," in *Mimesis: The Representation of Reality in Western Literature,* trans. Willard Trask (Princeton: Princeton University Press, 1953), 13, 19.

5. The word *periplus* means "a sailing round," either in the sense of circumnavigation or of a round trip with many ports of call, and *periploi* often described circular rather than linear voyage tracks.

6. For a summary of Wenamon's voyage, see Lionel Casson, *Travel in the Ancient World* (London: George Allen and Unwin, 1974), 39–43.

7. For a more detailed account of early *periploi,* see O. A. W. Dilke, *Greek and Roman Maps* (London: Thames and Hudson, 1985), 130–37.

8. For an account of this retracing, see Tim Severin, *The Jason Voyage: The Quest for the Golden Fleece* (London: Hutchinson, 1985). The word *replica* must be qualified in a number of ways because there is scant information about galleys of this era, much less of a specific ship first described in the oral tradition. For authoritative reviews of the evidence see J. S. Morrison and R. T. Williams, *Greek Oared Ships, 900–322 B.C.* (Cambridge: Cambridge University Press, 1968), hereafter cited in text, and Lionel Casson, *Ships and Seamanship in the Ancient World* (Princeton: Princeton University Press, 1971), hereafter cited in text. For more information on the assumptions used by the naval architect who designed *Argo,* see Colin Mudie, "Designing Replica Boats: The Boats of St. Brendan, Sinbad and Jason," in *Sailing into the Past: Proceedings of the International Seminar on Replicas of Ancient and Medieval Vessels* (Roskilde, Denmark: The Viking Ship Museum, Roskilde, 1986), 38–41 and 52–59.

9. Although the delay of the fleet at Aulis was part of the epic cycle, it is not clear that Homer knew about Agamemnon's intended sacrifice of his own daughter, Iphigenia. This brutal means of breaking the impasse that stalls the amassed fleet does appear in the *Cypria,* the epic that precedes the *Iliad* in narrative matter but was probably composed later; Aeschylus and Sophocles elaborated the incident, which provides a strong motive for Clytemnestra's later murder of Agamemnon. In Book 9 of the *Iliad,* Agamemnon twice refers to his daughter as if she were alive back in Mycenae, and no cause for Clytemnestra's anger appears in Book 11 of the *Odyssey.*

10. In the southeastern Sporades, the meltemi backs from northeast to north or even slightly northwest.

11. The divergent tracks of Menelaus and Odysseus, both blown offshore by strong gales from the northerly quadrant (northeast to northwest), are not as anomalous as they may seem. Pilot charts show that currents off Cape Malea are generally westerly at one knot but in the strait between Cythera and western Crete may be stronger and southerly or southwesterly in direction, especially in meltemi conditions; beyond the capes of western Crete, the prevailing wind is northwesterly, and the current runs from southeastward to eastward. Given these variables in wind and current direction, it is not unrealistic for Menelaus to reach the south coast of Crete and later Egypt while Odysseus first lands farther southwest, perhaps in Libya or Tunisia.

12. James S. Romm, *The Edges of the Earth in Ancient Thought: Geography, Exploration, and Fiction* (Princeton: Princeton University Press, 1992), 3, 5; hereafter cited in text. For further detail on Hellenistic debates about the *Odyssey* as a *periplus*, see chapter 5 and the epilogue, especially p. 218.

13. *The Cambridge Ancient History*, 3d ed., ed. I. E. S. Edwards, C. J. Gadd, N. G. L. Hammond, and E. Sollberger (Cambridge: Cambridge University Press, 1975), vol. II, pt. 2, 821.

14. For a compact survey of metallurgical resources in the Troad, see Eberhard Zangger, *The Flood from Heaven: Deciphering the Atlantis Legend* (New York: Morrow, 1992), 68–71; as the title indicates, Zangger also links Troy with Plato's Atlantis. Michael Wood's *In Search of the Trojan War* (New York and Oxford: Facts on File Publications, 1985) provides a readable overview of the Trojan excavations and their relationship with the epics.

15. See Victor Bérard, *Les navigations d'Ulysse*, 4 vols. (Paris: Libraire Armand Colin, 1927–1929) and Ernle Bradford, *Ulysses Found* (London: Hodder and Stoughton, 1964). Berard wrote many volumes on the subject during his life, but the one cited is the most comprehensive and includes earlier work.

16. See Samuel Butler, *The Authoress of the Odyssey* (1922; reprint, Chicago: University of Chicago Press, 1967). Three of L. G. Pocock's books developing his geographical theory are

extant: *Reality and Allegory in the Odyssey* (Amsterdam: 1959); *Odyssean Essays* (Oxford: Blackwell, 1965); and *The Sicilian Origin of the Odyssey: A Study of the Topographical Evidence* (Wellington, New Zealand: New Zealand University Press, 1957).

17. See Tim Severin, *The Ulysses Voyage: Sea Search for the Odyssey* (New York: Dutton, 1987); hereafter cited in text. This theory has the virtue of directness and simplicity, but it cannot account for the loss of geographical precision after Malea—in waters well known to Greek seafarers.

18. See Mauricio Obregón, *Ulysses Airborne* (New York: Harper and Row, 1971) and Gilbert Pillot, *The Secret Code of the Odyssey,* trans. Francis E. Albert (London: Abelard-Schuman, 1969).

19. Such topographic matches are possible because Mediterranean sea levels and coastlines have changed very little since ca. 2000 B.C., except in specific local areas, where the changes may be considerable through uplift, subsidence, or volcanic activity (e.g., Pozzuoli in the Bay of Naples, southeastern Sicily, and Thera/Santorini). See Tj. H. Van Andel and J. C. Shackleton, "Late Paleolithic and Mesolithic Coastlines of Greece and the Aegean," *Journal of Field Archaeology* 9 (1982): 445–54. Sailing times are precise east of Malea but questionable after it because the metrical formulae of oral composition—especially nine days—often replace more exact measures.

20. I observed and photographed the following examples of isomorphism, among many others, during a 77-day research voyage on the conditions of Mediterranean seafaring in the summer of 1986.

21. Maritime historians and classical scholars still debate whether Odysseus built a raft or a boat, but the latter view prevails.

22. Comparing modern observations of winds in the Mediterranean with those made by Aristotle (*Meteorologica,* Book 2) and by his student Theophrastos (*De Ventis*) in the late fourth century B.C., William Murray concludes that there is a striking correlation between them, especially in the Eastern Mediterranean. See William B. Murray, "Do Modern

Winds Equal Ancient Winds?" *Mediterranean Historical Review* 2 (1987): 139–67.

23. "Works and Days" in *Hesiod: The Homeric Hymns and Homerica,* Loeb Classical Library (Cambridge, Mass.: Harvard University Press, 1982), 49–53. Curiously, in the same passage on sailing seasons he does not seem to notice Etesians: "At that time the winds are steady, and the sea is harmless."

24. During the research voyage, our first meltemi shattered a dead calm just after midnight with a blast of 35 knots, creating chaos among the yachts moored along the quay in the exposed harbor at Mykonos.

25. I have observed this spectacular effect from clifftops in three Mediterranean locations, produced by a frontal westerly in northeastern Spain, by a sirocco on the north coast of Crete, and by a meltemi at Lindos on Rhodes. In other parts of the world I have sailed through milder downdrafts that disrupt the orderly synergy of wind and sails with an unforgettable chaos of flying booms and near capsizes both to port and starboard.

26. This passage seems to conflate two distinct meteorological phenomena: downdrafts and thunderheads. There is a slightly different emphasis in Richmond Lattimore's *Odyssey of Homer* (New York: Harper and Row, 1965):

> He spoke, and pulled the clouds together, in both hands gripping
> the trident, and staggered the sea, and let loose all the storm-blasts
> of all the winds together, and huddled under the cloud scuds
> land alike and the great water. Night sprang from heaven.
> East Wind and South Wind clashed together, and the bitter blown West Wind
> and the North Wind born in the bright air rolled up a heavy sea. (5: 291–96)

In either translation, phrases like "churned the waves into chaos" or "let loose the stormblasts of all the winds together" point to bursts of wind moving in all directions simultaneously, the characteristic of downdrafts. Clouds, on the other hand, suggest a thunderhead, but as it passes overhead the shifts in wind direction occur successively, not simultaneously.

27. During our rounding of Malea on the research voyage, we encountered a textbook example of a katabatic gale. A moderate to fresh northeasterly breeze of 12 to 18 knots became fiercer and fiercer as we approached the leeward side of the cape: 22 to 27 knots five miles offshore, 28 to 33 knots three miles offshore, and a gale of 34 to 40 knots two miles offshore, with gusts registering between 45 and 60 knots.

28. Although galleys were at the mercy of gales, their ability to sail to windward in milder conditions is unknown. If they could, Odysseus might have been home in a week. In retracing both Jason's and Odysseus's voyages, Tim Severin found it impracticable either to row or to sail the galley *Argo* against a headwind and generally adopted the ancient strategy of waiting for a favorable breeze. Yet there is some evidence that sailing to windward was known and practiced in similar vessels during the classical era. By comparing passages from Aristotle, Nicander, and Virgil, John Morrison postulates that beating to windward must have been known by the fourth century B.C., and Lionel Casson reaches a similar conclusion, without specifying the date, by collating Greek and Latin sources. He suggests, however, that ancient vessels could head no closer than seven compass points off the wind (nearly 79 degrees), and any drift to leeward at that angle would cancel progress against the wind (Morrison 312–13 and Casson, *Ships and Seamanship*, 273–74).

Chapter 3

When citing works related to Columbus and Cook, I deliberately use sources likely to be found in most libraries rather than multi-volume sets that may be available only in major university libraries, unless there is a compelling reason to do otherwise; thus, whenever possible I refer to the single-volume version of Morison's biography and editions with selections from Cook's voluminous journals. The larger works are listed in the bibliographical essay.

1. Eviatar Zerubavel, *Terra Cognita: The Mental Discovery of America* (New Brunswick: Rutgers University Press, 1992), 5; hereafter cited in text.

2. Cf. Edmundo O'Gorman, *The Invention of America: An Inquiry into the Historical Nature of the New World and the Meaning of Its History* (Bloomington: Indiana University Press, 1961).

3. For two elaborate treatments of the medieval background, see especially Valerie I. J. Flint, *The Imaginative Landscape of Christopher Columbus* (Princeton: Princeton University Press, 1992), hereafter cited in text, and Djelar Kadir, *Columbus and the Ends of the Earth: Europe's Prophetic Rhetoric as Conquering Ideology* (Berkeley: University of California Press, 1992).

4. For a succinct account of these diverging possibilities, see Felipe Fernandez-Armesto, *Before Columbus* (Philadelphia: University of Pennsylvania Press, 1987), 245–52; hereafter cited in text.

5. Some scholars find it improbable that the letter was begun in the midst of the great storm off the Azores; on the other hand, in that crisis Columbus did manage to write up his discoveries, seal that document in a barrel, and toss it overboard. For the full text of this letter see *Journals and Documents on the Life and Voyages of Christopher Columbus,* trans. and ed. Samuel Eliot Morison (New York: Heritage Press, 1963), hereafter cited in text, or *The Journal of Christopher Columbus,* trans. Cecil Jane (New York: Clarkson Potter, 1960), hereafter cited in text. The letter, as well as documents relating to the other voyages, also appears in an accessible selection from R. H. Major's 1872 Hakluyt Society edition of Columbus's letters and documents, entitled *Christopher Columbus: Four Voyages to the New World* (Gloucester, Mass.: Peter Smith, 1978).

6. Cf. Samuel Eliot Morison, *Admiral of the Ocean Sea: A Life of Christopher Columbus* (Boston: Little, Brown and Co., 1942), 104–8; hereafter cited in text; see also William D. Phillips Jr., and Carla Rahn Phillips, *The Worlds of Christopher Columbus* (Cambridge: Cambridge University Press, 1992), 134; hereafter cited in text.

7. In the following description of literary and cartographic sources for Columbus's cosmography, I am heavily indebted to Flint's excellent analysis, especially the first three chapters.

8. In the 1970s an Irish scholar-adventurer set out to prove that Saint Brendan's voyages were possible and that he could have reached America. See Tim Severin, *The Brendan Voyage* (New York: McGraw Hill, 1978).

9. Kirkpatrick Sale, a prominent detractor of the Columbus myth, argues cogently (if somewhat tendentiously) that Columbus knew he had discovered a previously unknown continent during his third voyage. See "What Columbus Died Believing: The True Geographic Concepts of the Great Discoverer," *Terrae Incognitae* 21 (1989): 9–10.

10. For elegant reproductions of some of the maps available to Columbus and his contemporaries, see Kenneth Nebenzahl, *Atlas of Columbus and the Great Discoveries* (Chicago: Rand McNally, 1990).

11. See Nebenzahl 22–25; Flint 164–68; and another article by Flint, "Columbus, 'El Romero,' and the so-called Columbus Map," *Terrae Incognitae* 24 (1992): 19–29. In the latter she speculates that the map/chart, with a provenance never firmly established, might have been Columbus's gift to Queen Isabella during his crucial meetings with her after the sovereigns' victory at Granada in January, 1492.

12. Joseph Conrad, "Geography and Some Explorers," in *Last Essays* (London: J. M. Dent and Sons, 1955), 2; hereafter cited in text as "Geography."

13. *Confronting Columbus: An Anthology,* ed. John Yewell, Chris Dodge, and Jan DeSirey (Jefferson, N.C.: McFarland and Co., 1992), xi, xii. Fortunately, the quincentennial year also saw the publication of two complementary scholarly books that trace the vicissitudes of Columbus's reputation in different ways: Claudia L. Bushman, *America Discovers Columbus: How an Italian Explorer Became an American Hero* (Hanover, N.H.: University Press of New England, 1992); and Ilan Stavans, *Imagining Columbus: The Literary Voyage* (New York: Twayne Publishers, 1992). See also an excellent survey of both the controversies and the publications generated by the quincentenary, written by two influential Columbus scholars: William D. Phillips Jr. and Carla Rahn Phillips, "The Impact of 1992 on Christopher Columbus," *The Mariner's Mirror* 78:4 (November 1992): 469–83.

14. See Hjalmar R. Holand, *Norse Discoveries and Explorations in America, 982–1362* (New York: Dover Publications, 1969) for an interpretation supporting the authenticity of the stone. For documentation of the map, see R. A. Skelton, Thomas E. Marston, and George D. Painter, *The Vinland Map and the Tartar Relation,* rev. ed. (New Haven: Yale University Press, 1996).

15. Cf. discussion of the oral tradition in chapter 2. For an authoritative treatment of the provenance, historicity, and artistic conventions of the sagas, see Jonas Kristjansson, *Eddas and Sagas: Iceland's Medieval Literature,* trans. Peter Foote (Reykjavik, Iceland: Islenska Bokmenntafelag, 1992). There is a concise summary of the voyages and a comparison of the two sagas in Tryggvi J. Oleson, *Early Voyages and Northern Approaches, 1000–1632* (New York: Oxford University Press, 1964), especially chapters 2 and 3. Samuel Eliot Morison provides a readable account of the enterprise and a helpful bibliographical essay in *The European Discovery of America: The Northern Voyages, A.D. 500–1600* (New York: Oxford University Press, 1971), ch. 3; hereafter cited in text. For a recent treatment of the geographical and nautical contexts of the voyages, see also *The Viking Voyages to North America,* ed. Birthe L. Clausen (Roskilde, Denmark: Viking Ship Museum, 1993).

16. Helge Ingstad, the chief excavator at L'Anse aux Meadows, provides an informal account of the project in *Westward to Vinland: The Discovery of Pre-Columbian Norse House-sites in North America,* trans. Erik J. Friis (New York: St. Martin's Press, 1969).

17. The note is quoted in *The Life of the Admiral Christopher Columbus by His Son Ferdinand,* trans. Benjamin Keen (New Brunswick: Rutgers University Press, 1959), 11; hereafter cited in text as Ferdinand. The most exhaustive (and exhausting) analysis of evidence and opinion consumes more than a hundred pages in Vilhjalmur Stefansson's *Ultima Thule: Further Mysteries of the Arctic* (New York: Macmillan, 1940), 109–222.

18. The Bristol voyages raise complicated questions in their own right. For some of the documents, see James A. Williamson,

The Voyages of the Cabots and the English Discovery of North America under Henry VII and Henry VIII (London: Argonaut Press, 1929), 8–10 and 18–19, as well as Morison 1971, 205–9. For an orderly discussion of the evidence, see David B. Quinn, *England and the Discovery of America, 1481–1620* (New York: Alfred A. Knopf, 1974), ch. 1.

19. David Waters, "Columbus's Portuguese Inheritance," *The Mariner's Mirror* 78:4 (November 1992): 385–405.

20. Richard W. Unger, "Ships of the Late Middle Ages" in *Maritime History, Volume 1: The Age of Discovery*, ed. John B. Hattendorf (Malabar, Fla.: Krieger Publishing, 1996), 35; hereafter cited in text. Unger's *The Ship in the Medieval Economy, 600–1600* (Montreal: McGill-Queen's University Press, 1980) is a standard work in the field. More recent books include Xavier Pastor, *The Ships of Christopher Columbus* (London: Conway Maritime Press, 1992) and Roger C. Smith, *Vanguard of Empire: Ships of Exploration in the Age of Columbus* (New York: Oxford University Press, 1993); the latter, which includes an extensive literature review and evaluates evidence from underwater archaeology, will become another standard work on this elusive subject. For the uninitiated, the beautiful illustrations in Bjorn Landstrom's *Columbus: The Story of Don Cristóbal Colón, Admiral of the Ocean* (New York: Macmillan, 1966) will be most helpful in providing a general idea of what the ships probably looked like.

21. Carla Rahn Phillips, "The Evolution of Spanish Ship Design from the Fifteenth to the Eighteenth Century," *The American Neptune* 53:4 (Fall 1993): 236. The rest of that article as well as another in the same issue by Eugene Lyon, "The *Niña*, the *Santa Cruz*, and Other Caravels as Described in the *Libro de Armadas* and Other Spanish Records," provides much information on recent evaluation of documentary resources. For a very helpful review of Spanish sources, see also Clinton R. Edwards, "Design and Construction of Fifteenth-Century Iberian Vessels: A Review," *The Mariner's Mirror* 78:4 (November 1992): 419–32.

22. For a balanced history of the landfall question, see John Parker, "The Columbus Landfall Problem: A Historical Perspective," in *In the Wake of Columbus: Islands and Controversy,*

ed. Louis De Vorsey Jr., and John Parker (Detroit: Wayne State University Press, 1985); hereafter cited in text. (The same material was published as volume 15 (1983) of *Terrae Incognitae*.) This excellent volume is the best introduction to the whole landfall question, which has generated a bibliography too massive to be cited here; it is best tracked through the pages of two scholarly journals, *Terrae Incognitae* (Society for the History of Discoveries) and *The Mariner's Mirror* (Society for Nautical Research), both of which contain extensive book reviews, notes, and bibliographies as well as articles on the subject.

23. Joseph Judge, "Where Columbus Found the New World," *National Geographic* 175:5 (November 1986): 568; more than forty pages of this issue are devoted to the landfall question and related Columbus material.

24. Philip L. Richardson and Roger A. Goldsmith, "The Columbus Landfall: Voyage Track Corrected for Winds and Currents," *Oceanus* 30:3 (Fall 1987): 3–10. See also Douglas T. Peck, *Cristoforo Colombo: God's Navigator* (Columbus, Wis.: Columbian Publishers, 1993).

25. Felipe Fernandez-Armesto, *Columbus* (Oxford: Oxford University Press, 1991), 81; hereafter cited in text.

26. David Henige, "Guanahaní the Elusive: The Columbus Landfall Debate in Historical Perspective," *The Mariner's Mirror* 78:4 (November 1992): 462. For a fuller exposition of the same argument, see his book, *In Search of Columbus: The Sources of the First Voyage* (Tucson: University of Arizona Press, 1991); hereafter cited in text.

27. Henige makes a similar point to introduce his elaborate critique of attempts to establish the landfall from evidence in the *Diario* but pushes the argument one stage too far, citing the doubts of Eratosthenes but forgetting the opposing arguments of Crates of Mallos, Polybius, and Strabo. In so doing he collapses the protracted debate between Alexandrian scholars and Stoics about the geography of the *Odyssey*—a debate that reverberated through the ancient world with more force than the Columbus landfall debate does now—into a single oversimplification: "Seeking Odysseus's route can be no more than a quest for a chimera since his adven-

tures are unmistakably set in the realm of fantasy" (159). For a concise summary of the ancient debate, see Romm (cited in chapter 2 notes) 183–96.

28. *The Diario of Christopher Columbus's First Voyage to America, 1492–1493; Abstracted by Fray Bartolomé de las Casas,* transcr. and transl. Oliver Dunn and James E. Kelley Jr. (Norman, Okla.: University of Oklahoma Press, 1989), 59–60; hereafter cited in text as *Diario.* Dunn and Kelley lineate their authoritative text to match the Spanish manuscript of the *Diario;* here those lines are run in. Their note indicates that the *veedor* was a representative of the crown on board, a kind of purser charged with accounting for the expected wealth of the Indies.

29. See "The Pinzón Version of the Discovery" in Morison 1963. For suggestions about the meaning of the light, see an extended review of Henige by James E. Kelley Jr., "Epistemology 101 for First Landfall Students: An Appreciation of an Important New Book," *Terrae Incognitae* 24 (1992): 102–5.

30. Henige dismisses the question of the light with absolute skepticism: "Whether Columbus saw a light, thought he did, or simply took advantage of the chance to say he did is unimportant in the sense that it is indeterminable" (179). Such a position may be reasonable in judging the authenticity of the sighting, but it dodges the broader rhetorical questions about the incident's implications for our reading; no one doubts that the light is in the *Diario,* no matter how, when, or why it got there.

31. Those wishing to dip into the measurement game and rationale for corrections should consult an article by Lt. John W. McElroy, USNR, Chief Navigating Officer of the Harvard Columbus Expedition, "The Ocean Navigation of Columbus on His First Voyage," *The American Neptune* 1:3 (July 1941), esp. 212–17. Also see James E. Kelley Jr., "In the Wake of Columbus on a Portolan Chart" in DeVorsey and Parker, 91 and 102–4, and Henige, 152–55.

32. Samuel Eliot Morison, *The European Discovery of America: The Southern Voyages,* A.D. *1492–1616* (New York: Oxford University Press, 1974), 57; hereafter cited in text; Paolo Emilio Taviani, *Columbus, the Great Adventure: His Life, His Times, and*

His Voyages, trans. Luciano F. Farina and Marc A. Beckwith (New York: Orion Books, 1991), 95; hereafter cited in text; Fernando-Armesto 1991, 79; Kelley, in DeVorsey and Parker, 104–8; and Phillips, 147–48.

33. For a concise summary of the expansion of the mutiny story and its primary sources, see David Henige, "The Mutinies on Columbus' First Voyage: Fact or Fiction?" *Terrae Incognitae* 23 (1991): 29–37.

34. In his writing about the incident, Morison assumes that the ship is lost in a relatively short time, but it is not clear on what basis, other than general seafaring experience with coral reefs (Morison 1942, 301; Morison 1974, 79). For the fullest account of the shipwreck, see his "The Route of Columbus along the North Coast of Haiti, and the Site of Navidad" in *Transactions of the American Philosophical Society,* New Series, vol. 31, pt. 4 (Philadelphia: American Philosophical Society, December 1940): 239–85.

35. For a moderate statement of this position, see Phillips 106–8.

36. See Henige 116–18 for a literalistic calculation of the improbabilities in this case; such overinterpretation misses the mark because we are clearly more in the realm of sailors' lore than of logbook reporting throughout this scene.

37. See Alan Moorhead, *The Fatal Impact: An Account of the Invasion of the South Pacific, 1767–1840* (New York: Harper and Row, 1966).

38. Lynne Withey, *Voyages of Discovery: Captain Cook and the Exploration of the Pacific* (New York: William Morrow, 1987), 11; hereafter cited in text. For surveys of Cook's reputation and treatment by artists and biographers see especially Bernard Smith, "Cook's Posthumous Reputation," and Michael E. Hoare, "Two Centuries' Perceptions of James Cook: George Forster to Beaglehole" in *Captain James Cook and His Times,* ed. Robin Fisher and Hugh Johnston (Seattle: University of Washington Press, 1979), 159–85 and 211–28; hereafter cited in text.

39. See Kevin Haydon, "Captain Cook's *Endeavour*: A New Replica of the Whitby Collier Will Retrace Cook's Voyages,"

and Jeffrey Mellefont, "Fitting Out the *Endeavour*" in *Sea History* 74 (Summer 1995): 30–34.

40. Hydrographic work done on board the *Endeavour* has been reproduced in *The Charts & Coastal Views of Captain Cook's Voyages,* vol. 1, *The Voyage of the "Endeavour" 1768–1771,* ed. Andrew David with assistance from Rudiger Joppien and Bernard Smith; Hakluyt Society Extra Series No. 43 (London: The Hakluyt Society, 1988).

41. The longitude problem has generated a bibliography far too extensive to explore here, apart from three suggestions. Raymond E. Ashley provides a concise but detailed survey in "The Search for Longitude," *The American Neptune* 51:4 (Fall 1991): 252–66. For a well-written informal history of the development of the chronometer, see Dava Sobel, *Longitude: The True Story of a Lone Genius Who Solved the Greatest Scientific Problem of His Time* (New York: Walker, 1995). One of the standard scholarly works on the subject is Derek Howse, *Greenwich Time and the Discovery of Longitude* (Oxford: Oxford University Press, 1980).

42. These volumes appeared in a series entitled *The Journals of Captain James Cook on His Voyages of Discovery.* The first volume is *The Voyage of the Endeavour, 1768–1771,* ed. J. C. Beaglehole (Cambridge: Published for the Hakluyt Society at the University Press, 1955); hereafter cited in text. Subsequent volumes covering the second and third voyages appeared in 1961 and 1967. Beaglehole also edited a companion journal from the first voyage, *The Endeavour Journal of Joseph Banks, 1768–71,* published in two volumes for the Trustees of the Public Library of New South Wales (Sydney: Angus and Robertson, 1962). As if he had not already done enough for the Captain, Beaglehole later wrote an elegant and definitive biography of Cook, published posthumously by his son: *The Life of Captain James Cook* (London: A and C Black, 1974); hereafter cited in text. It is also available in a paperback edition published by the Stanford University Press.

43. Beaglehole 1955, ccliii, and Beaglehole 1974, 439–40, 459–61, and 471.

44. Standard works on the opening of the Pacific include the book that led Beaglehole into his life's work, *The Exploration of the Pacific*, 3d ed. (Stanford: Stanford University Press, 1966), and a more recent trilogy by O. H. K. Spate published under the general title *The Pacific since Magellan* by the University of Minnesota Press: Volume I, *The Spanish Lake*, 1979; Volume II, *Monopolists and Freebooters*, 1983; and Volume III, *Paradise Found and Lost*, 1988.

45. For a succinct account of the Admiralty's role, see Glyn Williams, " 'To Make Discoveries of Countries Hitherto Unknown': The Admiralty and Pacific Exploration in the Eighteenth Century," *The Mariner's Mirror* 82:1 (February 1996): 14–27.

46. A. Grenfell Price, ed., *The Explorations of Captain James Cook in the Pacific as Told by Selections of His Own Journals, 1768–1779* (New York: Dover Publications, 1971), 19; hereafter cited in text as *Explorations.* Unlike many other inexpensive and accessible versions of the journals, this edition, although composed of selections and connecting commentary, goes back to Cook's original text that was being edited by J. C. Beaglehole for the four volumes of the Hakluyt Society edition.

47. The set of untoward circumstances leading to Cook's death in Kealakekua Bay on the west coast of the Big Island of Hawaii on 14 February 1779 has been told, retold, and analyzed many times, generating a bibliography of its own that is not relevant to this volume. For balanced accounts of that event, see either Beaglehole's *Life* or Withey's *Voyages of Discovery.*

48. For a discussion of Dalrymple's geographical theories and role in preparations for Cook's first voyage, see Beaglehole 1974, ch. 4, esp. 102–6 and 120–26.

49. David Fausett, "Historical and Literary Parallels in the Early Mapping of Australia," *Terrae Incognitae* 26 (1994): 27; for a broader context also see his *Writing the New World: Utopias and Imaginary Voyages of the Great Southern Land* (Syracuse: Syracuse University Press, 1993), ch. 6–11. For the evolution of mapping in the Pacific and reproductions of 200 maps, see Robert Clancy, *The Mapping of Terra Australis* (New South Wales, Australia: Universal Press, 1995).

50. For an overview of the connections between travel narratives and novels, see Percy G. Adams, *Travel Literature and the Evolution of the Novel* (Lexington: University of Kentucky Press, 1983).

51. Although Cook's diet was extraordinarily successful during his first voyage, its medical basis has been questioned in a number of ways. See Sir James Watt, "Medical Aspects and Consequences of Cook's Voyages" in Fisher and Johnston, 129–57, and Frances E. Cuppage, *James Cook and the Conquest of Scurvy* (Westport, Conn.: Greenwood Press [1994?]).

Chapter 4

1. The definitive treatment of Cooper's voyage fiction and its context in the first half of the nineteenth century is Thomas Philbrick's *James Fenimore Cooper and the Development of American Sea Fiction* (Cambridge, Mass.: Harvard University Press, 1961); hereafter cited in text.

2. Growing interest in the literature of the sea has borne fruit in the last decade with the publication of three volumes of criticism and literary history: *Literature and Lore of the Sea*, ed. Patricia Ann Carlson (Amsterdam: Rodopi, 1986); Bert Bender, *Sea Brothers: The Tradition of American Sea Fiction from Moby-Dick to the Present* (Philadelphia: University of Pennsylvania Press, 1988); and *America and the Sea: A Literary History*, ed. Haskell Springer (Athens, Ga.: University of Georgia Press, 1995). All three will be cited in text hereafter.

3. W. H. Auden, *The Enchaféd Flood, or the Romantic Iconography of the Sea* (New York: Random House, 1950), 13–14; hereafter cited in text.

4. Robert Foulke and Paul Smith, *An Anatomy of Literature* (New York: Harcourt, Brace, Jovanovich, 1972), 53–55. Our analysis of the form is largely indebted to the work of Northrop Frye, especially in his *Anatomy of Literature: Four Essays* (Princeton: Princeton University Press, 1957); hereafter cited in text.

5. Herman Melville, *Moby-Dick: An Authoritative Text*, Norton Critical Edition, ed. Harrison Hayford and Hershel Parker (New York: W. W. Norton, 1967), ch. 104, 379; for the conve-

nience of readers using other editions, all citations include chapter as well as page references.

6. For details about Melville's use (and abuse) of these sources, see Howard P. Vincent, *The Trying-Out of Moby-Dick* (Boston: Houghton Mifflin, 1949), esp. 126–35; hereafter cited in text. For a more detailed study of Melville's sources, see Merton M. Sealts Jr., *Melville's Reading: A Check-list of Books Owned and Borrowed* (Madison: University of Wisconsin Press, 1966) and Mary K. Bercaw, *Melville's Sources* (Evanston, Ill.: Northwestern University Press, 1987). For yet more detail about Melville's use of the Scoresby volume, see Mary K. Bercaw's analysis in *Melville Society Extracts* 70 (September 1987): 9–13.

7. See Stuart M. Frank, *Herman Melville's Picture Gallery: Sources and Types of the "Pictorial" Chapters in Moby-Dick* (Fairhaven, Mass.: Edward J. Lefkowicz, 1986).

8. For details, see *Narratives of the Wreck of the Whale-ship Essex,* ed. Robert Gibbings (New York: Dover Publications, 1989).

9. The text of Reynolds's story is available in a number of editions of *Moby-Dick,* including the Norton Critical Edition.

10. For an elaboration of this claim see Charles Feidelson Jr., *Symbolism and American Literature* (Chicago: University of Chicago Press, 1953), 28–35.

11. Warner Berthoff, *The Example of Melville* (Princeton: Princeton University Press, 1962), 78–89. For an interesting treatment of the sea as the central focus of the novel see Bender, ch. 2.

12. Herman Melville, *Mardi, and a Voyage Thither* (Boston: L. C. Page, 1923), 488.

13. For a specific typological interpretation of these encounters, see Auden 63–66.

14. Emilio De Grazia, "A Coming Indistinctly into View: A Familiar Review of *Moby-Dick*" in Carlson 142.

15. Willard Thorp, "Introduction" to *Herman Melville: Representative Selections* (New York: American Book Company, 1938), lxxiv–lxxv.

16. From *The Letters of Herman Melville,* ed. Merrell R. Davis and William H. Gilman (New Haven: Yale University Press, 1960) as reprinted in the Norton Critical Edition of *Moby Dick,* 557–58.

17. Lawrance Thompson, *Melville's Quarrel with God* (Princeton: Princeton University Press, 1952), 242–43.

18. It may be hard to believe that undergraduates could ever get so excited about literary interpretation, but the inscription in the flyleaf of my copy of *Melville's Quarrel with God* reads as follows: "This note is just to remind you of Thompson's Quarrel with the Melvillians, starting with the night that George Garrett and you and others ganged up on me—a full year before this was published!"

19. Reprinted in *By-Line: Ernest Hemingway, Selected Articles and Dispatches of Four Decades,* ed. William White (New York: Charles Scribner's Sons, 1967), 239–40.

20. See Carlos Baker, *Ernest Hemingway: A Life Story* (New York: Charles Scribner's Sons, 1969), 489–90.

21. Ernest Hemingway, *The Old Man and the Sea* (New York: Charles Scribner's Sons, 1952), 40, 50, and 105; hereafter cited in text as *Old Man.*

22. Stewart Sanderson, *Ernest Hemingway* (New York: Grove Press, 1961), 117.

23. Gerry Brenner, *The Old Man and the Sea: Story of a Common Man* (New York: Twayne Publishers, 1991), 38.

24. Tony Tanner, *The Reign of Wonder: Naivety and Reality in American Literature* (Cambridge: Cambridge University Press, 1965), 238–39.

25. Joseph Conrad, *The Nigger of the "Narcissus"* (London: J. M. Dent and Sons, 1950), 99.

Chapter 5

1. William McFee, *Watch Below* (New York: Random House, 1940), 38–39.

2. Joseph Conrad, "Legends" in *Last Essays* (London: J. M. Dent, 1955), 46.

3. Joseph Conrad, "Memorandum on the Scheme for Fitting Out a Sailing Ship . . ." in *Last Essays,* 69. For documentation of conditions in the last era of commercial sail, see my article, "Life in the Dying World of Sail, 1870–1910," *The Journal of*

British Studies 3:1 (November 1963): 105–36; reprinted in *Literature and Lore of the Sea,* ed. Patricia Ann Carlson (Amsterdam: Rodopi, 1986), 72–115.

4. Gerald Morgan, "The Book of the Ship *Narcissus*" in the Norton Critical Edition of *The Nigger of the "Narcissus,"* ed. Robert Kimbrough (New York: W. W. Norton, 1979), 203.

5. Joseph Conrad, *An Outcast of the Islands* (London: J. M. Dent, 1949), 12–13.

6. Joseph Conrad, "Poland Revisited," in *Notes on Life and Letters,* 161.

7. G. Jean-Aubry, *Joseph Conrad: Life and Letters* (Garden City, N.Y.: Doubleday, Page, 1927), I, 78.

8. Joseph Conrad, *The Nigger of the "Narcissus"* (London: J. M. Dent, 1950), 138; hereafter cited in text as *Nigger.*

9. Alfred Henry Alston, *Seamanship and Its Associated Duties in the Royal Navy,* 1st ed. (London, 1860), 249–50; hereafter cited in text. The same advice was included in subsequent editions of 1871, 1893, and 1902.

10. John Harland, *Seamanship in the Age of Sail: An Account of the Shiphandling of the Sailing Man-of-War 1600–1860, Based on Contemporary Sources* (Annapolis, Md.: Naval Institute Press, 1984), 214. This is the best source now in print for detailed information about handling square-rigged ships.

11. See Edmund A. Bojarski, "Conrad at the Crossroads: From Navigator to Novelist with Some New Biographical Mysteries," *The Texas Quarterly* (Winter 1968): 22.

12. Captains R. S. Cogle and R. K. Taylor, *The New Handbook for the Board of Trade Examinations,* 17th ed. (Liverpool, 1893), 134.

13. However, the American title was probably substituted by the publisher, Dodd, Mead, for other reasons, especially to avoid use of the word *nigger* in an American context.

14. For expanded detail on the problems of narration outlined here, see my "Postures of Belief in *The Nigger of the 'Narcissus,'*" included in the Norton Critical Edition of the novel, ed. Robert Kimbrough (New York: Norton, 1979), 308–21. See also two excellent and thorough treatments in Jakob Lothe, *Conrad's Narrative Method* (Oxford: Clarendon Press, 1989),

ch. 6, and Jeremy Hawthorn, *Joseph Conrad: Narrative Technique and Ideological Commitment* (Sevenoaks, Kent: Edward Arnold, 1992), part 1. In his first voyage novel Conrad is probably experimenting with various techniques for handling all the perspectives he needs to tell the story.

Bibliographic Essay

The historical and literary scholarship associated with the major figures treated in this volume—Homer, Columbus, Cook, Melville, Conrad, Hemingway—is broad and deep. It can hardly be contained in this brief essay, so I have adopted principles of inclusion that are rigorously selective. The reader will find here only works that meet three criteria: (1) they are essential to an understanding of the work discussed; (2) they are significant in relation to the genre of sea voyage narratives; and (3) they are reasonably accessible, either in libraries or in recent editions. Exceptions to these criteria will be noted in the essay.

The first three chapters are weighted more heavily in this essay for several reasons. They deal with complex materials from disciplines not always familiar to literary scholars, whereas the last three are clearly in *terrae cognitae* for those who study British and American fiction. Thus for Melville, Hemingway, and Conrad standard bibliographies, biographies, and especially pertinent works of scholarship are included, but critical studies are not unless they contribute significantly to our understanding of the story as a voyage narrative. All the rest may be recovered in the bibliographies and updated from the annual supplements published by the Modern Language Association.

The works mentioned in the postscript (chapter 6) are all included in the recommended reading list and would be superfluous in this essay. Inevitably, there is some duplication between works cited in the notes and those mentioned here, but I have tried to minimize redundancy by relegating those that deal with specific points to the notes and describing those with more general reference in this essay.

Bibliographies

Bibliographies related to voyage narratives fall into two quite distinct categories, those for sea literature aimed at general readers and those for maritime history compiled by professional scholars. In the first category are *Books of the Sea: An Introduction to Nautical Literature* by Charles L. Lewis (Annapolis and Westport, Conn.: Naval Institute Press and Greenwood Press, 1943); Frank Knight's *The Sea Story: Being a Guide to Nautical Reading from Ancient Times to the Close of the Sailing Ship Era* (London and New York: Macmillan and St. Martin's Press, 1958); and *Sea Fiction Guide* by Myron J. Smith and Robert G. Weller (Metuchen, N.J.: Scarecrow Press, 1976). By far the most comprehensive and useful specialized bibliography is *Adventures Afloat: A Nautical Bibliography*, 2 volumes, by Ernest W. Toy Jr. (Metuchen, N.J. and London: The Scarecrow Press, 1988), which covers works on every aspect of designing, building, sailing, racing, and navigating yachts "from the earliest writings through 1986"; with annotations, it is an indispensable source for tracking voyage narratives about sailing yachts. The exception to the general rule is the most recent and comprehensive bibliography of American sea literature in *America and the Sea: A Literary History* (described later), compiled by and for scholars with both primary and secondary sources.

In the second category, maritime history, there is a relatively complete and periodically updated major bibliography by Robert Greenhalgh Albion, *Naval and Maritime History: An Annotated Bibliography*, 4th ed., rev. and expanded (Mystic, Conn.: Munson Institute of American Maritime History, Marine Historical Association, 1972). This is an essential bibliographical tool with thorough but nevertheless selective coverage; Albion sets out "to separate the wheat and chaff" and settles on the following means of doing so: "It has seemed best to divide them [books on naval and maritime history] into three major categories—the shallow or superseded books not worth including, the large body of useful works, and the select minority of the most substantial and useful, indicated with an '*' " (vi). Many of the important books are annotated, and for our purposes, the sections on merchantmen and warships, captains and crews, exploration, original seafaring accounts, and sea routes are the most pertinent. The bibliography has been brought up to date by Benjamin W. Labaree in *A Supplement (1971–1986) to Robert G. Albion's Naval and Maritime History: An Annotated Bibliography*, 4th ed. (Mystic, Conn.: Munson Institute, 1988). He has followed Albion's pattern but has added sections on marine art, archaeology, and policy; annotations are fuller and more frequent.

Another general source for earlier works is *English Maritime Books Printed before 1801 Relating to Ships and Their Construction and Operation at Sea*, compiled by Thomas R. Adams and David W. Waters (Providence and Greenwich: John Carter Brown Library and National Maritime Museum, 1995). There are three good sources for later works in the reviews and bibliographies published by *The Mariner's Mirror* (London: Society for Nautical Research), *The American Neptune* (Salem, Mass.: Peabody Essex Museum), and *Terrae Incognitae: The Journal for the History of Discoveries* (Detroit: Wayne State University Press). For serious scholars, there are many other sources available in the printed catalogues of major maritime libraries like the John Carter Brown (Brown University), the James Ford Bell (University of Minnesota), G. Blunt White (Mystic Seaport Museum), and James Duncan Phillips (Peabody Essex Institute). For those with a special interest in yacht voyages, Charles A. Borden's *Sea Quest: Global Blue-Water Adventuring in Small Craft* (Philadelphia: MacRae Smith, 1967), although not a bibliography in form, provides a broad survey of the voyagers who have generated a prolific and growing collection of narratives.

Works on the Genre (Chapter 1)

There is a great disparity between the huge volume of writing about voyages and the trickle of scholarship devoted to those voyage accounts and stories as narratives belonging to a coherent genre. To be sure, maritime history is an established discipline with its own scholarly journals and professional organizations, but treatment of the history of sea literature has been minuscule and the study of voyage narratives in generic terms is just emerging from its infancy. The handful of scholarly books that appeared in the first half of the twentieth century viewed sea literature as a segment of much larger literary histories, as indicated by their titles.

The British Tar in Fact and Fiction: The Poetry, Pathos, and Humour of the Sailor's Life, by Charles N. Robinson and John Leyland (1909; reprint, Detroit: Omnigraphics, 1968) tries to bridge the gap between "naval history and historical literature." In addition to a historical survey of the British seaman as a character type, the authors provide useful chapters on Tudor and Jacobean drama, the sea novel in the eighteenth and nineteenth centuries, and sea poetry and art related to naval types. Some other surveys work clearly within the traditional framework of literary periods broadly or narrowly defined, like Anne Treneer's *The Sea in English Literature from Beowulf to Donne* (London: Houghton and Stoddard, 1926) and Geoffrey Atkinson's *The Extraordinary Voyage in French Literature from 1700 to 1720* (Paris: Edouard Champion, 1922). A few studies continue that tradition in the latter half of this century, particularly *The Sailor in English Fiction and Drama, 1550–1800,* by Harold Francis Watson (New York: AMS Press, 1966) and, most recently, *The Story of the Voyage: Sea Narratives in Eighteenth-Century England* by Philip Edwards (Cambridge: Cambridge University Press, 1994). Two continental studies round out this list of works on sea literature written in English, a German analysis of "seapieces" from the eighteenth through the twentieth centuries, Peter Krahe's *Literarische Seestücke: Darstellungen von Meer und Seefahrt in der englischen Literature des 18. bis 20. Jahrhunderts* (Hamburg and Bremerhaven: Ernst Kabel Verlag and Schiffahrtsmuseum, 1992) and a French analysis of American sea literature by Jeanne-Marie Santraud, *La Mer et le Roman Américain dans le Première Moitié du Dix-Neuvième Siécle* (Paris: Didier, 1972). The list is sparse in comparison to the massive bibliography accumulated around all of the individual writers treated in this book, and among these seven surveys only the Edwards volume focuses clearly on voyage narratives rather than the larger and more amorphous subject of sea literature.

The broader approach is characterized by *Literature and Lore of the Sea,* a collection of essays edited by Patricia Ann Carlson (Amsterdam: Rodopi, 1986). Subjects of the essays include maritime history, studies of specific works, influence among related writers, themes, images, literary conventions, and sea lore. *America and the Sea: A Literary History,* edited by Haskell Springer (Athens, Ga.: University of Georgia Press, 1995) also has different authors for each chapter but is more systematic in its sweeping survey of American sea literature. Organized both chronologically and by subjects, it includes chapters on periods in American literary history, genres broadly defined as movements in poetry and prose and more narrowly as sea types ("Personal Narratives, Journals, and Diaries"), major figures, regional and ethnic categories ("Great Lakes Maritime Fiction," "African-American Literature"), and related arts ("Hymns, Chanteys, and Sea Songs," "American Seascape Art"). Two other studies, both narrower in scope, have been influential in shaping attitudes toward American sea literature. Thomas Philbrick's *James Fenimore Cooper and the Development of American Sea Fiction* (Cambridge, Mass.: Harvard University Press, 1961) does precisely what its title suggests: "Viewed as a body, the hundreds of nautical novels and short stories that were produced in this country during the first half of the nineteenth century offer a revelation of the surprising depth and range of American interest in the sea and its affairs" (vii). Bert Bender's *Sea-Brothers: The Tradition of American Sea Fiction from Moby-Dick to the Present* (Philadelphia: University of Pennsylvania Press, 1988) continues Philbrick's in-depth study with chapters on Melville, Crane, Jack London, a number of writers dealing with the transition from sail to steam in the later decades of the nineteenth century, Hemingway, and Peter Matthiessen. Like Philbrick, Bender is interested in continuities: " . . . the sea's influence on American literature has been more profound and continuous than is presently accepted, exceeding even that of the inland frontier" (xi).

Another work that deals specifically with the sea's influence on literature is W. H. Auden's slim classic, *The Enchaféd Flood, or The Romantic Iconography of the Sea* (New York: Random House, [1950]), a volume that grew out of the Page-Barbour Lectures at the University of Virginia in 1949. In the first chapter he contrasts the sea and the desert as wastelands that compel human wandering; in the second he examines the sea, ship, and wind as image and symbol; and in the third he draws parallels between Don Quixote and Ishmael. Also very useful is Percy G. Adams's *Travel*

Literature and the Evolution of the Novel (Lexington, Ky.: University Press of Kentucky, 1983), a study of the larger category of literature that contains voyage narratives. Of particular interest is chapter 2, a broad survey and typology of travel literature before 1800; chapter 3 on the "truth-lie dichotomy"; chapter 4 on "realism and romanticism"; and chapter 5 on "the hero and his journey." The introduction to *Last Voyages—Cavendish, Hudson, Raleigh: The Original Narratives,* edited by Philip Edwards (Oxford: Clarendon Press, 1988), deals succinctly with the relation of historical and fictional elements in voyage narratives from a different perspective. Three anthologies of sea stories are also particularly useful: H. M. Tomlinson's *Great Sea Stories of All Nations* (Garden City, N.Y.: Garden City Publishing, 1937) for its foreword by a knowledgeable sea writer and worldwide table of contents; *The Oxford Book of Sea Stories,* selected by Tony Tanner (Oxford: Oxford University Press, 1994), for its thought-provoking introduction and fine selection; and *Short Stories of the Sea,* edited by George C. Solley and Eric Steinbaugh (Annapolis: Naval Institute Press, 1984), for its balanced and eminently teachable selection of stories.

There are too many related topics to examine adequately, from seamanship and navigation to cartography, but a few particularly useful surveys of these topics can be isolated from far larger bodies of more specialized works. For those unfamiliar with the history of navigation, a good starting point is a standard work by E. G. R. Taylor, *The Haven-Finding Art: A History of Navigation from Odysseus to Captain Cook* (1957; reprint, New York: American Elsevier, 1971, with an appendix on "Navigation in Medieval China" by Joseph Needham). It is strong on early navigation, particularly by Phoenicians, Greeks, Irishmen, and Norsemen; it works through the development of the art of navigation by the Portuguese, Spaniards, and English; the last part, entitled "towards mathematical navigation," deals with chart projections, the development of nautical tables, and the invention of a reliable chronometer. A more recent work that covers the same territory and brings it up to the present is *From Sails to Satellites: The Origin and Development of Navigational Science* by J. E. D. Williams, past president of the Royal Institute of Navigation (Oxford: Oxford University Press, 1993). A related volume is Derek Howse and Michael Sanderson's *The Sea Chart: An Historical Survey Based on the Collections in the National Maritime Museum* (New York: McGraw-Hill, 1973), with a brief historical introduction and commentaries on 60 reproduced charts; another volume with the same pattern is Thomas Suárez's *Shedding the Veil: Mapping the European Discovery of America and the World* (Singapore: World Scientific, 1992). A more specialized book on inaccurate charting is *Legendary Islands of the Ocean Sea* by Robert H. Fuson, professor emeritus of geography at the University of South Florida (Sarasota, Fla.: Pineapple Press, 1995). For background on narratives involving square-rigged ships, John H. Harland's *Seamanship in the Age of Sail: An Account of the Shiphandling of the Sailing Man-of-War, Based on Contemporary Sources* (Annapolis: Naval Institute Press, 1984) provides more than its title indicates, a virtual manual on square-rigger seamanship with profuse detail and wonderful illustrations by Mark Myers.

Works on Ancient Seafaring and the *Odyssey* (Chapter 2)

Scholars approaching the *Odyssey* find themselves almost inevitably enmeshed in an interdisciplinary study involving ancient history, archaeology, the history of oral and textual transmission, linguistics, and literary criticism. Those who study Odysseus's wanderings as a voyage narrative must also add marine archaeology, the history of ancient seamanship, navigation, and trade routes, ancient cartography, coastline geology, and meteorology. The bibliographical suggestions that follow are designed to serve as a rough chart through this labyrinth of subjects and disciplines for the uninitiated, with very few excursions into traditional Homeric scholarship and criticism, a realm mapped in the bibliographical resources of classical studies.

We begin with the standard histories of ancient seafaring, derived until a few decades ago almost entirely from archaeological and literary sources. Two works are preeminent, one American and the other British. Lionel Casson's *Ships and Seamanship in the Ancient World* (Princeton: Princeton University Press, 1971) is the most comprehensive survey, covering craft from prehistory through the late Roman and Byzantine navies, with further chapters on shipbuilding, rigging, sailing seasons, officers and men, small craft, markings and names, and harbors. The companion British volume is *Greek Oared Ships, 900–322 B.C.*

by J. S. Morrison and R. T. Williams (Cambridge: Cambridge University Press, 1968), which focuses more narrowly on oared vessels in the Homeric, Archaic, and Classical periods and includes close analysis of literary texts and an extensive catalogue of ship representations. As lifelong scholars of their subjects, both Casson and Morrison are prolific in quite distinct ways. Casson, a fine stylist like another noted maritime scholar, Samuel Eliot Morison, has written a number of books for a wider audience that deal with the same or related subjects, including *Travel in the Ancient World* (London: George Allen and Unwin, 1974), *Ancient Trade and Society* (Detroit: Wayne State University Press, 1984), *The Ancient Mariners: Seafarers and Sea Fighters of the Mediterranean in Ancient Times,* 2d ed. (Princeton: Princeton University Press, 1991), and *Ships and Seafaring in Ancient Times* (London: British Museum Press, 1994). He has also edited and translated a number of ancient voyage and travel texts, including *The Periplus Maris Erythraei* (Princeton: Princeton University Press, 1989). In recent years Morrison has focused his energies on founding and directing the Trireme Trust, which designed and joined the Greek Navy in building a replica of an Athenian trireme, the dominant warship of the fifth and fourth centuries B.C. He has written many monographs related to this project, as well as *The Athenian Trireme: The History and Reconstruction of an Ancient Greek Warship* (Cambridge: Cambridge University Press, 1986). A third major scholar of ancient seafaring, Lucien Basch, has written an extensive study of the iconographic sources for naval architecture in the ancient Mediterranean, *Le Musée Imaginaire de la Marine Antique* (Athens: Institut Hellenique pour la Preservation de la Tradition Nautique, 1987).

Three other broad surveys have less detail but provide a useful overview of the ancient maritime world, which has to be reconstructed mostly from indirect evidence. Walter Woodburn Hyde's *Ancient Greek Mariners* (New York: Oxford University Press, 1947) has useful chapters on the Argonaut's voyage, the vexed questions of Odyssean geography, and Greek colonial expansion. Jean Rouge's *Ships and Fleets of the Ancient Mediterranean,* translated from the French by Susan Fraser (Middletown, Conn.: Wesleyan University Press, 1981), is mostly concerned with the Roman era but has introductory chapters on the practices of ancient seafaring and the construction, rigging, and ballasting of ships. Fik Meijer's *A History of Seafaring in the Classical World*, originally written in Dutch (New York: St. Martin's Press, 1986), is the broadest of the three, covering the whole range of maritime activity in the Mediterranean from 3000 B.C. to the end of the Roman Empire. Also useful is *The Greeks and the Sea*, edited by Speros Vryonis Jr. (New York: New York University Press, 1993), a collection of papers presented at the Alexander Onassis Center, some of which deal with maritime activity in the Archaic era.

Archaeological evidence of various kinds, though scarce for ancient seafaring, has produced a number of useful surveys, including *Archaeology of the Boat: A New Introductory Study* by Basil Greenhill, Director of the National Maritime Museum, Greenwich (Middletown, Conn.: Wesleyan University Press, 1976), which contains an overview of the development of boats and a chapter on early Greek vessels by J. S. Morrison. Two other studies are more specifically directed to ancient seafaring: Paul Johnstone's *The Sea-Craft of Prehistory* (London: Routledge and Kegan Paul, 1980), like the Greenhill volume, surveys early types of water transport and then describes specific regional types in the Mediterranean and other parts of Europe, America, and Asia. With much narrower focus, Paul Forsythe Johnston's *Ship and Boat Models in Ancient Greece* (Annapolis: Naval Institute Press, 1985) studies what can be learned about the shape of ancient vessels from this important body of archaeological evidence. New dimensions in knowledge garnered from "hard" evidence have been established by the rapid development of underwater archaeology during the past three decades, leading one of its pioneers, George F. Bass, to edit *A History of Seafaring Based on Underwater Archaeology* (London and New York: Thames and Hudson and Walker and Co., 1972). The coverage stretches from the earliest watercraft through the age of European discovery to boats and ships used on American inland waterways, but the first two chapters on ancient seafaring in the Mediterranean are particularly relevant.

A study of the voyage narrative in the *Odyssey* also requires some understanding of the three periods in prehistory that are involved: the late Bronze Age for the siege of Troy, the troubled "Dark Age" when Mycenaean civilization collapsed, and the Archaic Age for the composition of the epic. The best place to start for an overview of these eras is *The Cambridge Ancient History*, 3d ed. (Cambridge: Cambridge University Press, 1975). Next, one might consult a classic study, Emily Vermeule's *Greece in the Bronze Age* (Chicago: University of Chicago Press, 1964, 1972) and move on to some of the many books written by M. I. Finley, professor of ancient history at Cambridge University: *The World of Odysseus* (New York: Viking, 1954); *The Ancient Greeks* (London and New York: Chatto and Windus, 1963); and *Early Greece: The Bronze and Archaic Ages* (London: Chatto and Windus, 1970). (All three are available in revised and inexpensive paperback editions.) Further exploration would lead to J. T. Hooker's *Mycenaean Greece* (London: Routledge and Kegan Paul, 1976) and V. R. d'A. Desborough's *The Greek Dark Ages* (London: Ernest Benn, 1972).

Speculative studies of the migrations that may have destroyed Mycenaean civilization include *The Rise of the Dorians* by Ivor Gray Nixon (Puckeridge, Herts.: Chancery Press, 1968) and *The Sea Peoples: Warriors of the Ancient Mediterranean*, rev. ed. (London: Thames & Hudson, 1985) by N. K. Sandars. Anthony Snodgrass's *Archaic Greece: The Age of Experiment* (London: J. M. Dent, 1980) deals with the era of the *Odyssey*'s composition. For the expansion of Greek civilization in the Mediterranean, see the first two chapters of Chester G. Starr's *The Influence of Sea Power on Ancient History* (New York: Oxford University Press, 1989) and John Boardman's *The Greeks Overseas: Their Early Colonies and Trade*, new and enlarged ed. (London: Thames and Hudson, 1980). For an informed summary of the complex historical and archaeological issues growing out of the excavation of Troy, read Michael Wood's *In Search of the Trojan War* (New York: Facts on File, 1985), a profusely illustrated and substantive book that grew out of the BBC series of the same name. Those issues are also addressed in the papers of the Greenbank Colloquium, *The Trojan War: Its Historicity and Context*, edited by Lin Foxhall and John K. Davies (Bristol: Bristol Classical Press, 1984).

For a preliminary orientation to the geographical context of the *Odyssey* voyage, see two slender atlases illustrating stages of human settlement in the ancient world. One is Michael Grant's *Ancient History Atlas*, with cartography by Arthur Banks (New York: Macmillan, 1971), which contains 87 maps. The second, *The Penguin Atlas of Ancient History*, by Colin McEvedy (London and

New York: Penguin, 1967) has descriptive text for each map and an interesting theoretical introduction. For more extended analyses of the beginnings of cartography in the ancient world, turn to O. A. W. Dilke's *Greek and Roman Maps* (London: Thames and Hudson, 1985) and volume I in the history of cartography series, *Cartography in Prehistoric, Ancient, and Medieval Europe and the Mediterranean,* edited by J. B. Harley and David Woodward (Chicago: University of Chicago Press, 1987); like most cartographic works with full-scale plates, the latter volume is expensive and should be consulted in a library. James S. Romm's *The Edges of the Earth in Ancient Thought: Geography, Exploration, and Fiction* (Princeton: Princeton University Press, 1992) forges strong connections between ancient geography and literary traditions with an interesting chapter on the boundaries of the earth and a section of another on the interpretation of the *Odyssey* voyage geography by ancient commentators. Eberhard Zangger's *The Flood from Heaven: Deciphering the Atlantis Legend* (New York: William Morrow, 1992) would not at first seem to pertain to the voyage, but it does, both theoretically by addressing links between myth and geography and directly by proposing an identification for one of the most puzzling *Odyssey* sites. That process of course raises questions discussed at some length in the chapter, with comments on a number of twentieth century titles devoted to establishing the voyage track (see notes 15–18). Another provocative book by Paul Veyne deals with questions of myth and geography, addressing the question directly in its title, *Did the Greeks Believe in Their Myths?: An Essay on the Constitutive Imagination,* translated by Paula Wissing (Chicago: University of Chicago Press, 1988).

Whatever attitude we take toward the geography of the voyage, understanding the conditions of ancient seafaring in the Mediterranean requires other scientific contexts, primarily geological, oceanographic, and meteorological. For well-written overviews of the first two, read Tjeerd van Andel's *Tales of an Old Ocean: Exploring the Deep-Sea World of the Geologist and Oceanographer* (New York: Norton, 1977) and *Ocean Science: Readings from Scientific American* (San Francisco: W. H. Freeman, 1977). Robert Raikes's *Water, Weather and Prehistory* (Atlantic Highlands, N.J.: Humanities Press, 1967) links water-produced geological changes with climatic shifts, and H. H. Lamb's *Climate, History and the Modern World* (London: Methuen, 1982) explains the factors causing climate change and analyzes significant changes throughout human history. Another volume edited by A. Harding, *Climatic Change in Later Pre-History* (Edinburgh: Edinburgh University Press, 1982), deals with the same issues. An unusual and valuable book connecting such contexts to puzzles in the ancient world is Mott T. Greene's *Natural Knowledge in Preclassical Antiquity* (Baltimore: Johns Hopkins University Press, 1992). Greene describes the book as "a series of meditations on the relationships between mythology and natural knowledge," and one of his essays tackles the relationship between volcanoes and the Cyclopes.

Finally, among the many volumes devoted to literary scholarship and criticism of the *Odyssey*, I would begin with a handful that have been particularly useful. For a short and cogent overview, William G. Thalmann's *The Odyssey: An Epic of Return* (New York: Twayne Publishers, 1992); for a summary of the pioneering work on the oral tradition done by Milman Parry and Albert Lord, G. S. Kirk's *The Songs of Homer* (Cambridge: Cambridge University Press, 1962); for more recent work on the oral tradition, John Miles Foley's *Traditional Oral Epic: The Odyssey, Beowulf, and the Serbo-Croatian Return Song* (Berkeley and Los Angeles: University of California Press, 1990), and for the interaction of writing and oral communication, Rosalind Thomas's *Literacy and Orality in Ancient Greece* (Cambridge: Cambridge University Press, 1992); for analysis of the *nostos*, Douglas G. Frame's *The Myth of the Return* (New Haven: Yale University Press, 1978); for the amalgamation of folktales with realistic voyage material, D. L. Page, *Folktales in Homer's Odyssey* (Cambridge, Mass.: Harvard University Press, 1973); for origins of tales of travel, *Homer's Odyssey* by John H. Finley Jr. (Cambridge, Mass.: Harvard University Press, 1978); and for a group of influential essays on the *Odyssey, Reading the Odyssey: Selected Interpretive Essays,* edited by Seth L. Schein (Princeton: Princeton University Press, 1996). All of these have bibliographies that suggest further reading.

Voyages of Discovery (Chapter 3)

As indicated in the introduction to this chapter, the quincentenary of 1992 was both a boon and a bane to Columbus scholarship, providing an opportunity for many good books to be published and simultaneously encouraging a mass of ephemera into print. The former have established a new plateau in the understanding of Columbus's enterprise of the Indies whereas the latter can safely be ignored. Those pertinent to our focus on voyage narratives rather than the wider implications of the enterprise join older substantive works that have proved their usefulness. Works focused on many specialized topics—the maps available to Columbus, his reputation, his ships, the site of the first landfall, and preceding contacts with America by Norse and Bristol voyagers—are discussed in the notes to chapter 3.

Columbus scholarship is complicated and extensive. Luckily, several bibliographers have tried to sort it out, and many biographers and recent scholars provide helpful bibliographies. The essential starting point is Foster Provost's *Columbus: An Annotated Guide to the Scholarship of His Life and Writings, 1750- 1988* (Detroit: published for the John Carter Brown Library by Omnigraphics, 1991). This bibliography is highly selective but provides a good survey of the history of Columbus scholarship. Provost's comments are sane and careful, and the bibliography is particularly useful for sections on the first voyage, navigation, Columbus's ships, and a bibliographical essay. Provost also compiled the *Columbus Dictionary* (Detroit: Omnigraphics, ca. 1991), which includes bibliographical references. *An Introductory Bibliography of Maritime References for the New World and the Spanish Empire Therein, 1492–1821,* 2d ed., compiled and edited by J. Bankston (Bisbee, Ariz.: Terrenate Associates, 1986) was undergoing revision in 1992. Another useful recent work is not a bibliography in format, *The Christopher Columbus Encyclopedia,* compiled by Silvio A. Bedini for an editorial board headed by David Buisseret (New York: Simon and Schuster, ca. 1992). It contains extensive articles by more than a hundred scholars, a number of which are particularly useful—especially those on Prince Henry ("the Navigator"), Icelandic sagas, imaginary geography, navigation, sailing directions, Columbus's ships, tides, and currents. All articles contain short, specific bibliographies. The comprehensive bibliography that will describe and evaluate the publishing splurge of 1992 has yet to appear.

Although biographies range far beyond our interests in the narratives of Columbus's voyages, they cannot be ignored. Among the many obstacles for any biographer are gaping holes in sources for his life, especially in Genoa and Portugal, and the lack of uncontaminated secondary documents. Fray Bartolomé de las Casas, who redacted and compressed the account of the first voyage we now know as the *Diario*, also summarized Columbus's prior life and preparations for that voyage in Book One of *History of the Indies*, a condensed version of his multivolume *Historia de las Indias*, translated and edited by Andree Collard (New York: Harper and Row, 1971). Las Casas began to write the *Historia* in 1527 and continued working on it until his death in 1566; regarded as subversive for its excoriation of Spanish treatment of Indians in the New World, the work was not published until 1875. The first biographer was Columbus's illegitimate son Ferdinand, whose *Historie* of his father's life has an equally tangled textual history; no manuscript is extant, and it was first published in Italian translation in 1571, more than 30 years after his death. Ferdinand's work is now available in a translation by Benjamin Keen, *The Life of the Admiral Christopher Columbus by His Son Ferdinand* (New Brunswick, N.J.: Rutgers University Press, 1959). Discrepancies between the accounts of the first voyage by Las Casas and by Ferdinand further complicate the task of determining historical truth. Modern biographers must juggle such questions of authenticity in most early documents relating to Columbus's life and the events of the first voyage in particular, but their nineteenth-century predecessors were less concerned with textual puzzles than with celebrating his achievements. Washington Irving's *A History of the Life and Voyages of Christopher Columbus*, 2 vols., new ed. revised and corrected by the author (New York: G. & C. & H. Carvill, 1831) is interesting because of its fullness of detail and because it was a primary source for the hagiography of Columbus in the United States. Nevertheless, it is based on many archival resources available to Irving in Madrid while he served as a diplomatic attaché and later foreign minister to Spain. As the title indicates, Justin Winsor's *Christopher Columbus and How He Received and Imparted the Spirit of Discovery* (New York: Houghton Mifflin, 1891), prepared for the quadricentennial of 1892, continued in the same vein of celebration. (See note 12 to chapter 3 for works dealing at length with Columbus's reputation throughout five hundred years.)

Even before the rash of political reevaluation in recent decades, twentieth-century biographers have been unwilling to idolize Columbus, although some admire his accomplishments; almost all are interested in adding to the story or revising it rather than simply retelling it for a latter-day audience. Pre-eminent among them is Samuel Eliot Morison, America's most prolific maritime historian, who devoted much of his attention to Columbus. His *Admiral of the Ocean Sea: A Life of Christopher Columbus*, 2 vols. (Boston: Little, Brown, 1942) is the result of the Harvard Columbus Expedition, which resailed the route of the first voyage, and thorough archival research. As might be expected, it is the best source for nautical detail on the voyages, and it has full notes and bibliographical surveys at the end of each chapter; beyond that, Morison's uncluttered and ebullient style makes the book a "good read." Somewhat confusingly, a single volume with the same title and publisher appeared simul-taneously, condensing the former by omitting notes altogether and shortening nautical chapters, especially a long prefatory chapter on "Ships and Sailing"; chapter IX on "Niña, Pinta, and Santa Maria"; chapter X on "Officers and Men"; and chapter XIII on "How Columbus Navigated." "Otherwise the two editions are identical," writes Morison. Some of the same material also appears in succinct form in *Christopher Columbus, Mariner* (New York: New American Library, 1955), a paperback designed to accompany a CBS miniseries. Morison also provides detailed accounts of each of the four voyages in *The European Discovery of America: The Southern Voyages, A.D. 1492–1616* (New York: Oxford University Press, 1974).

Those interested in the nautical aspects of the voyages may also want to consult a beautifully designed and illustrated book, *Columbus: The Story of Don Cristóbal Colón, Admiral of the Ocean, and His Four Voyages Westward to the Indies According to Con-temporary Sources, Retold and Illustrated by Bjorn Landstrom* (New York: Macmillan, 1966). The title indicates the bent of the volume, and the illustrations of ships, navigational instruments, and maps bring the fifteenth-century maritime world alive. In many ways comparable is Paolo Emilio Taviani's *I Viaggi di Colombo*, 2 vols. (Novara, Italy: Instituto Geographico de Agostini, 1984), a profusely illustrated account of the four voyages that is being translated into English. Like Morison, Taviani is a prolific Columbus scholar whose *Christopher Columbus: The Grand Design*, edited by John Gilbert (London: Orbis, 1985) ranks as a comparable major biography of this century. This translation, done collaboratively by the author and William Weaver, shortens the original two-volume Italian study, *Cristoforo Colombo: la genesi della grande scoperta* (1974, 1980, and 1982) significantly by compressing the first part, a life, from more than 563 pages to only 217. The second part consists of discursive, detailed notes on each chapter of the life, and even in this volume exceeds the life itself in length. Because Taviani concentrates on what led up to the first voyage and nothing beyond, his sharp focus also allows broad exploration of related subjects ranging from Henry the Navigator and Norse voyages to Columbus's "seafaring genius." The translation sometimes falters, but the book is richly illustrated with color plates. Also like Morison, Taviani has produced a much smaller volume for public consumption, *Columbus: The Great Adventure; His Life, His Times, and His Voyages* translated by Luciano F. Farina and Marc A. Beckwith (New York: Orion Books, ca. 1991).

Both Morison and Taviani provide biographies in varying scales to suit the scholar's or reader's taste, but one of the best of the pre-quincentennial crop follows the British tradition established by Lytton Strachey during the Bloomsbury Group's heyday. Felipe Fernández-Armesto's *Columbus* (Oxford: Oxford University Press, 1991) is as succinct as its title. Using primary sources almost exclusively, Fernández-Armesto eschews detail unless it is illustrative and covers the same life span that has usually produced volumes in a mere 218 pages. Unlike many other writers of the 1990s, he is not a revisionist with an agenda so much as a minimalist: "This book has been written in the belief that readers want unadorned facts about Columbus, as far as these can be elicited. I have tried to say nothing which cannot be verified—or in some cases reasonably inferred—from unimpeachable sources" (vii–viii). The result is not a comprehensive biography so much as a poignant portrait of a complicated human being.

The question of sources is always problematic in Columbus studies, and not many are "unimpeachable." Prime among the suspects is the key document for the first voyage, the *Diario* that has been variously amended, redacted, and translated by many hands. These difficulties have been discussed in chapter 3, but here one crucial book will help any reader sort them out in detail, David Henige's *In Search of Columbus: The Sources for the First Voyage* (Tucson, Ariz.: University of Arizona Press, 1991). Henige's task is an onerous one because it involves questioning every assumption that previous scholars, biographers, and translators have used in dealing with the enigmatic record of Columbus's first voyage. His rigorous textual analysis considers every detail relevant to the authenticity (or lack of it) of the *Diario* and other documents related to the first voyage. One leaves the acid bath cleansed of misconceptions but, unfortunately, still in pursuit of an authentic text that may never be attainable. Margarita Zamora provides another analysis of these same problems in *Reading Columbus* (Berkeley and Los Angeles: University of California Press, 1993), as well as an assessment of their ideological implications; an appendix prints the original text and a translation of a previously unknown letter of 4 March 1493 to Ferdinand and Isabella describing the first voyage (presumably written by Columbus). The Las Casas manuscript of the *Diario* is based on Columbus's lost journal, the original of which was in the possession of Ferdinand and Isabella, with one copy made for Columbus, also lost. Las Casas both summarized and quoted from the journal; his manuscript was produced in the 1530s but then disappeared and was not found until ca. 1790 by Martín Fernández de Navarrete in the library of the Duke of Infantado; it is now in the National Library in Madrid. By general agreement, the best version we have is the translation by Oliver Dunn and James E. Kelley Jr., *The Diario of Christopher Columbus's First Voyage to America, 1492–1493*, abstracted by Fray Bartolomé de las Casas (Norman, Okla.: University of Oklahoma Press, 1989). This is a full scholarly edition with transcription and translation on facing pages, a concordance for the transcription, footnotes discussing variants in other editions, and an index. None of the published editions prior to this one reproduce the Las Casas manuscript precisely, including peculiarities of spelling, punctuation, marginal notes, and canceled text.

If not for an authoritative text, earlier editions are still worth consulting for ancillary material. Among them is Cecil Jane's *The Voyages of Christopher Columbus: Being the Journals of his First and Third, and the Letters Concerning His First and Last Voyages, to which Is Added the Account of His Second Voyage Written by Andres Bernaldez* (London: Argonaut Press, 1930).

The documents are preceded by a monograph-length introduction of 130 pages. The Jane translation, somewhat modified by

L. A. Vigneras, appeared again in a later American edition, *The Journal of Christopher Columbus*, translated by Cecil Jane with an appendix by R. A. Skelton (New York: Clarkson N. Potter, 1960). This elegantly printed and illustrated edition includes 90 illustrations from prints and maps of the period. In a short introduction, Vigneras outlines the textual history of the journal and explains his own practice of modifying Jane's translation, which he claims is the best English version to date. Robert H. Fuson's translation, *The Log of Christopher Columbus* (Camden, Maine: International Marine, 1987) takes even more liberties with the text of the *Diario*, filling in gaps with passages from Las Casas's *Historia* and Ferdinand's *Historie* (discussed earlier), modernizing archaic expressions, converting the confusing Spanish miles and leagues to nautical miles, and replacing the third person with the first for rhetorical effect. However, this edition contains useful material on ships, navigation, and landfall theories. Two other collections of contemporary documents are especially valuable to serious students of Columbus's voyages, one translated and edited by Jane and the other by Morison. The former is *Select Documents Illustrating the Four Voyages of Columbus, Including Those Contained in R. H. Major's Select Letters of Christopher Columbus*, 2 vols. (London: The Hakluyt Society, 1930). Volume I contains a long introduction on "The Objective of Columbus," notes on the documents, a bibliography, and four documents, only one of which, a letter of Columbus, relates to the first voyage. The introduction is really a monograph of 150 pages full of elaborate argumentation about Columbus's knowledge and state of mind before the first voyage. It is clearly dated now, but the documents and their translations still have value to the extent that they are not duplicated elsewhere. Some of these documents are also available in a less expensive bilingual edition based on Major's larger collection for the Hakluyt Society, *Christopher Columbus: Four Voyages to the New World, Letters and Selected Documents*, translated and edited by R. H. Major (Gloucester, Mass.: Peter Smith, 1978). The other important collection of documents is *Journals and Other Documents on the Life and Voyages of Christopher Columbus*, translated and edited by Samuel Eliot Morison; illustrated by Lima de Freitas (New York: Heritage Press, 1963). It is organized in five parts, one devoted to preliminaries, and the other four to supporting materials on each of the voyages. It contains many documents crucial to an understanding of the first voyage, including the Toscanelli correspondence about the geographical assumptions of the voyage, the capitulations from Ferdinand and Isabella related to the voyage, and Columbus's letter to them after his return.

Among the many volumes dealing with matters beyond biography and text, seven are particularly useful for those interested in the nautical aspects of the Columbian enterprise. The first is a work by two noted Columbus scholars, William D. Phillips Jr. and Carla Rahn Phillips, appropriately entitled *The Worlds of Christopher Columbus* (Cambridge: Cambridge University Press, 1992). It can best be described as a compendium of useful contexts surrounding the prelude to the voyages, biographical data relevant to the conception of the voyages, and the implications of the discoveries. Particularly valuable is the chapter on "Tools of Expansion," which assesses the combination of ships, navigational instruments and techniques, and knowledge of winds and currents that made the first voyage feasible. Two authoritative works on the wider significance of ships in the European political economy expand the core emphasis of the Phillips' chapter. Richard W. Unger's *The Ship in the Medieval Economy, 600–1600* (Montreal: McGill-Queen's University Press, 1980) focuses on the relationship between the economy and technical change, while Roger C. Smith's *Vanguard of Empire: Ships of Exploration* (New York: Oxford University Press, 1993) relates the successes of Iberian sea power to the versatility of caravels and naos.

An older volume by George E. Nunn, *The Geographical Conceptions of Columbus: A Critical Consideration of Four Problems* (New York: American Geographical Society, 1924), although now outdated in its conclusions, is historically important in creating a focus on three controversies that would resound throughout the remainder of the century—Columbus's measurements of distance, his belief that he had reached Asia, and his knowledge of the winds and currents of the Atlantic. A fourth controversy still raging—the site of the landfall—was first intelligently approached in a collection edited by Louis De Vorsey Jr. and John Parker, *In the Wake of Columbus: Islands and Controversy* (Detroit: Wayne State Univ. Press, 1985). Previously published as vol. 15 of *Terrae Incognitae*, this volume devoted entirely to the landfall problem begins with a historical survey by John Parker, includes a discussion of *Diario* problems by Robert Fuson, and ends with a segment of the *Diario* translated by Oliver Dunn. In between various landfall theories are presented by Pieter Verhoog, Oliver Dunn, James Kelley, Arne Molander, and Robert Power. (For further bibliography on the controversy see notes 21–25 to chapter 3.) The broadest scholarly treatment of the geographical conceptions that set Columbus sailing westward can be found in Valerie J. Flint's *The Imaginative Landscape of Christopher Columbus* (Princeton: Princeton University Press, 1992). Flint meticulously tracks every element of Columbus's geographical inheritance and concludes that it is more medieval than modern, which helps explain his stubborn persistence in the belief that he had reached the outskirts of Asia rather than discovered a New World. A companion volume with a narrower ideological thesis is Djelal Kadir's *Columbus and the Ends of the Earth: Europe's Prophetic Rhetoric as a Conquering Ideology* (Berkeley: University of California Press, 1992). Five of these eight are works published in 1992 and 1993, representing the best of the quincentennial harvest.

Scholars who focus on Columbus alone sometimes assume that he invented Atlantic exploration and the idea of sailing west to reach the Indies. A healthy corrective to such myopia lies in building a context around his enterprise, starting with a survey of earlier voyages. One might begin with G. V. Scammell's *The World Encompassed: The First European Maritime Empires, c. 800–1650* (Berkeley: University of California Press, 1981), which surveys Norse, Hanseatic, Venetian, Genoese, Portuguese, Spanish, Dutch, French, and English maritime enterprises. An excellent more recent work growing out of the first NEH Seminar on Maritime History at the John Carter Brown Library is *Maritime History, Volume 1: The Age of Discovery*, edited by John B. Hattendorf (Malabar, Florida: Krieger Publishing, 1986), which covers much of the same territory with a maritime emphasis. Tryggvi J. Oleson's *Early Voyages and Northern Approaches, 1000–1632* (Toronto: McClelland and Stewart, 1964) provides expanded treatment for the Norse voyages, and *The Viking Voyages to North America*, edited by Birthe L. Clausen (Roskilde, Denmark: Viking Ship Museum, 1993), is a recent, succinct account of Viking ships, seamanship, and settlements. Those who want to focus on the transition from Mediterranean to Atlantic maritime activity should consult Felipe Fernández-Armesto's *Before Columbus: Exploration and Colonization from the Mediterranean to the Atlantic, 1229–1492* (Philadelphia: University of Pennsylvania Press, 1987). Portuguese voyages are examined in detail in Morison's monograph, *Portuguese Voyages to America in the Fifteenth Century* (New York: Octagon Books, 1973). For more information on specific transatlantic voyages, turn to another sweeping survey, Morison's monumental *The European Discovery of America*, 2 vols. (New York: Oxford University Press, 1971, 1974). The first volume covers the northern voyages (500–1600) and the second, the southern voyages (1492–1616); each chapter is heavily annotated and provided with bibliographical references. A new edition with selected material from this work appeared in a single volume, *The Great Explorers: The European Discovery of America* (New York: Oxford University Press, 1978).

The role of England in early transatlantic ventures has been documented thoroughly in many volumes by a pioneering scholar, James A. Williamson, whose work includes *The Cabot Voyages and Bristol Discovery under Henry VII* (Cambridge: Hakluyt Society, 1962). That work has been continued by other notable scholars like David B. Quinn in *England and the Discovery of America, 1481–1620* (New York: Alfred A. Knopf, 1974) and Kenneth R. Andrews in *Trade, Plunder and Settlement: Maritime Enterprise and the Genesis of the British Empire, 1480–1630* (Cambridge: Cambridge University Press, 1984). Another context is provided by Boies Penrose's *Travel and Discovery in the Renaissance, 1420–1620* (Cambridge, Mass.: Harvard University Press, 1952), which has chapters on Henry the Navigator, Portuguese voyages, and Columbus's voyages. For those who want the broadest context, two elegant coffee-table books by notable scholars are well worth looking at. One is J. H. Parry's *The Discovery of the Sea* (New York: Dial Press, 1974), beautifully printed and generously illustrated, which covers the whole era encompassed in chapter three, from the Portuguese voyages preceding Columbus through the exploration of the Pacific by Cook and others. The second is the result of collaboration by W. P. Cumming, R. A. Skelton, and D. B. Quinn, *The Discovery of North America* (London: Elek Books, 1971), also an attractive book in appearance, quality of printing, and especially abundant and wonderful illustrations; it does have minimal scholarly apparatus tucked in the back, and of course is written by three of the world's best scholars on the subject. It covers the whole subject from Irish and Norse voyages through the first settlements in North America in the seventeenth century. Finally, one should not leave the Columbian era without brushing against its most spectacular aftermath, Magellan's circumnavigation (1519–1522), completed less than two decades after Columbus's fourth voyage. Magellan bibliography is of course a subject in itself, but one can get a good sense of the voyage from a recent interesting and readable biography, Tim Joyner's *Magellan* (Camden, Maine: International Marine, 1992); on the same topic, one can also read *Magellan's Voyage around the World: Three Contemporary Accounts [by] Antonio Pigafetta, Maximilian of Transylvania [and] Gaspar Correia*, edited by Charles E. Newell (Evanston: Northwestern University Press, 1962).

The essential bibliography on Cook's voyages can all be attributed to one incredibly industrious and prolific scholar. Armed with what J. C. Beaglehole edited and wrote, one could not go far wrong in assessing the importance of Cook's exploration of the Pacific. Beaglehole, professor of history at Victoria University in Wellington, New Zealand, began the central work of his life with the publication of the first edition of *The Exploration of the Pacific* in 1934, a volume now in its third edition (Stanford, Calif.: Stanford University Press, 1966). Collaborating with R. A. Skelton, curator of the British Museum map room and honorary secretary of the Hakluyt Society, Beaglehole spent 20 years sorting out the authentic work of Cook that had been buried for nearly two centuries in a barrage of partial, doctored, and pirated editions, beginning with the one commissioned by the Admiralty that enraged Cook for its inaccuracies and inflated rhetoric, John Hawkesworth's *An Account of the Voyages Undertaken by the order of His Present Majesty for Making Discoveries in the Southern Hemisphere* (1773). Beaglehole restored the accurate text of the first voyage in the initial volume, *The Voyage of the Endeavour, 1768–1771* (Cambridge: Hakluyt Society, 1955), first of a series under the general title *The Journals of Captain James Cook on His Voyages of Discovery*. The second volume, *The Voyage of the Resolution and Adventure, 1772–1775*, appeared in 1961; and the third, *The Voyage of the Resolution and Discovery*, appeared in 1967. During the same years Beaglehole edited a complementary source for the first voyage, *The Endeavour Journal of Joseph Banks, 1768–1771*, 2 vols. (Sydney: Trustees of the Public Library of New South Wales in association with Angus and Robertson, 1962), providing another perspective through the eyes of the highly educated, literate chief scientist for the voyage. When Beaglehole retired from the university in 1967, he turned his hand to Cook's biography and had corrected typescript through the first two voyages before he died in 1971; his son, T. H. Beaglehole, completed the work, *The Life of Captain James Cook* (London: Hakluyt Society, 1974), also available in a paperback edition (Stanford, Calif.: Stanford University Press, 1974).

All of Beaglehole's editions are amply illustrated with color plates, drawings, and sketch maps, and two other major publishing ventures make the visual record of Cook's voyages extraordinarily complete. *The Art of Captain Cook's Voyages*, 3 vols., edited by Rudiger Joppien and Bernard Smith (New Haven: Yale University Press, 1985–1988) documents the voyages with a text and a "Descriptive Catalogue of all known original drawings and paintings of peoples, places, artefacts and events and original engravings associated with the voyages." The same editors, in association with chief editor Andrew David, are currently engaged in another three-volume series under the general title *The Charts and Coastal Views of Captain James Cook's Voyages* (London: Hakluyt Society in association with the Australian Academy of the Humanities, vol. 1, 1988, and vol. 2, 1992), superbly produced in atlas size to convey the skill with which Cook and his artists performed their hydrographic charge from the Admiralty.

Unfortunately, the multivolume Beaglehole editions and complementary volumes of art and charts are seldom found outside of major university libraries. To my knowledge, no inexpensive and authoritative complete edition of any voyage is currently available, although several of many ancillary accounts by other hands have been reprinted, including John Ledyard's *A Journal of Captain Cook's Last Voyage to the Pacific Ocean,* edited by James Kenneth Munford (Corvallis, Oreg.: Oregon State University Press, 1963), and John Rickman's *Journal of Captain Cook's Last Voyage to the Pacific Ocean* (Northern Israel: Da Capo Press, 1967). For the most part we must depend upon composite editions summarizing the voyages. In many ways the best of these is *The Explorations of Captain James Cook in the Pacific, as Told by Selections of His Own Journals, 1768–1779,* edited by A. Grenfell Price (New York: Dover, 1971), particularly because it uses Beaglehole's text (to the extent that had been completed) for its selections and has succinct summaries of much of the omitted material. Everyman's Library has had an edition in print since 1906, based on the editorial work of John Barrow in 1860, *Captain Cook's Voyages of*

Discovery (London and New York: Dent and Dutton, 1967); the same text is the basis for *Captain Cook: Voyages of Discovery* (Chicago: Academy Chicago Publishers, 1993). Other editions include *Three Voyages Round the World Made by Captain James Cook*, edited by Charles R. Low (New York: Burt, n.d.), *The Voyages of Captain James Cook Round the World* (New York: Chanticleer Press, 1949), *Seventy North to Fifty South: The Story of Captain Cook's Last Voyage*, condensed, edited, and annotated by Paul W. Dale (Englewood Cliffs, N.J.: Prentice-Hall, 1969), and Richard Hough's retelling of the third voyage, *The Last Voyage of Captain James Cook* (New York: William Morrow, 1979).

As one might expect from the repeated publication of versions of Cook's journals, the secondary bibliography is also massive, and the Mitchell Library of Sydney undertook the publication of a comprehensive annotated *Bibliography of Captain James Cook, R.N., F.R.S., Circumnavigator,* 2d ed. (Sydney: Council of the Library of New South Wales, 1970). It includes the voyages, collected and individual works by Cook not related to the voyages, personal and imaginative works on the life of Cook, and other bibliographies. Those without access to this work can consult the bibliography in Beaglehole's *Life* and bibliographical references in other, more recent, volumes. The most useful is Lynn Withey's *Voyages of Discovery: Captain Cook and the Exploration of the Pacific* (New York: William Morrow, 1987), also available in paperback (Berkeley: University of California Press, 1989); this volume combines background material, biography, and an analysis of the significance of the voyages. Another helpful book is a compendium of 12 papers originally delivered at a conference on Cook at Simon Fraser University in 1978, *Captain James Cook and His Times,* edited by Robin Fisher and Hugh Johnston (Seattle: University of Washington Press, 1979). In the same year a British Museum Yearbook, *Captain Cook and the South Pacific* (London: British Museum Publications, 1979), contains five papers, including one of special interest on Cook's views of ancient Pacific voyaging. Also relevant for our purposes are two volumes by seaman-scholars. *Captain James Cook,* by Alan Villiers (New York: Scribners, 1967) was simultaneously published in London by Hodder and Stoughton with a more revealing title, *Captain Cook, the Seaman's Seaman,* and Frank Knight's *Captain Cook and the Voyage of the Endeavour* was written by a prolific nautical author.

Again, as in the case of Columbus, it would be unwise to focus solely on Cook's three voyages without reference to the broader context of what has been called "the second age of discovery." Here one might begin with a slim volume from the British scholar who wrote many books on maritime history, James A. Williamson's *Cook and the Opening of the Pacific* (London: Hodder and Stoughton, 1946). Next one might look at *The Pacific Basin: A History of Geographical Exploration,* edited by Herman R. Friis (New York: American Geographical Society, 1967). Also useful is *Background to Discovery: Pacific Exploration from Dampier to Cook,* edited by Derek Howse (Berkeley: University of California Press, ca. 1990), which has six chapters dealing with various aspects of the enterprise, including two on navigation and hydrographic art. Another very useful kind of background is provided by David Fausett's *Writing the New World: Imaginary Voyages and Utopias of the Great Southern Land* (Syracuse: Syracuse University Press, 1993), a volume that explores the relationships between literary and historical material related to *Terra Australis Incognita* in detail. It might well be read in conjunction with the Romm and Flint volumes mentioned earlier in this essay in relation to the *Odyssey* and Columbus. For more detail on voyages by other explorers see John Dunmore's *French Explorers in the Pacific,* 2 vols. (Oxford: Clarendon Press, 1965–1969) and Günter Shilder's *Australia Unveiled: The Share of the Dutch Navigators in the Discovery of Australia,* translated by Olaf Richter (Amsterdam: Theatrum Orbis Terrarum, 1976). Two other background volumes describing voyages that had great influence on English perceptions of the Pacific are easily accessible: William Dampier's *A New Voyage Round the World* (New York: Dover, 1968) and Richard Walter's *A Voyage Round the World in the Years 1740–1744,* by George Anson, edited by Glyndwr Williams (Oxford: Oxford University Press, 1974); this volume is also available in a Dover edition. The larger subject of Pacific exploration also has its comprehensive magnum opus that no one should ignore, a trilogy by O. H. K. Spate published by the University of Minnesota Press under the series title, *The Pacific since Magellan*: volume 1, *The Spanish Lake* (1979); volume 2, *Monopolists and Freebooters* (1983); and volume 3, *Paradise Found and Lost* (1988). Finally, consider also *Maritime History, volume 2: The Eighteenth Century* (Melbourne, Fla.: Krieger Publishing, 1997), edited by John B. Hattendorf, which contains the lectures of scholars who participated in the second NEH Summer Institute on Maritime History at the John Carter Brown Library.

The Sea Quest (Chapter 4)

Scholars were slow to recognize the need for careful editing of nineteenth- and twentieth-century texts until this century, when it became apparent that texts of major writers in the modern era needed just as much scrutiny as older works. Luckily, Melville has received that textual attention in the collected edition published by the Northwestern University Press and the Newberry Library, with Harrison Hayford, Hershel Parker, and G. Thomas Tanselle as editors. *Moby-Dick* is volume 6 in the series entitled *The Writings of Herman Melville* (1988); in addition to the text, the volume contains a voluminous editorial appendix with a long historical note, a record of the textual process, and many related documents, including Melville's notes on the story of the whaleship *Essex* and the crew memorandum from the *Acushnet*. Hayford and Parker had earlier produced a Norton Critical Edition of *Moby-Dick* (New York: Norton, 1967), which also has an extensive textual history, material on whaling, reviews and letters related to the novel, analogues and sources, and a selection of criticism. More editions than can be counted are available, of course—including a beautiful Modern Library Edition illustrated by Rockwell Kent (New York: Random House, 1982) and a heavily annotated edition by Luther S. Mansfield and Howard P. Vincent (Putney, Vt.: Hendricks House, 1952)—but the Hayford and Parker work sets the standard by which all others are measured.

Melville scholars have been well served for a generation by Leon Howard's *Herman Melville: A Biography* (Berkeley: University of California Press, 1951), but sustained interest in major writers like Melville inevitably leads to an accumulation of new material, including the publication of two new biographies in a single year. One of them is the long-expected work of lifetime Melville scholar Hershel Parker, *Herman Melville: A Biography* (Baltimore: Johns Hopkins University Press, 1996); the other, also the work of a scholar who has written two previous books about Melville, is Laurie Robertson-Lorant's *Melville: A Biography* (New York: Clarkson Potter, 1996). Older works also provide a variety of specialized biographical and source studies, including Jay Leyda's comprehensive *The Melville Log: A Documentary Life of Herman Melville, 1819–1891*, 2 vols. (New York: Harcourt Brace, 1951), which documents what Melville did and wrote, day by day, throughout his life. *Melville's Reading: A Check-List of Books Owned and Borrowed*, by Merton M. Sealts Jr. (Madison: University of Wisconsin Press, 1966), provides a succinct history of Melville's wide reading and a description of volumes in his library. Howard P. Vincent's classic source study, *The Trying-Out of Moby-Dick* (Boston: Houghton Mifflin, 1949) tracks Melville's sources through the novel, chapter by chapter, including his borrowings from "five chief whaling authorities." Until recently there was no comparable source study for the "pictorial" chapters of *Moby-Dick* (55–57), but Stuart Frank has filled that gap with *Herman Melville's Picture Gallery: Sources and Types of the "Pictorial" Chapters of Moby-Dick* (Fairhaven, Mass.: Edward J. Lefkowicz, 1986). In it Frank, who is director of the Kendall Whaling Museum in Sharon, Massachusetts, expertly selects and reproduces the representations of whales that Melville might have encountered in the galleries and bookstalls of London, Paris, New York, and Boston in 1849 and 1850. An elegantly printed and illustrated book of related interest is Elizabeth A. Schultz's *Unpainted to the Last: Moby-Dick and Twentieth-Century Art* (Lawrence, Kans.: University Press of Kansas, 1995), which studies not pictorial sources for the novel but subsequent art created by it. Another prime source, *Narratives of the Wreck of the Whale-Ship Essex* (New York: Dover, 1989), includes accounts of the disastrous encounter with a whale by Owen Chase, first mate; Thomas Chapple, second mate; and Captain James Pollard. The whole story of the sinking of the *Essex* and its influence on *Moby-Dick* is told in Thomas Farel Heffernan's *Stove by a Whale: Owen Chase and the Essex* (Middletown, Conn.: Wesleyan University Press, 1981); one appendix reproduces Melville's markings in his copy of Owen Chase's *Narrative* of 1821. Mary K. Bercaw's *Melville's Sources* (1987) (Evanston, Illinois: Northwestern University Press, 1987) is a more recent and extremely detailed source study.

Bibliographies are a standard feature in most scholarly and critical books on Melville, and Brian Higgins's *Herman Melville, an Annotated Bibliography, Volume I: 1846–1930* (Boston: G. K. Hall, 1979) is particularly useful as a guide through the voluminous secondary material that has accumulated, but it stops before the flood of publications and should be supplemented by *Herman Melville: A Reference Bibliography*, compiled by Beatrice Ricks and Joseph Adams (Boston: G. K. Hall, 1973). The most useful and entertaining bibliographical tool is still *Moby-Dick as Doubloon: Essays and Extracts, 1851–1970*, edited by Hershel Parker and Harrison Hayford (New York: Norton, 1970), which scours reviews and criticism for more than a century since the novel's publication to produce a representative sampling of its reception and acclaim, or lack of it; the volume closes with an annotated bibliography of selected secondary books and articles from 1921 through 1969. A more recent book picks up the same lead, *The Critical Response to Herman Melville's Moby-Dick*, edited by Kevin J. Hayes (Westport, Conn.: Greenwood Press, 1994), with a chronological arrangement of criticism and reviews from the nineteenth century to the present. Two more hefty volumes include masses of secondary material and criticism. One is *A Companion to Melville Studies*, edited by John Bryant (New York: Greenwood Press, 1986), containing 25 articles dealing with Melville's biography, work, thought, art, and reputation. The other is *Critical Essays on Herman Melville's Moby-Dick*, edited by Brian Higgins and Hershel Parker (New York: G. K. Hall, 1992), with a full array of reviews, articles, essays, and studies of literary influences and affinities. Melville scholarship and bibliography have assumed proportions appropriate to the whale, and it is not surprising that Robert L. Gale has compiled *A Herman Melville Encyclopedia* (Westport, Conn.: Greenwood Press, 1995).

Renewed interest in Melville after World War II also produced a splurge of criticism to complement biographical and scholarly studies. Among the books that caught attention was Charles Olson's *Call Me Ishmael* (New York: Grove Press, 1947), which, like D. H. Lawrence's earlier *Studies in Classic American Literature* (New York: Doubleday, 1953; first published in 1923), prefigured a whole line of passionate reinterpretations of the novel. Equally influential and probably more useful is a triad of books that appeared at the turn of the decade: Richard Chase's *Herman Melville: A Critical Study* (New York: Macmillan, 1949); Newton Arvin's *Herman Melville* (New York: Sloan, 1950); and W. H. Auden's *The Enchaféd Flood, or the Romantic Iconography of the Sea* (New York: Random House, 1950), much of which is devoted to

Moby-Dick. By this time it was clear that the floodgates of critical interest in Melville had opened. They have not yet closed, so those unfamiliar with the intricacies of Melville criticism should consult *Approaches to Teaching Melville's Moby-Dick,* edited by Martin Bickman (New York: Modern Language Association, 1985). This remarkable volume, although designed for college teachers who must deal with the huge, intractable novel in the classroom, is in fact the best introduction to the relevant scholarship and criticism for the uninitiated.

I have found a number of critical books to be particularly useful, either for general perspective or for a specific focus on voyage narratives. This short list includes Lawrence Thompson's *Melville's Quarrel with God* (Princeton: Princeton University Press, 1952), which scoops up details in the text, integrates them, and draws from them an analysis of Melville's use of indirection. A decade later Warner Berthoff's *The Example of Melville* (Princeton: Princeton University Press, 1962) and James Guetti's *The Limits of Metaphor: A Study of Melville, Conrad, and Faulkner* (Ithaca, N.Y.: Cornell University Press, 1967) deal with central questions of Melville's use of language and techniques of narration. For diverging theories of the meaning (or lack of it) in the whale, see Paul Brodtkorb's *Ishmael's White World: A Phenomenological Reading of Moby-Dick* (New Haven: Yale University Press, 1965); see also Robert Zoellner's *The Salt-Sea Mastodon: a Reading of Moby-Dick* (Berkeley: University of California Press, 1973) and William B. Dillingham's *Melville's Later Novels* (Athens, Ga.: University of Georgia Press, 1986). Three more books fit the special focus of this study of voyage narratives: Leon F. Seltzer's *The Vision of Melville and Conrad: A Comparative Study* (Athens, Ohio: Ohio University Press, 1970) outlines the tenuous connection between these two major novelists of the sea; Peter Knox-Shaw's *The Explorer in English Fiction* (New York: St. Martin's, 1986) relates features of historical voyage journals to a number of novels, including *Moby-Dick;* and Christopher Sten's *Sounding the Whale: Moby-Dick as Epic Novel* (Kent, Ohio: Kent State University Press, 1996) studies the quest and examines the relationship between *Moby-Dick* and the *Odyssey.*

Compared to *Moby-Dick, The Old Man and the Sea* is a mite on the eye of the leviathan, but it too has generated a substantial bibliography. Luckily, this one is easier to manage. One might choose to begin with Gerry Brenner's *The Old Man and the Sea: Story of a Common Man* (New York: Twayne, 1991), a slim but comprehensive volume that sketches the literary, biographical, and historical context of the novella, provides a thorough reading, and concludes with a selected, annotated bibliography. After this overview, one should turn to Hemingway's Beaglehole, Carlos Baker, a prolific biographer and critic who devoted much of his life to Hemingway scholarship (although I remember him in an oddly irrelevant context, as an advisor for my senior thesis on E. M. Forster at Princeton). His massive *Ernest Hemingway: A Life Story* (New York: Charles Scribner's Sons, 1969) remains a standard biography, although it has been supplemented by a much more informal account related to some aspects of *The Old Man and the Sea:* Norberto Fuentes's *Hemingway in Cuba,* translated by Consuelo E. Corwin with an introduction by Gabriel García Márquez (Secaucus, N.J.: Lyle Stuart, 1984) and two new biographies. Baker also edited *Ernest Hemingway: Selected Letters, 1917–1961* (New York: Charles Scribner's Sons, 1981) and two very useful earlier anthologies of criticism, *Hemingway and His Critics: An International Anthology* (New York: Hill and Wang, 1961) and *Ernest Hemingway: Critiques of Four Major Novels* (New York: Charles Scribner's Sons, 1962), which contains five articles on *The Old Man and the Sea.* Just as Beaglehole began his life's work on Cook with *The Exploration of the Pacific,* Baker's first foray into Hemingway criticism appeared in 1952, the year of *The Old Man and the Sea's* publication, and was subsequently revised four times as his biographical work proceeded: *Hemingway: the Writer as Artist,* 4th ed. (Princeton: Princeton University Press, 1972). The next big biography was Jeffrey Meyers's *Hemingway: A Biography* (New York: Harper and Row, 1985), soon followed by Kenneth S. Lynn's simply titled *Hemingway* (New York: Simon and Schuster, 1987). Both were due, certainly, to create new perspectives on Hemingway's life and work after time had leavened many of the legends about Hemingway that were very much alive when Baker had written.

Princeton also published the standard bibliography for Hemingway studies, Audre Hanneman's *Ernest Hemingway: A Comprehensive Bibliography* (Princeton: Princeton University Press, 1967) and a *Supplement* (1975), covering work through 1973. Additions are most easily tracked in the *Hemingway Review,* published by Ohio Northern University, Ada, Ohio. Those seeking wider comparative contexts for the novella in the short fiction will find Paul Smith's *A Reader's Guide to the Short Stories of Ernest Hemingway* (Boston: G. K. Hall, 1989) invaluable for its concise summaries of sources and critical opinion and its targeted bibliographies for each story. Serious students may also want to consult Jo August's *Catalogue of the Ernest Hemingway Collection at the John F. Kennedy Library*, 2 vols. (Boston: G. K. Hall, 1982). For most readers there is plenty of more accessible criticism in print, often in paperback. Here one might begin with Philip Young's *Ernest Hemingway*, originally published—like Baker's first book—in the same year as *The Old Man and the Sea* but later revised as *Ernest Hemingway: A Reconsideration* (University Park, Pa.: Pennsylvania State University Press, 1966). Other works particularly relevant to interpretation of *The Old Man and the Sea* include Sheridan Baker's *Ernest Hemingway: An Introduction and Interpretation* (New York: Holt, Rinehart and Winston, 1967); Delbert Wylder's *Hemingway's Heroes* (Albuquerque: University of New Mexico Press, 1969); Ben Stoltzfus's *Gide and Hemingway: Rebels against God* (Port Washington, N.Y.: Kennikat Press, 1978); and Wirt Williams's *The Tragic Art of Ernest Hemingway* (Baton Rouge: Louisiana State University Press, 1981).

Voyages of Endurance (Chapter 5)

Conrad scholarship and criticism, like that devoted to Melville, is rich and complex, but here the key to the kingdom lies in a traditional tripartite division of his work into novels and stories dealing with the Far East, with politics, and with the sea; only the latter is our concern. Although all such divisions by topic are superficial, in this case they are initially helpful because Conrad's many voyage narratives share the characteristics of the genre and help define its potentialities. *The Nigger of the "Narcissus,"* although a masterpiece in itself, is his first work in the genre. For those unfamiliar with the terms and conditions of seafaring under sail, the best approach to the novella is through the Norton Critical Edition, *The Nigger of the "Narcissus": An Authoritative Text, Backgrounds and Sources, Reviews and Criticism,* edited by Robert Kimbrough (New York: W. W. Norton, 1979), which lives up to its extended title and also provides a useful glossary of nautical terms, ship diagrams, and an essay on seamanship. Since World War II, the standard edition of Conrad's works has been the Dent Collected edition, more for accessibility than demonstrated authenticity, but it is gradually being replaced by a new, authoritative, and scholarly edition (still in progress) undertaken by the Cambridge University Press, with *The Nigger of the "Narcissus,"* edited by Kenneth W. Davis and Donald W. Rude. Prior to this major undertaking, the most important study of the *Nigger* text was one of the earliest, John D. Gordan's *Joseph Conrad: The Making of a Novelist* (New York: Russell and Russell, 1963), originally published by the Harvard University Press in 1940.

Conrad scholarship and criticism revived after World War II and have never faltered since, producing a steady stream of major books. Among many Conrad biographies, two works generated at the same time, one American and one Polish, have largely replaced the earlier work of G. Jean-Aubry and Jocelyn Baines. The first is Frederick R. Karl's massive *Joseph Conrad, The Three Lives: A Biography* (London: Faber and Faber, 1979), and the second is Zladislaw Najder's *Joseph Conrad: A Chronicle* (Cambridge: Cambridge University Press, 1983). Owen Knowles's *A Conrad Chronology* (Boston: G. K. Hall, 1990), somewhat comparable to Jay Leyda's *Melville Log*, helps us keep track of Conrad's activities month by month. In addition, an eight-volume edition of *The Collected Letters of Joseph Conrad*, edited by Frederick R. Karl and Laurence Davies, is beyond the midpoint with the publication of the fifth volume (Cambridge: Cambridge University Press, 1996). With all this activity Conrad bibliographies have grown, too, from an initial slender volume compiled by Kenneth A. Lohf and Eugene P. Sheehy, *Joseph Conrad at Mid-Century: Editions and Studies, 1895–1955* (Minneapolis: University of Minnesota Press, 1957), to Theodore G. Ehrsam's heftier *A Bibliography of Joseph Conrad* (Metuchen, N.J.: Scarecrow Press, 1969) to the positively fat *Joseph Conrad: An Annotated Bibliography of Writings about Him*, compiled by Bruce E. Teets and Helmut E. Gerber (De Kalb, Ill.: Northern Illinois University Press, 1971). Two decades later, another volume was obviously due, and Owen Knowles has provided it in *An Annotated Critical Bibliography of Joseph Conrad* (New York: St. Martin's, 1992).

At the same time a four-volume compendium of criticism edited by Keith Carabine, *Joseph Conrad: Critical Assessments*

(Robertsbridge, East Sussex: Helm Information, 1992) provides more than 2,900 pages to fill in some of the gaps, with significant material on *The Nigger of the "Narcissus."* In addition to the Norton Critical Edition mentioned earlier, some other collections of criticism focus on the novella, such as *Twentieth Century Interpretations of The Nigger of the "Narcissus,"* edited by John R. Palmer (Englewood Cliffs, N.J.: Prentice-Hall, 1969). Yet the most important extended analyses of the novel remain embedded in two major books separated by several decades, Albert J. Guerard's *Conrad the Novelist* (Cambridge, Mass.: Harvard University Press, 1958) and Ian Watt's *Conrad in the Nineteenth Century* (London: Chatto and Windus, 1980); both employ the techniques of refined textual criticism, with an archetypal bent in Guerard's case and a historical one in Watt's.

Between and just beyond these two seamarks lie many smaller but useful critical treatments of the novella, embedded in books like Donald C. Yelton's *Mimesis and Metaphor: An Inquiry into the Genesis and Scope of Conrad's Symbolic Imagery* (The Hague: Mouton, 1967); Bruce Johnson's *Conrad's Models of Mind* (Minneapolis: University of Minnesota Press, 1971); H. M. Daleski's *Joseph Conrad: The Way of Dispossession* (London: Faber and Faber, 1977); Jacques Berthoud's *Joseph Conrad: The Major Phase* (Cambridge: Cambridge University Press, 1978); Daniel R. Schwarz's *Joseph Conrad: Almayer's Folly to Under Western Eyes* (London: Macmillan, 1980); William Bonney's *Thorns and Arabesques: Contexts for Conrad's Fiction* (Baltimore: Johns Hopkins University Press, 1980); and Adam Gillon's *Joseph Conrad* (Boston: Twayne, 1982).

Beyond Watt, a number of books are especially useful. For dealing with the problems of narration in Conrad, see especially Aaron Fogel, *Conrad's Poetics of Dialogue* (Cambridge, Mass.: Harvard University Press, 1985); Jacob Lothe's *Conrad's Narrative Method* (Oxford: Clarendon Press, 1989); Richard Ambrosini's *Conrad's Fiction as Critical Discourse* (Cambridge: Cambridge University Press, 1991); and Jeremy Hawthorn's *Joseph Conrad: Narrative Technique and Ideological Commitment* (Sevenoaks, Kent: Hodder and Stoughton, 1992). Another crucial line of criticism dealing with the anomalies of *The Nigger of the "Narcissus"* text begins with a seminal study by Cedric Watts, *The Deceptive Text: An Introduction to Covert Plots* (New York: Barnes and Noble,

1984) and continues with Kenneth Graham's *Indirections in the Novel: James, Conrad, and Forster* (Cambridge: Cambridge University Press, 1988) and Mark A. Wollaeger's *Joseph Conrad and the Fictions of Skepticism* (Stanford, Calif.: Stanford University Press, 1990).

Several books have special relevance to this study. Unfortunately, the one book devoted to Conrad's nautical context, C. F. Burgess's *The Fellowship of the Craft: Conrad on Ships and Seamen and the Sea* (Port Washington, N.Y.: Kennikat Press, 1976), is organized in such a way that it is of very little use in interpreting any of Conrad's voyage narratives. Another is Paul Bruss's *Conrad's Early Sea Fiction: The Novelist as Navigator* (Lewisburg, Penn.: Bucknell University Press, 1979), which has a full chapter on the *Nigger* as a "new metaphor." The missing book, alas, is one that Alan Villiers was writing when he died, combining his own extensive sea experience with a lifelong reading of Conrad's voyage fiction.

Recommended Reading

Since this list cannot be comprehensive, it is designed to be representative of the wide variety of narratives encompassed by the genre. Thus most classic literary narratives are included, but only a sampling of many other types appears, gathered from the abundance of voyage narratives published in England from the sixteenth through the eighteenth centuries and in America during the nineteenth century, from the spate of yacht voyages published in both countries during the twentieth century, and from the growing number of narratives about seafaring under steam or diesel power. If some of the reader's favorite titles do not appear, the same may be said of the author's. For further reading suggestions, consult the bibliographies described in the bibliographical essay.

The original date of publication is indicated in parentheses immediately following the title; details on the reprinted work then follow. Most influential titles have been republished a number of times, so many editions are available. For the convenience of the reader, publication information is provided for a less expensive edition with reliable text when such an edition is available.

Apollonius of Rhodes. *The Voyage of Argo: The Argonautica* (ca. 260–240 B.C.), Trans. by E. V. Rieu. Harmondsworth, Middlesex: Penguin, 1959.

Banks, Joseph. *The Endeavour Journal of Joseph Banks* (1768–71). Ed. J. C. Beaglehole. Sydney: Trustees of the Public Library of New South Wales in association with Angus and Robertson, 1962.

Barth, John. *The Last Voyage of Somebody the Sailor* (1991). Boston: Little Brown, 1991.

———. *Sabbatical: A Romance* (1982). Harmondsworth, Middlesex: Penguin, 1982.

———. *The Tidewater Tales: A Novel* (1987). New York: G. P. Putnam's Sons, 1987.

Belloc, Hilaire. *The Cruise of the "Nona"* (1925). London: Century Publishing, 1983.

Bligh, William. *The Mutiny on the HMS Bounty* (1790). New York: New American Library, 1961.

Blunden, Godfrey. *Charco Harbor*. London: Weidenfield and Nicolson, 1958.

Bradford, Ernle. *The Journeying Moon* (1958). London: Grafton, 1987.

———. *Ulysses Found* (1963). New York: Harcourt Brace, 1964.

Brassey, Anne. *Around the World in the Yacht "Sunbeam," Our Home on the Ocean for Eleven Months* (1878). New York: Henry Holt, 5 eds., 1878–1891. Many other American editions were published between 1878 and 1904.

Buckley, Christopher. *Steaming to Bamboola* (1982). New York: Viking Penguin USA, 1982.

Bullen, Frank T. *The Cruise of the Cachalot: Round the World After Sperm Whales* (1899). New York: Dodd, Mead, 1947.

Bushnell, O. A. *The Return of Lono: A Novel of Captain Cook's Last voyage*. Boston: Little, Brown, 1956.

Brinkley, William. *The Last Ship*. New York: Viking, 1988.

Carlisle, Henry. *The Jonah Man* (1984). New York: Knopf, 1984.

———. *Voyage to the First of December* (1972). New York: G. P. Putnam's Sons, 1972.

Cartier, Jacques. *First Voyage to Canada* (1534). *The Voyages of Jacques Cartier* (1534–1536). Toronto: University of Toronto Press, 1993.

Casson, Lionel, trans. and ed. *The Periplus Maris Erythraei* (ca. A.D. 60). Princeton: Princeton University Press, 1989.

Chichester, Sir Francis. *Gypsy Moth Circles the World* (1967). New York: Pocket Books, 1968.

Childers, Erskine. *The Riddle of the Sands* (1903). New York: David McKay, 1977.

Coleridge, Samuel Taylor. *The Rime of the Ancient Mariner* (1798). New York: Atheneum, 1992.

Columbus, Christopher. *The Diario of Christopher Columbus's First Voyage to America 1492–1493* (ca. 1530–1540). Abstracted by Fray Bartolomé de las Casas. Trans. and ed. by Oliver Dunn and James E. Kelley Jr. Norman, Okla.: University of Oklahoma Press, 1989.

———. *The Journal of Christopher Columbus* (1530–1540). Trans. Cecil Jane. New York: Clarkson N. Potter, 1960.

———. *The Log of Christopher Columbus* (1530–1540). Trans. Robert H. Fuson. Camden, Maine: International Marine Publishing Company, 1987.

Conrad, Joseph. *Lord Jim* (1900). Harmondsworth, Middlesex: Penguin, 1949.

———. *The Mirror of the Sea* (1906). London: J. M. Dent, 1946.

———. *The Nigger of the "Narcissus"/Typhoon and Other Stories* (1897 and 1903). Harmondsworth, Middlesex: Penguin, 1963.

———. *The Shadow-Line and Two Other Tales: Typhoon and The Secret Sharer* (1917). Garden City, N.Y.: Doubleday Anchor, 1959.

———. *"Youth," "Heart of Darkness," and "The End of the Tether"* (1903). Garden City: Doubleday Anchor, 1959.

Cook, James. *Captain Cook: Voyages of Discovery* (1768–1779). Chicago: Academy Chicago, 1993.

———. *The Explorations of Captain James Cook in the Pacific: As Told by Selections of His Own Journals, 1768–1779*. Ed. A. Grenfell Price (1957). New York: Dover, 1971.

———. *The Journals of Captain James Cook on his Voyages of Discovery*, 4 vols. Ed. J. C. Beaglehole. Cambridge: Hakluyt Society at the Cambridge University Press, 1955–1974.

———. *Voyages of Discovery* (1768–1779). Ed. John Barrow (1906). London: Dent. New York, Dutton, 1967.

(N.B. This is a small selection of various editions of Cook's voyages. Authoritative editions of the journals of Cook and Banks are those edited by J. C. Beaglehole, but some of the others listed may be more accessible.)

Cooper, James Fenimore. *Afloat and Ashore, or The Adventures of Miles Wallingford* (1844). New York: Dodd Mead, 1956.

———. *The Pilot: A Tale of the Sea* (1824). Ed. Kay Seymour House. Albany: State University of New York Press, 1986.

———. *The Sea-Lions, or, The Lost Sealers* (1849). Ed. Warren S. Walker. Lincoln, Nebr.: University of Nebraska Press, 1965.

———. *Sea Tales: The Pilot, The Red Rover* (1824, 1827, respectively). Albany: State University of New York Press, 1986, 1990.

(N.B. Cooper wrote eleven sea novels; these are representative of various periods and styles.)

Dampier, William. *A New Voyage Round the World* (1697). New York: Dover, 1968.

Dana, Richard Henry. *Two Years Before the Mast* (1840). Harmondsworth, Middlesex: Penguin, 1981.

Darwin, Charles. *The Voyage of the Beagle* (1839). Garden City: Doubleday, 1962.

Defoe, Daniel. *Captain Singleton* (1720). London and New York: J. M. Dent and E. P. Dutton, 1951.

———. *The Life and Adventures of Robinson Crusoe* (1719). Boston: Houghton Mifflin, 1968.

de Hartog, Jan. *The Call of the Sea* (1966). New York: Atheneum, 1966.

———. *The Captain.* New York: Atheneum, 1966.

Edwards, Philip. *Last Voyages—Cavendish, Hudson, Raleigh: The Original Narratives* (1988). Oxford: Clarendon Press, 1988.

Ellsberg, Edward. *Hell on Ice: The Saga of the "Jeannette"* (1938). New York: Dodd, Mead, 1938.

Forester, C. S. *Captain Horatio Hornblower* (1937). Garden City: Sun Dial, 1944.

———. *The Indomitable Hornblower.* Includes *Commodore Hornblower* (1945), *Lord Hornblower* (1946), and *Admiral Hornblower in the West Indies* (1957, 1958). Boston: Little, Brown, n.d.

Gerbault, Alain. *Firecrest Round the World.* Includes *The Fight of the Firecrest* (1926) and *In Quest of the Sun* (1929). New York: David McKay, 1981.

Golding, William. *Close Quarters* (1987). London: Faber and Faber, 1988.

———. *Fire Down Below* (1989). London: Faber and Faber, 1989.

———. *Rites of Passage* (1980). London: Faber and Faber, 1982.

(N.B. These three form a trilogy dealing with a single voyage in the Napoleonic era and should be read in a sequence based on the original date of publication.)

Hakluyt. *Voyages and Discoveries: The Principal Navigations, Voyages, Traffiques and Discoveries of the English Nation* (1598–1600). Ed. and abridged Jack Beeching. London: Penguin, 1972.

Hayden, Sterling. *Voyage: A Novel of 1896* (1976). New York: Avon, 1976.

———. *Wanderer* (1963). New York: Avon, 1978.

Heaps, Leo, ed. *Log of the Centurion, Based on the Original Papers of Captain Philip Saumavez on Board HMS Centurion, Lord Anson's Flagship during His Circumnavigation 1740–44* (1973). New York: Macmillan, 1973.

Hemingway, Ernest. *The Old Man and the Sea* (1952). New York: Charles Scribner's Sons, 1952.

Heyerdahl, Thor. *Kon-Tiki: Across the Pacific by Raft* (1950). Chicago: Rand McNally, 1950.

———. *The Ra Expeditions* (1971). Garden City: Doubleday, 1971.

———. *The Tigris Expedition* (1980). Garden City: Doubleday, 1981.

Homer. *The Illustrated Odyssey* (ca. 750–725 B.C.). Trans. E. V. Rieu. London: Sidgwick and Jackson, 1980.

————. *The Odyssey.* Trans. Robert Fagles. New York: Viking Penguin USA, 1996.

————. *The Odyssey* (ca. 750–725 B.C). Trans. Robert Fitzgerald. Garden City: Anchor, 1963.

————. *The Odyssey of Homer* (ca. 750–725 B.C.). Trans. Richmond Lattimore. New York: Harper and Row, 1965, 1967.

(N.B. All four translations are respected by scholars who prefer one or the other for specific reasons. The newest translation, by Robert Fagles, is direct and powerful in English, falling somewhere between Lattimore and Fitzgerald in its relationship to the Greek text. Fitzgerald is lively and idiomatic in English; Lattimore follows the original Greek very closely; Rieu, in prose, is accompanied by profuse and beautiful illustrations in this edition.)

Johnson, Charles. *Middle Passage* (1990). New York: Atheneum, 1990.

Kane, Herb. *Voyage: The Discovery of Hawaii* (1976). Honolulu: Island Heritage, 1976.

Kent, Rockwell. *N by E* (1930). Chicago: Lakeside Press, 1930.

Kingsley, Charles. *Westward Ho!* (1855). New York: Scribner, 1948.

Kipling, Rudyard. *Captains Courageous* (1897). New York: Bantam, 1982.

Knight, E. F. *The Cruise of the Alerte* (1890). London: Rupert Hart-Davis, 1952.

————. *The Cruise of the Falcon* (1884). New York: Arno, 1967.

Lallemand, Ferdinand. *The Cruise of The Dolphin* (1955). London: Methuen, 1957.

Ledyard, John. *A Journal of Captain Cook's Last Voyage to the Pacific Ocean and in Quest of a North-west Passage between Asia and America, Performed in the Years 1776, 1777, 1778, and 1779* (1963). Quadrangle Books, 1963.

Lewis, David. *Ice Bird: The First Single-Handed Voyage to Antarctica* (1975). New York, W. W. Norton, 1976.

London, Jack. *Cruise of the Snark* (1911). New York: Macmillan, 1936.

————. *The Sea Wolf* (1904). Ed. Matthew J. Bruccoli. Boston: Macmillan, 1958.

Magellan. *Magellan's Voyage around the World: Three Contemporary Accounts by Antonio Pigafetta, Maximilian of Transylvania and Gaspar Correia* (1519–1522). Ed. Charles E. Nowell. Evanston: Northwestern University Press, 1962.

Márquez, Gabriel García. *The Story of a Shipwrecked Sailor* (1970). New York: Alfred A. Knopf, 1986.

Marryat, Captain. *Mr. Midshipman Easy* (1836). London: Thomas Nelson, n.d.

Masefield, John. *The Bird of Dawning* (1933). London: William Heinemann, 1933.

————. *Victorious Troy or The Hurrying Angel* (1935). New York: Macmillan, 1935.

Matthiessen, Peter. *Far Tortuga* (1975). New York: Random House, 1975.

McFee, William. *Watch Below* (1940). New York: Random House, 1940.

McPhee, John. *Looking for a Ship* (1990). New York: Noonday Press, 1990.

Melville, Herman. *Billy Budd*. Ed. Milton R. Stern. Indianapolis: Bobbs-Merrill, 1981.

————. *Billy Budd Sailor: An Inside Narrative* (1924). Ed. Harrison Hayford and Merton M. Sealts Jr. Chicago: University of Chicago Press, 1962. Melville composed the manuscript between 1886 and his death in 1891, leaving a semifinished draft that remained unpublished before the standard edition of his works.

————. *Great Short Works of Herman Melville* (1969). Ed. Warner Berthoff. New York: Perennial Classic, 1969.

————. *Moby-Dick or, The Whale* (1851). Edited by Charles Feidelson Jr. Indianapolis: Bobbs-Merrill, 1964.

————. *Moby-Dick or, The Whale*. Ed. Harrison Hayford and Hershel Parker. New York: Norton, 1967.

————. *Redburn: His First Voyage* (1849). Garden City: Doubleday Anchor, 1957.

————. *White-Jacket or The World in a Man-of-War* (1850). Ed. Hennig Cohen. New York: Holt, Rinehart and Winston, 1967.

Monsarrat, Nicholas. *The Cruel Sea* (1951). New York: Penguin, 1983.

————. *The Master Mariner: Running Proud* (1978). New York: William Morrow, 1979.

Mostert, Noel. *Supership* (1974). New York: Warner Books, 1974.

Muncaster, Claude. *Rolling Round the Horn* (1933). London: Rich and Cowan, 1933.

Nordhoff, Charles, and James Norman Hall. *The Bounty Trilogy*. Including *Mutiny on the Bounty*, *Men Against the Sea*, and *Pitcairn's Island* (1932). Boston: Little, Brown, 1951.

Novak, Skip. *One Watch at a Time* (1988). New York: W. W. Norton, 1988.

Nowell, Charles E. *Magellan's Voyage Around the World* (1519–1522). From papers of Antonio Pigafetta, Maximilian of Transylvania, and Gaspar Correia. Evanston: Northwestern University Press, 1962.

O'Brian, Patrick. *The Commodore* (1995). New York: W. W. Norton, 1995.

————.*Master and Commander* (1970). New York: W. W. Norton, 1990.

————. *The Yellow Admiral* (1996). New York: W. W. Norton, 1996.

(N.B. O'Brian's Aubrey-Maturin series of novels about the Royal Navy during the Napoleonic wars contains 18 titles; only the first and two most recent titles are listed here.)

O'Neill, Eugene. *Seven Plays of the Sea* (1919). New York: Vintage Books, 1972.

The Periplus Maris Erythraei (ca. A.D. 60). Princeton: Princeton University Press, 1989.

Pigafetta, Antonio. *Magellan's Voyage: A Narrative Account of the First Circumnavigation* (1519–1522). New Haven: Yale, 1969.

Pillot, Gilbert. *The Secret Code of the Odyssey: Did the Greeks Sail the Atlantic?* (1972). New York: Abelard-Schuman, 1972.

Poe, Edgar Allan. *Arthur Gordon Pym, Benito Cereno, and Related Writings* (1838). Ed. John Seelye. Philadelphia: Lippincott, 1967.

Porter, Katherine Anne. *Ship of Fools* (1945). Boston: Little, Brown, 1962.

Reiner, Larry. *Minute of Silence* (1990). Phoenix, Arizona: Integra Press, 1990.

Rickman, John. *Journal of Captain Cook's Last Voyage to the Pacific Ocean* (1781). N. Israel: Da Capo Press, 1967.

Roth, Hal. *The Longest Race* (1983). New York: W. W. Norton, 1983.

Schildt, Goran. *In the Wake of Ulysses* (1953). New York: Dodd Mead, 1953.

Scott, Sir Walter. *The Pirate* (1821). Edinburgh: Constable, 1821.

Severin, Tim. *The Brendan Voyage* (1978). New York: McGraw-Hill, 1978.

———. *The China Voyage: A Pacific Quest by Bamboo Raft* (1994). London: Little Brown, 1994.

———. *The Jason Voyage: The Quest for the Golden Fleece* (1985). London: Hutchinson, 1985.

———. *The Sinbad Voyage* (1982). New York: G. P. Putnam's Sons, 1983.

———. *The Ulysses Voyage: Sea Search for the Odyssey* (1987). New York: E. P. Dutton, 1987.

Slocum, Joshua. *Sailing Alone around the World* (1900). New York: Dover, 1956.

———. *The Voyages of Joshua Slocum* (1958). Ed. Walter Teller. Dobbs Ferry, N.Y.: Sheridan House, 1985.

Solley, George C., and Eric Steinbaugh, eds. *Short Stories of the Sea* (1984). Annapolis: Naval Institute Press, 1984. Contains 31 stories, including "Benito Cereno," "The Open Boat," and "Youth."

Stevenson, Robert Louis. *Treasure Island* (1906). New York: Current Literature Publishing Co., 1906.

Stone, Robert. *Outerbridge Reach* (1992). New York: Ticknor and Fields, 1992.

Tanner, Tony, ed. *The Oxford Book of Sea Stories* (1994). Oxford: Oxford University Press, 1994. Contains 27 stories, including those by Irving, Poe, Melville, Crane, Conrad, Fitzgerald, Hemingway, and Faulkner.

Tomlinson H. M. *Gallions Reach* (1927). London: Rupert Hart-Davis, 1955.

———, ed. *Great Sea Stories of All Nations* (1930). Garden City: Garden City Publishing, 1937.

———. *Out of Soundings* (1931). New York: Harper, 1931.

Traven, B. *The Death Ship* (1926). New York: Knopf, 1934.

Vancouver, George. *A Voyage of Discovery to the North Pacific Ocean and round the World, 1791–1795,* 4 vols. (1984). Ed. W. Kaye Lamb. London: Hakluyt Society, 1984.

Verne, Jules. *Twenty-Thousand Leagues under the Sea.* (1870). New York: A. L. Burt.

Villiers, A. J. *By Way of Cape Horn* (1930). Garden City: Garden City Publishing, 1930.

———. *The Cruise of the Conrad* (1937). New York: Scribner, 1937.

———. *Great Sea Stories* (1959). New York: Dell, 1959.

Virgil. *The Aeneid of Virgil* (19 B.C.). Verse translation by Allen Mandelbaum. New York: Bantam, 1971.

Walcott, Derek. *Omeros* (1990). New York: Farrar Straus Giroux, 1990.

Walter, Richard. *Anson's Voyage round the World in the Years 1740–44* (1748). New York: Dover, 1974.

Wilson, Derek. *The World Encompassed: Francis Drake and His Great Voyage* (1577–1580). New York: Harper and Row, 1977.

Worsley, F. A. *Shackleton's Boat Journey* (1916). New York: W. W. Norton and Co., 1977.

Wouk, Herman. *The Caine Mutiny* (1951). Garden City: Doubleday, 1952.

Wroth, Lawrence. *The Voyages of Giovanni da Verrazzano 1524–1528.* New Haven: Pierpont Morgan Library by Yale University Press, 1970.

INDEX

(Author's Note: For the convenience of the reader, this index lists titles of major primary works after the name of the author, sometimes in shortened form; in most cases, publication information for editions currently available appears in the list of recommended reading. Secondary works are indexed by author only because titles and publication information appear in notes or the bibliographical essay; exceptions to this rule apply to works particularly important for an understanding of sea literature or voyage narratives. Substantive material in notes is indexed by author, topic, or both. Ship names and places particularly important to the text are indexed independently of the texts that refer to them, but characters in texts are not indexed separately.)

The Author

Robert Foulke has degrees from Princeton and the University of Minnesota and has taught at Minnesota, Trinity College, and Skidmore College, where he chaired the Department of English for a decade. In the process of maritime research he has been a Fulbright Fellow at the University of London, a Visiting Associate at Clare Hall, Cambridge University, a Visiting Fellow in the English Department at Princeton University, and a Fellow at the John Carter Brown Library, Brown University. An avid sailor long before he became a scholar of sea literature and maritime history, he has raced on the lakes of the Midwest, cruised offshore and along the coasts of New England, Nova Scotia, and Japan, as well as founding and directing a sailing school on Lake George. In the Navy he first served in a boat unit during the Korean War, then became Sailing Officer at the U.S. Naval Academy and skipper of a 44–foot yawl in the 1954 Bermuda race. He has taught for the Williams College Program in American Maritime Studies at Mystic Seaport and the Sea Education Association, both ashore in Woods Hole and at sea on the schooner *Westward,* and has taken Skidmore students to sea under sail for courses in sea literature, maritime history, nautical science, and oceanography. His publications include *An Anatomy of Literature* and articles on voyage narratives in *The Journal of British Studies, Modern Fiction Studies, Conradiana, The Log of Mystic Seaport, The Literature and Lore of the Sea, Oceans, The Great Circle, Conrad's Literary Career, Bermuda Journal of Archaeology and Maritime History,* and *The American Neptune.*

The Editor

R onald Gottesman is professor of English at the University
of Southern California.